Timothy B. Beresford

PEARL HARBOR
AMAZING FACTS!

BY TIMOTHY B. BENFORD

AMERICAN BOOK PUBLISHERS
New Jersey

ALSO BY TIMOTHY B. BENFORD

NONFICTION

The Ultimate World War II Quiz Book

World War II Flashback

The World War II Quiz & Fact Book, Vol. I

The World War II Quiz & Fact Book, Vol. II

The Space Program Quiz & Fact Book

The Royal Family Quiz & Fact Book

TRUE CRIME

Righteous Carnage
The List family murders in Westfield, NJ

NOVELS

Hitler's Daughter
Wants to occupy The White House

The Ardennes Tapes
Pray that somebody listens

PEARL HARBOR AMAZING FACTS　　　　　TIMOTHY B. BENFORD

For Marilyn, yet again

FIRST EDITION: May 2001

Design, layout, and computer typesetting by the author.

Library of Congress Cataloging in Publication Data

Benford, Timothy B.
   Pearl Harbor Amazing Facts

Includes photos and bibliography

ISBN 0-9710560-0-5

INTRODUCTION

In its broadest sense the Japanese attack on U.S. military installations in Pearl Harbor and throughout Oahu is, and always will be, spoken of and remembered under the singular, collective, umbrella of Pearl Harbor. Correctly or not, everything that happened on that fateful, historic, December 7, 1941 in the Hawaiian Islands is identified as part of the Pearl Harbor attack. That seemingly limited reference conjures up all events on what President Franklin D. Roosevelt called the "…date which will live in infamy".

Consequently, as has commonly been the historical reference for nearly six decades, the broad usage here of "Pearl Harbor" does not in any way diminish for one iota the suffering or heroic actions of military and civilian personnel who came under attack at EWA, Hickam, Wheeler, Ford Island, Schofield, Honolulu or anywhere else in Hawaii. The material in this book covers the entire attack in its broadest scope. But forevermore these events will be referenced and remembered as being part of the attack on Pearl Harbor.

ACKNOWLEDGEMENTS: With great appreciation I thank the following for their specific and individual contributions to this work: Ellsworth Boyd, for permission to reprint in toto his copyrighted article/interview in World War II magazine with Capt. Briggs concerning the "East wind, rain" message, starting on page 24; William Hughes, and the members of the USS Utah (BB-31/AG-16) Association for their assistance and permission to reprint the Utah copy on page 220; Mrs. Joan Mecteau for her father's (Cecil "Mac" McCloud) original copy of the USS Nevada Log; George Schroth for his exclusive, not previously published photos; Mrs. Joan Nemick, for the information about the discovery and burial of her relative, Pfc. Peter Giacalone in 1997; ISSHO Kikaku, a Japan-based non-profit organization which researches Japan-related issues, and the late James and Mari Michner for their encouragement, urging and advice so many years ago when this book was just an idea.

CONTENTS

NOTE: *"Pearl Harbor Amazing Facts" contains several hundred interesting, unusual, amazing facts, brief vignettes, anecdotes, coincidences, warnings, and individual items of interest plus 50 photos (several not previously published) throughout this book. Only significant, larger and key items are noted here for quick reference.*

TIME WAS RUNING OUT:
 A chronological timetable of warnings, events, and missed
opportunities leading up to December 7, 1941.................................11

THE MARTIN-BELLINGER REPORT...............................15

"EAST WIND, RAIN", was it ever sent by Tokyo? Was it
intercepted by U.S. codebreakers?..24

DECEMBER 7, 1941: The minute-by-minute events prior to,
during, and immediately after the attack..............................33

"AIR RAID PEARL HARBOR. THIS IS NO DRILL"
Or was it "this is not drill? Who sent the famous message?..........46

COMPARATIVE TIMES: WASHINGTON AND OAHU..........49

SHIPS PRESENT AT PEARL HARBOR:
he complete list of all U.S. Navy ships in and around Pearl
Harbor the day of the attack...51

DECEMBER 7 LOG OF THE USS NEVADA (verbatim)..........57

PRESIDENT ROOSEVELT'S ADDRESS TO CONGRESS
complete text of the December 8, Date of Infamy speech.............66

KIDO BUTAI, the complete list of Japanese ships which
made up the Pearl Harbor strike force..............................…….107

FATE OF THE JAPANESE PLANNERS of the attack............…..104

BIOGRAPHIES of key figures related to the attack…………….111

WWII STILL IN THE NEWS……………………………….…..137

USS ARIZONA (BB-39) COMPLETE CASUALTY LIST…......140

BIBLIOGRAPHY…………....…………………………………241-247

APPENDICES:

SPECIAL BONUS WORLD WAR II FACTS:

Amazing WWII facts before and after the Pearl Harbor attack, plus fascinating items of interest from all theaters of operation, appear throughout the book and in the appendix, some significant ones:

- 20 LARGEST BATTLESHIPS, ALL NATIONS, IN WWII.............61

- DISPOSITION OF U.S. BATTLESHIPS, 1895-1944......................63

- 30 WWII SHIP MEMORIALS YOU CAN VISIT.......................206

- 25 LARGEST U.S. AIRCRAFT CARRIERS IN WWII..................226

- 20 TOP U.S. SUBMARINE COMMANDERS IN WWII..............230

- 20 TOP U-BOAT COMMANDERS IN WWII...........................231

- 50 TOP FIGHTER PILOTS, ALL NATIONS, IN WWII..............232

- 10 FASTEST FIGHTER PLANES IN WWII.............................234

FOREWARD

Did FDR know? It would be remiss to write a book about the December 7, 1941 Japanese surprise attack on Pearl Harbor and military installations on Oahu, Hawaii, without acknowledging many people still wonder about that question. Despite all the official investigations and enormous number of books and articles written, these inquiries have, in some ways, only added fuel to the fire.

Until the Kennedy Assassination in 1963 and, to some degree, the later revelations about the 1947 Roswell "Flying Saucer" incident, the most consuming conspiracy theory held by many Americans was Pearl Harbor. The premise being that President Franklin D. Roosevelt knew in advance that the Japanese were going to attack Pearl Harbor and he let it happen so the U.S. could get into the war against the Axis powers without having fired the first shot. Six decades have passed since Roosevelt's "date which will live in infamy" and the Pearl Harbor conspiracy remains alive.

Traditionalists believe that history has correctly recorded that Pearl Harbor happened because we were not properly prepared, ignored significant intelligence, misread other clues and, perhaps most of all, couldn't really believe the Japanese would be so bold as to cross the Pacific and attack in Hawaii. The most convincing traditionalist interpretation of the attack are the two works of Gordon Prange: *At Dawn We Slept* and *Dec. 7, 1941*. Both are based on extensive research by Prange and paint a picture that places the blame for the attack primarily upon the commanders in Hawaii.

Revisionists and believers in a conspiracy point to what can only be considered an unbelievable number of missed opportunities to thwart the attack and conclude Roosevelt did not want the attack prevented. Their reasoning is that a surprise Japanese attack would be America's ticket to the Big Show in Europe so we could join the British against Japan's ally, the Nazis. This theory is best advanced in *Infamy* by John Toland. Considered one of the foremost scholars of World War II, Infamy (as is true of Prange's book) is one of most extensively researched books on the attack. It take's the revisionist position.

In the opening section of *Pearl Harbor Amazing Facts* which follows, we have chronicled many of the key instances and events that revisionists point to as supporting their theories. For those who approach this book with an uncommitted, open mind, it would be impossible to read these items and not conclude they raise an issue of reasonable doubt.

Despite this author's personal opinion, I have no intention of playing Monday Morning Quarterback in this book or taking sides with either camp in this ongoing debate. Furthermore I would not presume to elevate my research of Pearl Harbor to the extraordinary academic achievements of Gordon Prange or John Toland.

Therefore it will be for you, the reader, to ingest and consider what is written here and form your own opinions. I would, however, strongly urge any serious consideration of these facts to also read the Prange and Toland books as well as any number of others in the bibliography.

Timothy B. Benford
Mountainside, N.J.
May, 2001

Japanese Ambassador Kichisaburo Nomrua (right) and Special Envoy Saburo Kurusu check the time as they wait in an outer office at the State Department building in Washington, D.C. to see U.S. Secretary of State Cordell Hull on Sunday afternoon, December 7, 1941. Purpose of the meeting was to present the U.S. with the 14-part message Tokyo had sent them about relations with the United States. They did not know that Pearl Harbor had already been attacked. *--National Archives photo*

TIME WAS RUNNING OUT!

Prior to hostilities in 1941 the U.S. had only eight Purple decoding machines, even though U.S. Army Colonel William Friedman had broken the code and designed the first machine more than 14 months before the surprise Japanese attack on Pearl Harbor. One machine was originally slated for Admiral Husband E. Kimmel or General Walter C. Short in Hawaii, the U.S. Navy and Army commanding officers on Oahu. Four were based in Washington, with the Navy and Army having two each. One was sent to General MacArthur in the Philippines and two others went to London in exchange for the Ultra intelligence the British were getting from their captured German Enigma machines. When both Washington and London expressed strong interest in acquiring an additional machine, Hawaii was bypassed and a third machine was sent to the British.

After reading the first 13-parts of the 14-part message Tokyo sent to its ambassadors in Washington on December 6 President Franklin Delano Roosevelt reportedly declared: "This means war."

If a Purple decoding machine had been available in Hawaii would Admiral Kimmel or General Short have had the same reaction?

- The 14th, and final part of the message, which was not decoded by American codebreakers in Washington until the morning of December 7, set "1 P.M. Eastern Standard Time today" (7:30 A.M. in Honolulu) as the precise time Tokyo instructed its ambassadors to deliver the message.
- Instead of alerting Pearl Harbor via military communications' channels, Washington sent Kimmel and Short a Western Union Telegram (in code) advising them of the 7:30 A.M. local time ultimatum. It reached the Western Union office in Honolulu 22 minutes before the attack, but for obvious reasons, wasn't delivered until four hours later. It took another three hours before the message was decoded by intelligence officers.

11

U.S. Ambassador to Japan, Joseph W. Grew sent a dispatch to the U.S. State Department eleven months before the Japanese attack on Pearl Harbor that said a member of his staff had been told by another diplomat that Japanese military forces planned a surprise attack on Pearl Harbor.   *--U.S. Government photo*

★ **January 1941:** "My Peruvian colleague told a member of my staff that he heard ... that Japanese military forces planned ... to attempt a surprise attack on Pearl Harbor."

Considered one of the most remarkable dispatches ever sent by a United States diplomat, U.S. ambassador to Japan Joseph C. Grew sent the above to the State Department within a month after Admiral Yamamoto *first disclosed to* anyone his bold plan for attacking Pearl Harbor. However, it received only token interest in official circles since Japanese fiction writers had used the theme of attacking Pearl Harbor for several years and the report was considered just an unfounded rumor based on such tales.

Nonetheless, on February 1, 1941, the Office of Naval Intelligence paraphrased the ambassador's dispatch and forwarded it to Admiral Husband E. Kimmel in Hawaii. Grew's "colleague" was Peruvian Minister Richardo Rivera Schreiber. The American Embassy staff member mentioned was Third Secretary Max Bishop.

★ **January 24, 1941:** "The security of the U.S. Pacific Fleet while in Pearl Harbor, and of the Pearl Harbor Naval Base itself, has been under renewed study by the Navy Department and forces afloat for the past several weeks. This reexamination has been, in part, prompted by the increased gravity of the situation with respect to Japan, and by reports from abroad of successful bombing and torpedo plane attacks on ships while in bases. If war eventuates with Japan, it is believed easily possible that hostilities would be initiated by a surprise attack upon the fleet or the naval base at Pearl Harbor... In my opinion the inherent possibilities of a major disaster to the fleet or naval base warrant taking every step, as rapidly as can be done, that will increase the joint readiness of the Army and Navy to withstand a raid of the character mentioned above."

The above is excerpted from a letter by Secretary of the Navy Frank Knox to Secretary of War Henry L. Stimson some 11 months before the attack. It was actually written for Secretary Knox by Rear Admiral Richmond Kelly Turner and approved by Admiral Harold R. Stark before Knox signed it.

★ **February 1941:** "It must be remembered too that a single submarine attack may indicate the presence of a considerable surface force ... accompanied by a carrier." Remarks from Admiral Kimmel to Rear Admiral Claude C. Bloch, the man he appointed as naval base defense commander for Pearl Harbor. At 6:45 A.M on December 7, Kimmel's comments rang true when the destroyer USS Ward (DD-139) depth-charged and sank a Japanese submarine more than an hour before the attack, and a second sub was sunk at 0700 by a Catalina flying boat.

★ **February 11, 1941:** Ten months before Japan's surprise attack Admiral Kimmel, Commander In Chief of the U.S. Fleet in Hawaii, issued a letter to his command that said in part. "A declaration of war might be preceded by... a surprise attack on ships in Pearl Harbor . . . a surprise submarine attack on ships in operating area ... [or] a combination of these two."

★ **February 18, 1941:** "I feel that a surprise attack (submarine, air or combined) on Pearl Harbor is a possibility." Letter from Admiral Kimmel to Admiral Stark. Kimmel had taken over command of the U.S. fleet in Hawaii earlier that month.

★ **February 25, 1941:** "In view of the Japanese situation, the Navy is concerned with the security of the fleet in Hawaii.... They are in the situation where they must guard against a surprise or trick attack. . . . We also have information regarding the possible use of torpedo planes. There is the possible introduction of Japanese carrier-based planes." Remarks by General George C. Marshall, U.S. Army Chief of Staff in Washington. Eight days later Marshall urged the Army commander in Hawaii, General Walter G. Short, to send as "a matter of first priority" a review of defenses against possible air attack.

==

FACT: A September 1941 Gallup Poll reflected that 70 percent of the American population was willing to risk war with Japan, up from a July poll which had shown 51 percent held that attitude.

★ **March 1941:** Rear Admiral Patrick N. L. Bellinger and Major General Frederick L. Martin authored the prophetic Martin-Bellinger Report for defending U.S. military installations in Hawaii. Both officers were based in Oahu. So incredible was their work, and containing an extraordinary number of actual, specific warnings of events which came to pass, that the so-named Martin-Bellinger Report is considered one of the most far-sighted advance military planning documents in history. Highlights and observations follow:

EXCERPTED FROM
THE PROPHETIC MARTIN-BELLINGER REPORT

* A successful, sudden raid against our ships and naval installations on Oahu might prevent effective offensive action by our forces in the Western Pacific for a long period.

* It appears possible that Orange [the U.S. codename for Japan] submarines and/or an Orange fast raiding force might arrive in Hawaiian waters with no prior warning from our intelligence service.

* Orange might send into this area one or more submarines and/or one or more fast raiding forces composed of carriers supported by fast cruisers.

* A declaration of war might be preceded by: A surprise submarine attack on ships in the operating area. A surprise attack on Oahu, including ships and installations in Pearl Harbor. It appears that the most likely and dangerous form of attack on Oahu would be an air attack ... such an attack would most likely be launched from one or more carriers which would probably approach inside of three hundred miles.

* Any single submarine attack might indicate the presence of a considerable undiscovered surface force...

* In a dawn air attack there is a high probability that it could be delivered as a complete surprise...

15

★ **April 1, 1941**: "Personnel of your Naval Intelligence Service should be advised that because of the fact that from past experience shows [sic] the Axis Powers often begin activities in a particular field on Saturdays and Sundays or on national holidays of the country concerned they should take steps on such days to see that proper watches and precautions are in effect."

--War warning issued by U.S. Naval Intelligence, Washington, D.C.

★ **April 23, 1941:** During a conversation during which President Roosevelt's Secretary of War, Henry L. Stimson speculated about the safety of U.S. military forces in Hawaii in the event of hostilities with Japan, Army Chief of Staff General George C. Marshall confidently replied, "The Japs wouldn't dare attack Hawaii."

★ **May 12, 1941:** Some seven months before the attack the U.S. Army and Navy held what the military described as "the greatest war drills ever staged" in the Hawaiian Islands. Army bombers "attacked" enemy aircraft carriers several hundred miles at sea just as one carrier was preparing to launch planes against the islands. In an ironic note, a formation of 21 B-17s landed on Oahu from the mainland while the "attack' was under way. The war games, detailed and complex, consisted of many phases and options and continued for two weeks, with the team representing the United States forces gaining the upper hand. The Navy had held similar games involving a Pearl Harbor attack by enemy aircraft carriers as far back as 1933.

**FACT** : The first published account of a Japanese surprise attack on the U.S. fleet based at Pearl Harbor appeared in the 1925 novel *The Great Pacific War* by author Hector C. Bywater, 16 years before the Day of Infamy. The work of fiction was reportedly widely read by officers at in the Japanese Navy War College throughout the 1930s. Some historians have questioned whether this novel inspired or played any part in Admiral Isoroku Yamamoto's eventual plan for the actual Dec. 7, 1941 attack.

★ **June 13, 1941:** "The only real answer was for the fleet not to be in Pearl Harbor when the attack came." That statement was made by Admiral Husband E. Kimmel, during a Washington meeting with Chief of Naval Operations Admiral Harold R. Stark and Secretary of the Navy Frank Knox. Kimmel had said the congestion of ships, fuel oil storage, and repair facilities in Pearl Harbor invited "an attack, particularly from the air." With the fleet in port it would take at least three hours to sortie, he noted.

★ **June 1941:** The United States government ordered all German and Italian consulates in the U.S. closed. Japan, as the third member of the Tripartite Pact, expected its consulates (including the one in Oahu), to also be closed. This eventuality caused concern among Admiral Yamamoto's superiors in the Imperial Japanese Navy General Staff. They feared that such action would greatly limit Japanese espionage activities on the U.S. Fleet and thereby necessitate a cancellation of the Pearl Harbor attack. However, the U.S. never issued an order to close the Japanese consulates, and they continued to function up to the moment of the attack.

★ **July 1941:** Lt. Colonel Kendall (Whoch) Fielder became the intelligence officer (G-2) on the staff of General Short. Fielder had no prior intelligence duty and had not previously served under Short.

★ **July 10, 1941:** "Our most likely enemy, Orange, can probably employ a maximum of six carriers against Oahu.... The early morning attack is, therefore, the best plan of action to the enemy." This accurate statement was contained in a report submitted by Colonel William E. Farthing, commander of the Fifth Bombardment Group, Hickam Field, Oahu, Hawaii. The purpose of "the Farthing Report" was to analyze the use of bombardment aviation as a defense for Hawaii.

★ **August 12, 1941:** "An attack upon these [Hawaiian] islands is not impossible and in certain situations not be improbable." Excerpt from an address by General Short at the University of Hawaii.

★ **September 10, 1941:** General Short made a strong request to the U.S. War Department for bombproof aircraft facilities, which he said would be "vital to the continued functioning of the Hawaiian Air Force during an attack on Oahu." The request was denied.

★ **September 20, 1941:** Major General Martin, commander of the Hawaiian Air Force, submitted a plan calling for joint Army-Navy exercise drills to specifically train against a potential Japanese carrier-based air attack. Martin proposed that the war games take place November 17-22. At the time Martin made the request the Japanese were themselves considering November 16 or 23 as the date for the attack. Martin's request was not acted on favorably.

★ **November 7, 1941:** U.S. Secretary of State Cordell Hull, responding to a cabinet meeting question from President Roosevelt, stated: "Relations were extremely critical, and we should be on the lookout for a military attack anywhere by Japan at any time."

★ **November 7, 1941:** Exactly one month before the attack Admiral Stark, CNO rejected another request from Admiral Kimmel that the battleships USS North Carolina (BB-55) and USS Washington (BB-56) plus more destroyers, be sent to Pearl Harbor to join the fleet: "Things seem to be moving steadily toward crisis in the Pacific," Stark wrote, adding, "A month may see literally anything."

★ **November 25, 1941:** "The President predicted that we were likely to be attacked perhaps next Monday...the question was how we should maneuver them into the position of firing the first shot." Diary entry of Secretary of War Henry L. Stimson, covering discussions which took place earlier that day at a Cabinet meeting over the possibility of war with Japan.

★ **November 27, 1941:** Washington sent what became known as the "war warning" message to U.S. forces in the Pacific, saying in part: "An aggressive move by Japan is expected within the next few days."

★ **November 28, 1941:** Admiral Kimmel issued an order stating that any submerged submarine operating in the designated restricted waters around Pearl Harbor should be considered hostile and sunk.

★ **December 1941:** General Hein Ter Poorten, commander of the Netherlands East Indies Army, advised the U.S. military observer in Java, Brigadier General Elliott Thorpe, in early December that Japan would attack Hawaii, the Philippines, Malaya, and Thailand shortly. He further noted (*incorrectly) that the signal for hostilities against the U.S. would be the message "East wind, rain," which U.S. code breakers were aware of because it and other coded "winds" references were found in a November 29 message Tokyo sent to its ambassadors in Washington. General Thorpe sent this Information to Washington along with three other messages on the same subject. *Washington's reply requested he send no further information on the subject!* (italics by author).

AUTHOR'S NOTE: See expanded information further on about both the East Wind, Rain and other "winds" messages [*The inclusion of "East wind, rain" in a radio weather report, according to the intercepted Nov. 29 Japanese transmission, would indicate that relations between Japan and the U.S. was in danger, not the start of hostilities].

★ **December 2, 1941:** When the Matson Lines passenger liner Lurline made port in Honolulu after a passage from California, her officers reported to the U.S. Navy that they had accidentally picked up a series of unidentifiable high-frequency transmissions from Tokyo and low-frequency replies from ships that they had plotted to be closing in on Hawaii.

★ **December 2, 1941:** Lieutenant Ellsworth A. Hosner and another staff member of the 12th Naval District Intelligence Office (San Francisco) detected radio signals in the Pacific they thought could be from the Japanese fleet (which had been missing since late November). Their commander, Captain Richard T. McCullough, a friend of President Roosevelt, was advised. These two officers continued to track the signals and on December 6 correctly established that the position was about 400 miles north of Oahu.

★ **December 2, 1941:** *"Do you mean to say that they [the Japanese fleet] could be rounding Diamond Head this minute and you wouldn't know?"* Question posed by Admiral Husband E. Kimmel to his intelligence officer on Oahu on December 2, 1941, five days before the infamous attack, when the officer informed Kimmel that the Japanese carrier force that left its home waters in late November was still "missing" to U.S. plotters. Post card scene above is Waikiki Beach, circa 1941.   ---author's collection

★ **December 3, 1941:** "Pearl Harbor will never be attacked from the air." So said Admiral Charles H. McMorris.

★ **December 4, 1941:** Admiral William F. Halsey's task force was advised that a submarine had been reported on December 4 just south of Hawaii.

★ **December 5, 1941:** The first contact U.S. naval forces operating out of Pearl Harbor had with Japanese ships that would be involved in the Pearl Harbor attack on December 7 actually came two days earlier. On December 5, the destroyers USS Selfridge (DD-357) and USS Ralph Talbot (DD-390) made underwater contact with what the Talbot commander reported as a submarine about five miles off Pearl Harbor. He requested permission to depth-charge but was denied such authority by his land-based superiors with the explanation that the readings he was getting were more probably from a blackish than a sub. "If this is a blackfish, it has a motorboat up its stern!" he reportedly responded.

★ **December 6, 1941:** On seeing the U.S. Fleet all lit up in Pearl Harbor the evening before the attack General Short exclaimed, "What a target that would make!" The general, his wife, and his intelligence officer, Lieutenant Colonel Fielder, were returning home after attending a party.

★ **December 6, 1941:** "The Japanese will not go to war with the United States. We are too big, too powerful, and too strong," boast made to other officers on Oahu by Vice Admiral William Satterlee Pye, the second-highest-ranking U.S. Navy officer at Pearl Harbor, (outranked only by Admiral Husband E. Kimmel). While in the War Plans Division in Washington, Pye drafted the U.S. Navy's war plan for the Pacific.

★ **December 6, 1941:** While at the office of U.S. Naval Intelligence in Washington, Captain Johan Ranneft, the Dutch naval attaché, was told that two Japanese aircraft carriers were proceeding east between Japan and Hawaii. He asked where they were, and an officer pointed to a wall map and indicated a position between 300 and 400 miles northwest of Honolulu. (NOTE: This incident is one of several that noted Pearl Harbor historian-authors Gordon Prange and John Toland disagree about. Toland reports it as fact in *Infamy*, whereas Prange dismisses it in *Pearl Harbor, The Verdict of History*.)

★ **December 6, 1941:** An article on the editorial pages of the *Washington Evening Star* that day noted: "ALLIED FLEETS ON TWENTY-FOUR HOUR WATCH TO MEET SURPRISE JAPANESE ATTACK IN FAR EAST".

★ **December 6, 1941:** Admiral Kimmel, in a meeting with aides, updated a memorandum titled "Steps to Be Taken in Case of American-Japanese War Within the Next Twenty-Four Hours."

★ **December 6, 1941:** "War is imminent. You may run into a war during your flight" Statement by Major General Henry H. (Hap) Arnold to members of the 38th and 88th Reconnaissance Squadrons, who were about to leave the U.S. to deliver several B- 17s to the Philippines. Their flight plan called for a scheduled fuel stop at Oahu, Hawaii, around 8 A.M.. on December 7.

★ **December 6, 1941:** "If we are going into a war, why don't we have machine guns?" Question to General Arnold from Major Truman H. Landon during the above briefing. To conserve fuel, the planes had been stripped of weaponry.

★ **December 6, 1941:** "The United States Navy can defeat the Japanese Navy at any place and at any time", so stated U.S. Senator Owen Brewster of Maine, during a speech at the ribbon-cutting ceremonies for a new building in San Juan, Puerto Rico at the Naval Air Station base there.

★ **December 6, 1941:** "They [Japan] will attack right here." The prophetic statement by Ensign Fred Hall, the assistant communications officer aboard the USS Vestal (AR-4), was interjected into a conversation among officers in the ship's wardroom. However, nobody bothered to ask Hall when the attack would take place. At 7:55 the following morning Hall was the officer of the deck and pulled what may have been the first general-quarters alarm on any ship in Pearl Harbor.

★ **December 6, 1941:** "This means war." Statement by President Roosevelt to his aide Harry Hopkins after reading the first 13 parts of the Tokyo message U.S. intelligence intercepted en route to the Japanese ambassadors in Washington, on December 6, 1941. The fourteenth part was yet to come. The copy FDR read was not the official communication which would not be delivered until the following day, but the quick result of U.S. Purple Code-breaking activity. At 0715 the morning of December 6 the U.S. Naval Station on Bainbridge Island, Washington state, intercepted a message from the Foreign Ministry in Tokyo to Ambassador Kichisaburo Nomura in Washington, D.C. and immediately forwarded it to the Navy Department (in Washington) where it was decoded. The message advised Nomura that he would receive a reply to the November 26 U.S. proposals presented by Secretary of State Cordell Hull. Transmission of the fourteen-part message from Japan, (in code but in English!) began at 0800 and was intercepted by the Bainbridge station hardly three minutes later. The U.S. had been reading the Japanese Purple code since 1939 when it intercepted and broke a March message between Tokyo and Berlin.

★ **December 7, 1941:** After reading the 14th and final part of the Japanese message and noting that the 1 P.M. deadline in the nation's capital would be 7:30 A.M. in Hawaii, three intelligence officers correctly concluded that it suggested the outbreak of hostilities against Pearl Harbor was nearly certain. The officers were U.S. Army Colonel Rufus S. Bratton, Commander Arthur H. McCollum, and Lieutenant Commander A D. Kramer, both of Naval Intelligence.

★ **December 7, 1941:** "No, thanks, Betty, I feel I can get it through quickly enough." Reply from General George C. Marshall to Admiral Harold R (Betty) Stark's telephone call offer to send the following message, marked First Priority-Secret to Pearl Harbor through the U.S. Navy's rapid transmission system that Stark had offered.

> *"The Japanese are presenting at 1 P.M. Eastern Standard time today what amounts to an ultimatum. Also they are under orders to destroy their code machine immediately. Just what significance the hour set may have we do not know, but be on the alert accordingly."*

After turning down Stark's offer to send the message via the Navy's rapid transmission system, Marshall had it sent, in code, via Western Union. Admiral Kimmel and General Short did not receive the decoded version until seven hours after the attack had begun.

"EAST WIND RAIN"
"Higashi no kaze ame"

Was this infamous coded message ever actually sent by Tokyo and intercepted by U.S. military intelligence? Absolutely, according to Ralph T. Briggs, the 27-year-old U.S. Navy Petty Officer who reportedly detected and interpreted it and immediately sent it to his superiors. Ellsworth Boyd, a colleague and friend of this author, knew Briggs and discussed the Winds message with him a number of times, eventually writing a feature article which appeared in the November, 2000 issue of *World War II* magazine. That article is presented herewith in toto, courtesy of Ellsworth Boyd.

By Ellsworth Boyd

Each year around December 7, when most people are contemplating the Christmas holidays, students of World War II debate the "what ifs" of the Japanese attack on Pearl Harbor. High on the list of these what ifs is the debate over what would have happened that fateful morning if Pearl's defenders had been ready for the Japanese attack. While many think that the Japanese attack was inevitable, Ralph T. Briggs believes that had events prior to the attack taken a slightly different course, Pearl Harbor would have been ready for the attack, he would have become famous and the United States could have avoided the worst military disaster in its history.

In 1941 Ralph T. Briggs was a 27-year-old U.S. Navy communications intelligence (COMINT) technician working at an intercept station. A Navy man since 1934, first in the reserve and then the Regular Navy, Petty Officer 1st Class Briggs was serving on a cruiser stationed off Panama when he was given secret orders to report to Washington, D.C.

Once he arrived in Washington, he joined seven other radiomen who became crack COMINT operators and along the way "earned a reputation for being oddballs," as Briggs put it. They were named the "On the Roof Gang," a reference to the steel, reinforced concrete blockhouse on top of the old Navy Department Building in Washington, D.C., where they were instructed. Trained by the Office of Naval Intelligence and Department of Naval Communications, as U.S. relations with Japan worsened, the radiomen were warned that they were subject to transfer to the Pacific or Far East at a moment's notice.

Briggs had a superb memory and excelled at his new assignment. He soon became one of the Navy's best at intercepting secret radio messages that were encoded into Tokyo's weather broadcasts. Trained to intercept and read Japanese telegraphic Kata Kana and some Hira Gana (square and round character) writing, Briggs was on watch at the Cheltenham, Md., intercept station early on the morning of December 4, 1941, when he received the startling and unexpected "East Wind Rain" message.

"We had been anticipating the tip-off code phrase for the impending Japanese diplomatic break with Great Britain including attacks on Thailand, Malaya and the Dutch East Indies," Briggs said. "Nishi no kaze hare, meaning 'West Wind Clear.' There also was a possible 'North Wind Cloudy' message, which meant war with Russia. But I did a double take after I copied *Higashi no kaze ame*, which means 'East Wind Rain' in Japanese. This was their code that warned there would be a break with the United States. It was a war warning message."

With his heart pounding and adrenaline flowing, Briggs immediately checked his supervisor's classified instructions to be sure of the message's meaning. Sure enough, this was one of the warning messages sent to select Japanese embassies, consulates and agents, telling them to destroy classified documents and prepare for war with the United States.

First Briggs sent a teletype the East Wind Rain message, which the Navy designated "Winds Code Execute," to Naval Intelligence headquarters in Washington. Then he made two carbon copies plus an entry in his log sheet that included the Japanese characters, the time, date and frequency of the message. Briggs was careful to closely follow procedures for recording such information,

Commander Mitsuo Fuchida, the leader of the air attack on Pearl Harbor, was en route to Hiroshima by plane on August 6, 1945 and saw the mushroom cloud rise above the destroyed city when the U.S. dropped the atom bomb. Fuchida was also aboard the battleship USS Missouri (BB-63) to witness the surrender ceremonies that September. He is believed to be the only person to be present *at all three* historic events. After the war he became a convert to Christianity and frequently visited the Unite States. Photo above was taken the day before Japan surrendered.

–Author's collection

just as he had been trained.

"I was the only COMINT operator on my watch section, consisting of six to seven men-midnight to 8 a.m., who understood the significance of the code *Higashi no kaze ame*," Briggs said. "The message I had intercepted meant war with the United States. After I sent the teletype, I phoned station chief Daryl Wigle, who lived at Cheltenham, and got him out of bed. He came up later and checked the log sheet and the station copy of the intercept and confirmed to me that I came up with 'the real McCoy.'"

The Winds Code Execute message was received in Washington's Navy Department by the watch officer, who immediately notified Lt. Comdr. A.D. Kramer, head of the translation section of the Navy's COMINT unit. When Kramer saw Briggs' message from Cheltenham, he lept from his chair and rushed into Cmdr. Laurence Safford's office with the news. His hands shook as he thrust the long yellow teletype paper at Safford, exclaiming, "This is it!"

Safford was a brilliant and innovative man. Recognized as the Navy's foremost cryptanalyst, he had founded COMINT and designed a new cipher machine that was superior to others in use at the time.

After Kramer handed Safford the message, he read the whole thing, more than 200 words of combined news and weather, with the Winds Code Execute message appearing right in the middle of the text. Safford immediately sent the original teletype containing the message to his superior officer, Rear Admiral Leigh Noyes, Director of Naval Communications. A few moments later, Safford breathed a sigh of relief when verification of "message received" came from Noyes. Flushed with success, Safford a message to his men: "Well done! Discontinue coverage of the target."

Briggs believed that he had hit upon a vital piece of intelligence that was now traveling up through the highest channels in the government. Unfortunately, he was wrong. The information in Briggs' message was not acted upon, and early on the morning of December 7, 1941, Japanese dive bombers launched a surprise attack on Pearl Harbor that destroyed a good portion of the U.S.

Pacific Fleet. Not long after the last Japanese plane had returned to its aircraft carrier and word of the attack reached Washington, heretofore isolationist Americans were clamoring for the heads of those responsible for the surprise.

Rear Admiral Husband E. Kimmel, who was commander in chief of the U.S. Pacific Fleet, and Major General Walter C. Short, the U.S. Army commander at Pearl Harbor, were cast as the disaster's principal scapegoats. In the eyes of many, those two men were responsible for America's 2,403 dead, 1,178 wounded, 19 ships sunk or damaged and 265 aircraft lost. Both Kimmel and military leaders in Washington, were relieved of their commands and reduced in rank on charges of dereliction of duty and for "making errors in judgment."

Kimmel, under a steady barrage of criticism by the public, the military and the Washington bureaucracy, accepted the blame, saying, "I stand ready at any time to accept the consequences of my acts." Although a court-martial was suggested, the Roosevelt administration wanted to avoid making a public spectacle at such a sensitive time. Negative publicity and the disclosure of military secrets were two of many reasons such a procedure was frowned upon. On February 19, 1942, less than two months after Pearl Harbor, Kimmel's request for retirement was granted.

Kimmel, who had resolved to take the blame, completely changed his attitude, however, when someone told him about the Winds Code Execute message. Warned that the people in Washington would destroy him if he sought to publicize the message, Kimmel said: "That's a chance I'll have to take. My mind is made up."

First, Kimmel requested a retroactive court-martial, a request that was promptly denied. Meanwhile, Frank Knox, secretary of the Navy, opened another Pearl Harbor inquiry under the direction of Admiral Thomas C. Hart. Kimmel was instructed *that he* could have counsel, introduce and cross-examine witnesses and present matters pertinent to the inquiry, a major boost to his hopes for vindication.

In the fall of 1943, Kimmel hired a lawyer and began a probe

28

in which Safford would play a major role. Up to that point, Safford had condemned Kimmel for dereliction of duty. But he did a complete turnabout when he discovered that none of the intercepted Japanese messages that had come through his office, including the Winds Code Execute message, had been transmitted to Kimmel prior to the attack. He was outraged by this and became determined to help Kimmel, even if it threatened his own career.

Safford assisted Kimmel's lawyers in their efforts to locate the Winds Code Execute message. Searching through the Navy's secret files, one of Kimmel's legal aides found 43 Japanese messages that should have gone to Kimmel prior to the Pearl Harbor attack. The Winds message was not among them. It was gone, nowhere to be found. No one could say if it had been lost or destroyed. The fact that the message existed was brought out in court, but without actual proof, testimonies carried tittle weight.

The late Percy L. Greaves, Jr., former chief of the minority staff of the Joint Congressional Investigation of the Pearl Harbor Attack, wrote in *The Seeds and Fruits of Infamy*: "Captain* Safford suffered the torments of hell as he stuck to telling the truth. Had it not been for him, the cover-up boys would have buried the truth where it could not be found. It was he who provided Admiral Kimmel with the ammunition to fight. It was he who located and replaced many of the vital intercepts the cover-up boys thought had all been destroyed. He sacrificed his own career, but he refused to sacrifice that of Briggs." (*AUTHOR'S NOTE: at the time of the Pearl Harbor attack Stafford was a Commander. He became a captain later in his career)

Kramer backed up Safford, saying he had seen the intercept, but Noyes denied ever receiving the Winds message. When the Pearl Harbor inquiries were over and Kimmel had been exonerated, one question still lingered: why was Ralph Briggs not called in to testify during at least one of the many hearings? Safford took a beating during cross-examination as the words "alleged" and "actual existence," referring to the Winds message, were repeated by the opposing counsel and some of the Congressional Committee members. Safford's charges of a frame-up of Kimmel were renounced and his career jeopardized.

In a brief meeting, Safford had asked Briggs if he would be willing to appear as a witness at the hearings. Briggs wholeheartedly agreed. But a day later, Captain John S. Harper, commanding officer of the Naval Security Station, called Briggs in and ordered him not to confer with Safford anymore on the Winds subject. He also ordered Briggs not to appear as a witness at any of the hearings. Harper told Briggs, "Perhaps someday you'll understand the reason for this."

Briggs was confused when he left Harper's office. He did not want to disobey orders and jeopardize his career. He felt he had to talk to Safford one more time. Briggs telephoned Safford and told him what happened. The captain expressed regret for Briggs' being called on the carpet. Safford said the decision to prevent Briggs' testimony could have originated from someone on the staff of the joint Congressional Committee. He concluded that a higher authority probably had been responsible for canceling further rebuttal witnesses. Safford never identified the higher authority or what channel had been used to pass orders down to Harper. Why were there such eager efforts to cover up the truth? And what happened to the message?

"I believe Roosevelt knew in advance about a Japanese attack. The trend in America was not to get involved. We even had the America First Committee. We had no incentive, no excuse to get in. We needed to be hit first. There was a cover-up, a fast cover-up. There's no proof that Roosevelt knew something was about to happen, but I think he did. He knew almost everything that was going on. The military bent over to keep Roosevelt informed, from Chief of Staff General George C. Marshall on down. I have no reason to believe that Roosevelt didn't know about an attack. War was imminent. Marshall was running everything, and Secretary of War Henry L. Stimson, Secretary of State Cordell Hull and Secretary of the Navy Henry Knox were there with him.

"Of all the books written about Pearl Harbor," remarked Briggs, "one of the best is *Infamy: Pearl Harbor and Its Aftermath*, by John Toland. Toland, one of America's most respected historians, wrote a revealing, documented account of the events surrounding the attack, including the events surrounding my interception of the East Winds Rain message. In 1986, in the book's seventh paperback edition, Toland added a postscript from his interviews with two prominent Japanese naval officers of that era. They both confirmed that the Winds message was received on the East Coast of the United States on 4 December, 1941"

Briggs' transcription of the acted upon, the commanders at Pearl Harbor could have been alerted to the pending Japanese attack. Had the U.S. Pacific Fleet escaped destruction that Sunday morning, the entire course of the war could have been different, and today Ralph Briggs would probably be as well known as Paul Revere.

AUTHOR'S NOTE: THE OTHER WINDS MESSAGES

The much discussed "East wind, rain" message was actually one of three "winds" messages U.S. codebreakers were on the alert for after November 19, 1941 when the U.S. intercepted an advisory from Tokyo telling its Washington ambassador:

". . .In case of emergency (danger of cutting off our diplomatic relations), and the cutting off of international communications, the following warning will be added in the middle of the daily Japanese language short wave news broadcast.

*(1) **East wind, rain** (Higashi no kaze ame) would mean Japanese and U.S. relations were in danger;*

*(2) **North wind, cloudy** (Kita no kaze kumori) would indicate Japanese and U.S.S.R. relations were in danger;*

*(3) **West wind, clear** (Nishi no kaze hare) would warn that Japanese and British relations were in danger.*

Tokyo also advised: "The above will be repeated five times and included at the beginning and end. Relay to Rio de Janeiro, Buenos Aires, Mexico City, San Francisco". Admiral Kimmel in Hawaii and the 14th Naval District were promptly made aware of the intercepted Nov. 29 "winds" messages.

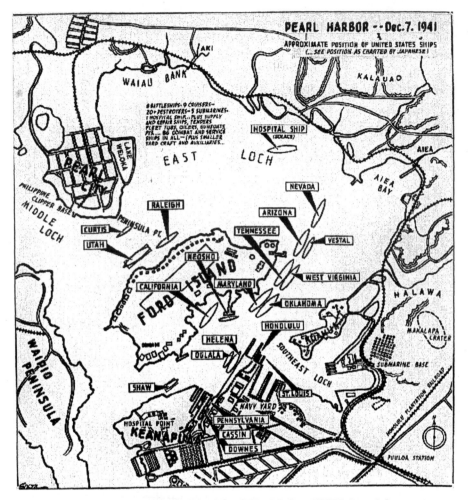

APPROXIMATE POSITION OF U.S. SHIPS: After Pearl Harbor, critics repeatedly asked why the U.S. fleet was in port rather than out at sea. The simple answer was a critical fuel shortage. Admiral Kimmel wanted to keep two task forces at sea at all times while a third remained in port. All fuel had to be brought to Hawaii from the U.S. mainland, and only four of the Pacific fleet's tankers were capable of fueling ships at sea. As an example of fuel consumption, a single destroyer at sea was capable of consuming its entire fuel supply in thirty hours.

MINUTE BY MINUTE EVENTS OF DECEMBER 7, 1941

Considering fast-breaking action commensurate with the Japanese surprise attack on Oahu on Sunday morning, December 7, 1941, it is remarkable that so many individuals had the wherewithal to note precise times of events. The record below, though far from totally inclusive, has been compiled from various published time frames. It is also be noted that the number of enemy aircraft reported shot down exceeds the actual Japanese losses. This is the result of more than one ship firing at the same target and all believing that its fire was responsible for downing the aircraft. In the days after the attack it was determined that one quarter of all guns on all armed ships in Pearl Harbor actually fired at the enemy during the surprise attack.

0342, Ensign R. C. McCloy, officer of the deck aboard the minesweeper USS Condor (Amc-14) observes a white wave to port in restricted waters near the entrance to Pearl Harbor. McCloy and Quartermaster B.C. Utterick alternately watch the wave through binoculars and determine if it was being caused by the submerged periscope of a submarine. He reports the sighting to patrol destroyer USS Ward (DD-139) under the command of Lt. William W. Outerbridge. The message is taken by Lt. (jg) Oscar Goepner who awakens Outerbridge. McCloy thus, became the first American in Hawaii to sight elements of the Japanese Kido Butai attack force. The time in Washington, D.C. is 9:12 A.M. the morning of Dec.7;

0458, Submarine and antitorpedo net gates across the entrance to Pearl Harbor are opened to admit approaching Minesweepers USS Crossbill (AMc-9) and USS Condor (Amc-14). The time is logged with the notation " Gate open--white lights." [The Crossbill would not pass through until ten minutes later and the Condor not until 0532. Furthermore, the gates continued to remain open because the Navy ocean tug USS Keosanqua (AT-38) was expected to enter the harbor at approximately 0615. The protective submarine and antitorpedo nets were open for more than one hour];

0610, 220 miles north of Oahu Admiral Nagumo commences launching from six aircraft carriers 220 miles north of Oahu of the 183 planes in the 1st attack wave. Two aircraft are lost during the takeoff process;

0615, Approximately 200 miles south of Oahu the aircraft carrier USS Enterprise (CV-6) launches the first two of 18 aircraft to scout ahead and then land at Ford Island, Pearl Harbor, before the remaining 16 planes are launched. Estimated time of arrival is two hours later. ETA for Enterprise at Pearl Harbor is eight hours later;

0630, Destroyer USS Ward (DD-139) is alerted that a second submarine sighting near the entrance to Pearl Harbor has been made by the supply ship USS Antares (AKS-3). A U.S. Navy PBY patrol plane is ordered to join the search and hunt;

0645, USS Ward (DD-139) sights and opens fire on what it identifies as a submarine in the restricted defensive sea area and reports hitting the sub's conning tower. The Ward also drops depth charges and the PBY joins in the attack as well;

0653, USS Ward (DD-139) immediately reports the incident to the 14th Naval District watch officer, stating: "We have attacked, fired upon and dropped depth charges upon submarine operating in defensive sea area";

0700, Flight Leader Commander Mitsuo Fuchida heading the first wave attack planes heading towards Oahu, picks up the music being broadcast by radio station KGMB and directs his pilots to home in on the radio station's beam;

0702, U.S. Army Private's George Elliott and Joseph Lockhard, on duty at the Opana Radar Station, observe what they conclude is a flight of unidentified at 132 miles north of Oahu and bearing in;

0710, Elliott reports the sighting by phone to Lt. Kermit Tyler at the Fort Shafter Information Center. The officer had only been posted to his duty 4 days earlier and though he was the only officer on duty at the time, he was still in training. During a lengthy, detailed conversation which lasted about ten minutes, Lt. Tyler told Elliott he believed the aircraft sighting of unidentified planes was, in fact, a flight of B-17s scheduled to arrive from the mainland that morning. Tyler also tells Elliott they should shut down the Opana Radar Station. Nonetheless, Elliott and Lockhard continue to observe and plot incoming flight as they feel it is good training;

Lord Louis Mountbatten, first row center, cousin of the reigning British King, George V, visited the Hawaiian Islands in 1941 as commander of the British aircraft carrier Illustrious. The four American officers seen here with him would forever be linked to December 7, 1941: General Walter C. Short, U.S. Army commander; Admiral Husband E. Kimmel, U.S. Navy commander; General Frederick L. Martin, commander of the Hawaiian Air Force; and Admiral Patrick N. L. Bellinger (see Martin-Bellinger Report).   *--U.S. Army photo*

0715, The message confirming the submarine attack by the USS Ward (DD-139), logged as having been sent at 0653, was delayed in decoding and is finally received by Lt. Comdr. Harold Kaminski, watch officer at the 14th Naval District and thereafter to Commander Vincent Murphy, Admiral Kimmel's duty officer;

0715, The second wave of Japanese attack aircraft, totaling 168 planes, are launched from the six aircraft carriers;

0733, General George C. Marshall's RCA telegram from Washington to General Walter Short in Hawaii, is received and logged in Honolulu. Since the message is not flagged as priority, RCA messenger Tadao Fuchikami simply slots it into the appropriate place for delivery during his route;

0739, The Opana Radar Station loses radar contact with the large blip of aircraft approximately 20 miles off the coast of Oahu. The situation is a result of interference caused by surrounding hills;

0740, First Wave of Japanese aircraft makes visual contact with Oahu's North Shore and begins deployment for attack;

0748, A Japanese Zero strafes the Kaneohe Naval Air Station. This action is approximately seven minutes before the air raid on ships in Pearl Harbor commences;

0749, Commander Fuchida gives the "To, To, To" attack command (abbreviation for *totsugekiseyo*, Japanese word loosely translated to mean "charge") to planes over Pearl Harbor;

0753, First Wave, Commander Fuchida, excited that total surprise has been achieved, orders that the fleet be informed via the prearranged coded signal "Tora, Tora, Tora" (Tiger, Tiger, Tiger);

0753, Almost simultaneously, Ewa Field, the U.S. Marine base on Oahu, is under attack as parked aircraft are bombed and strafed;

0755, Less than two minutes after Fuchida's "Tora, Tora, Tora, and the attack on Ewa, all U.S. military installations on Oahu come under fire as Japanese dive bombers strike airfields at Kaneohe, Ford Island, Hickam, Bellows, Wheeler, and Japanese torpedo planes begin their runs at Battleship Row and other ships in Pearl Harbor;

0755, The former battleship USS Utah (AG-16), by this time in its life functioning as a target ship, is hit by torpedo. The Utah had returned to Pearl Harbor from sea duty on Dec. 5;

0755, Japanese aircraft strafe Fort Kamehameha;

0757, Torpedo detonates beneath the minelayer USS Oglala (CM-4) briefly lifting the ship;

0758, The historic and famous *"AIR RAID PEARL HARBOR. THIS IS NOT DRILL"* message is broadcast from Hawaii; to the world. But who actually sent it? Rear Admiral Patrick Bellinger? Or Lieutenant Commander Logan C. Ramsey? The controversy is explored further on in this book;

0758, The light cruiser USS Helena (CL-50) shudders after an explosion on her starboard side;

0758, The seaplane tender, destroyer, USS Hulbert (AVD-6) takes credit for shooting down an enemy plane;

0759, One of three American submarines at Pearl Harbor, the USS Dolphin (SS-169) commences action against enemy aircraft;

0800, (1330 in Washington) While having lunch, Army Chief of Staff General George C. Marshall learns of the Japanese attack in a telephone call from Colonel John R. Deane, secretary to the General Staff;

0800, Aboard the USS Nevada (BB-36) the battleship's band, under the direction Oden McMillan, begins playing as colors are raised, and continues through the final notes of "The Star Spangled Banner" while under attack. McMillan reportedly picked up the tempo somewhat as enemy fire hit the ship;

0800, A Japanese torpedo misses both the light cruisers USS Raleigh (CL-7) and USS Detroit (CL-8), but it fails to explode, as it passes between them;

0800, The oiler USS Ramapo (AO-12): reports shooting down a Japanese plane;

0800, The scheduled fuel stop at Oahu by a squadron of Army B-17 bombers en route to the Philippines from the mainland, and the advance scouting aircraft from carrier USS Enterprise (CV-6) are both caught between enemy and friendly fire as they attempt to land at Ford Island. The B-17's, from the 38th and 88th Reconnaissance Squadrons, had been stripped of weaponry to conserve fuel;

0802, USS Nevada (BB-36) opens fire on torpedo planes approaching portside, hitting two planes. Single torpedo hits port bow, tearing large huge hole;

0802, The minesweeper USS Grebe (AM-43) identifies incoming aircraft as Japanese;

0802, Patrol gunboat USS Sacramento (PG-19) reports an assist in shooting down an attacking Japanese plane;

0804, Radio station KGMB interrupted its programming with an announcement that military personnel should report for duty at once, but no mention is made of the air raid;

0805, Light cruiser USS Raleigh (CL-7) develops a serious port list after being hit by a torpedo;

0805, Repair ship USS Vestal (AR-4) moored outboard of battleship USS Arizona (BB-39) commences firing at incoming aircraft;

0805, Admiral Husband E. Kimmel, arrives at U.S. Pacific Fleet Headquarters;

0805, Battleship USS California (BB-44) is hit by two torpedoes;

0805, Destroyer USS Blue (DD-387) commences firing at enemy aircraft;

0808, Radio station KGMB again interrupts regular Sunday morning music programming with an announcement that "All Army, Navy, and Marine personnel report to duty";

0808, High level bombers unleash armor piercing, delayed action ordnance from altitude of 10,000 feet, resulting in hits along Battleship Row;

0810, Battleship USS Arizona (BB-39) forward magazines explode, instantly killing hundreds of men. The ship sinks the battleship in less than ten minutes;

0810, (1340 in Washington) President Franklin D. Roosevelt receives a telephone call from Secretary of the Navy Frank Knox telling the President that Pearl Harbor was under an air attack by the Japanese;

0810, USS Nesoho (AO-23) joins in the firing at enemy aircraft;

0812, Army General Walter G. Short orders a message alerting all military personnel in the Pacific Fleet and Washington that, "Hostilities with Japan commenced with air raid on Pearl Harbor";

0813, At Fort Kamehameha on Oahu, U.S. Army troops commence firing at enemy aircraft attacking the base;

0815, Radio station KGMB breaks into its programming for the third time, advising military personnel to report for duty;

0816, U.S. Pacific Fleet Headquarters repeats the message received from General Short, advising all ships that "Hostilities with Japan commenced with an air raid on Pearl";

0817, Destroyer USS Helm (DD-388) is the first destroyer to clear Pearl Harbor and quickly sights a Japanese midget submarine attempting, with difficulty, to enter the harbor. The destroyer fires upon the sub but fails to score a hit. The enemy sub manages to evade the destroyer and escape;

0820, Aboard the mortally wounded battleship USS Arizona (BB-39) all offensive firing ceases;

0825, Battleship USS California (BB-44) begins engaging enemy aircraft;

0825, Firing a BAR (Browning Automatic Rifle) Lt. Stephen Saltzman and Sgt. Lowell Klatt fire at and shot down an attacking Japanese plane strafing Schofield Barracks;

0826, Responding to a call for assistance from Hickam Field, three Honolulu Fire Department civilian firefighters are killed and 6 others are wounded;

0827, Destroyer USS Monaghan (DD-354) gets up sufficient steam pressure to get under way;

0829, Battleship USS California (BB-44) commences a serious list;

0830, Destroyer minesweeper USS Zane (DMS-14) confirms sighting of a submarine inside Pearl Harbor;

0830, Another destroyer, USS Henley (DD-391) gets under way;

0830, Radio station KGMB makes fourth announcement that military personnel should report for duty, but again makes no mention of the attack in progress;

0830, At Bellows Field a single Japanese plane strafes buildings before joining the departing First Wave of the Japanese attack;

0832, Based on the confirmation by the US Zane (DMS-14) U.S. Pacific Fleet Headquarters advises all ships it has reports of a Japanese midget submarine inside Pearl Harbor;

0835, (1405 in Washington) Japanese ambassadors Nomura and Kurusu arrive late at the U.S. State Department for their scheduled meeting with Secretary of State Cordell Hull;

0835, Oiler USS Neosho (AO-23), half loaded with high octane aviation fuel, successfully gets under way to put distance between itself, Battleship Row, and oil tank depot at Ford Island;

0836, Seaplane tender USS Curtiss (AV-4) sights and commences firing at Japanese midget submarine periscope about 700 yards off her starboard quarter;

0838, Japanese midget sub fires torpedo within the confines of Pearl Harbor but the ordnance fails to find a target;

0839, Destroyer USS Monaghan (DD-354) begins firing at, and sets a course directly for, the Japanese midget submarine already under fire from USS Curtiss (AV-4). The destroyer rams the sub and drops depth charges as she passes over it;

===

THE ANNUAL SOCIAL EVENT TO BE SEEN AT ON OAHU

Ann Etzler's Cabaret, a popular annual charity dinner dance was held the evening of December 6, 1941 at the Schofield Officers' Club. It was the last peacetime social event in Hawaii until 1945.

USS Oklahoma (BB-37), which with USS Arizona (BB-39) was one of two battleships permanently lost in the attack, was the first ship in Pearl Harbor hit by a Japanese torpedo (fired by pilot Inichi Goto). Oklahoma received five torpedo hits, which caused her to capsize within fifteen minutes after the attack had begun. BB-37 lost 415 officers and enlisted men. The 29,000-ton, 583-ft. long BB-37 entered service in 1915.　　　*–U.S. Navy photo*

___FACT:___ Joseph C. Grew was the U.S. Ambassador to Japan for nearly a decade and was the ranking member of the diplomatic corps when Pearl Harbor was attacked. Partially deaf, he never managed to master Japanese. However, his wife, Alice, spoke it fluently. She was the granddaughter of Commodore Perry.

0840, Battleship USS Nevada (BB-36) gets under way. It is the only battleship to do so on December 7;

0840, Radio station KGMB finally informs listeners that an air attack was under way and the planes carried the Japanese Rising Sun insignia [NOTE: various sources differ on the number of previous times KGMB interrupted programming because of the attack, but all agree that 0840 was the time it confirmed the attack was by Japanese aircraft].

0850, Second Wave of attacking Japanese aircraft begin deploying over Pearl Harbor and military installations throughout Oahu;

0852, (1452 in Washington) White House Press Secretary Steve Early reads a statement by President Roosevelt to the three major news wire services, Associated Press, United Press International, and International News Service, officially informing the American people and the world: "The Japs have attacked Pearl Harbor, all military activities on Oahu Island. A second air-attack is reported on Manila air and naval bases;"

0853, Aircraft in the Second Wave of the Japanese attack are sighted over Pearl Harbor and the USS Curtiss (AV-4) is among the first ships to commence firing;

0854, Lieutenant Commander Shigekazu Shimazaki, commander of the Second Wave, gives the order to attack;

0855, Destroyers USS Conyngham (DD-371), Tucker (DD-374), and the repair ship USS Medusa (AR-1) commence firing at Second Wave;

0900, Battleship USS California (BB-44) shakes violently from an "undetermined cause", either a bomb or torpedo;

0900, The small seaplane tender USS Avocet (AVP-4) escapes being hit as five bombs fall approximately 50 yards from ship but fail to explode;

0905, A badly shot-up Japanese plane from the Akagi, piloted by Lt. Mimori Suzuki, crashes into a crane aboard the Seaplane tender USS Curtiss (AV-4) after weathering a hail of gunfire;

0907, Battleship USS Pennsylvania (BB-38) hit on starboard side by bomb killing 15 men and setting off fires aboard the USS Cassin (DD-372) and USS Downes (DD-375) berthed near the battleship;

0908, USS Curtiss (AV-4) reports shooting down another plane as it passes over the seaplane tender;

0908, Light cruiser USS Raleigh (CL-7) is hit by bomb that totally penetrates several decks and explodes on harbor bottom, missing more than 3,000 gallons of aviation fuel below decks by approximately ten feet;

0908, Destroyer USS Conyngham (DD-371) shoots down plane that crashes near Schofield Barracks;

0909, Light cruiser USS Helena (CL-50) shoots down dive bomber which crashes near Hospital Point;

0910, Battleship USS Nevada (BB-36), underway and attempting to escape, is deliberately grounded near Hospital Point to avoid being sunk at the entrance and thereby blocking the harbor;

0911, Destroyer USS Dale (DD-353) reports shooting down a Japanese dive bomber;

0913, Seaplane tender USS Curtiss (AV-4) has the remarkable distinction of reporting it shot down three attacking Japanese aircraft in rapid order, two of which were dive bombers;

0930, Ammunition magazines and other ordnance aboard the destroyers USS Cassin (DD-372) and Downes (DD-375) start a repeating series of explosions;

0930, In one of the single most memorable events during the attack, the destroyer USS Shaw (DD-373) experiences a tremendous explosion;

1005, The 72-year-old territorial Governor of Hawaii, Joseph E. Poindexter contacts *The Honolulu Star Bulletin* and other news media to announce that a state of emergency exists for the entire territory of Hawaii. An hour and ten minutes later he reads a Proclamation of Emergency over radio station KGU. At 1625 that afternoon Marshall Law is proclaimed;

1100, Commander Mitsuo Fuchida observes damage the attack has caused to the U.S. fleet at Pearl Harbor and departs area to rejoin the aircraft carrier Kagi. He lands at 1300 and unsuccessfully pleads with Admiral Nagumo for a third wave. Instead, Nagumo withdraws from the area and heads home;

1458, Western Union messenger Tadao Fuchikami delivers the message from Washington, regarding ultimatum from Japan to be given at 1300 Washington time. Decoded it eventually reaches General Short. The attack had been over hours earlier.

★ ★

HALSEY'S GUT FEELINGS UPON RETURNING TO PEARL

When Rear Admiral William F. Halsey stood on the bridge of his flagship, the aircraft carrier USS Enterprise (CV-6), as Captain George Murray guided its return to Pearl Harbor and they saw destruction of the US. Fleet, it filled all present with rage. Halsey blurted out a remark all agreed with: "Before we're through with 'em, the Japanese language will be spoken only in hell!"

AUTHOR'S NOTE: *In the 1950s Halsey was involved in an unsuccessful effort to save the Enterprise from going to the scrap heap in Kearney, NJ. for recycling. By chance, I happened to be at a pier on lunch break the day in 1958 when the Enterprise passed under the 8th St. train bridge in Bayonne, N.J., as it headed up Newark Bay toward the scrap yard.*

"AIR RAID, PEARL HARBOR"
WHO REALLY SENT IT?

In the several decades since the attack, Rear Admiral Patrick Bellinger has been widely credited with the historic 7:58 A.M. message telling the world: "AIR RAID, PEARL HARBOR - THIS IS NO DRILL!" Bellinger is named as the officer who first sent out word of the attack in no less than three historic, well researched and detailed works: Samuel Eliot Morison's epic *The Two-Ocean War*; Walter Lord's *Day of Infamy* and Lieutenant Colonel Eddy Bauer's 24-volume *Illustrated World War II Encyclopedia*.

However, no less than two very credible giants in historical research (and particularly Pearl Harbor), Gordon Prange, in *At Dawn We Slept*, and John Toland in *Infamy*, both credit Lieutenant Commander Logan C. Ramsey with sending the message out, also at 7:58 A.M. In the Ramsey message "NO DRILL" is replaced by "NOT DRILL." It is interesting to note (and add to the confusion) that Ramsey was, coincidentally, with a Lieutenant Richard *Ballinger* near the radio room of the Ford Island command center at this point in the attack and reportedly ran into the room to order radiomen on duty to send out the message. Meanwhile, there are at least two other messages from other sources, similar in content, which were reportedly communicated at approximately the same time: At 7:58 an unidentified caller reached CINCPAC headquarters in Pearl Harbor and stated "Enemy air raid, not drill". At 8 A.M. Commander Vincent Murphy, at CINCPAC, sent out the message "Air raid on Pearl Harbor. This is no drill".

Bellinger is credited with the message that was picked up by a West Coast radio station and carried across the country.

==

ONE MUST TRY TO SAVE FACE, MUSN'T ONE?

Japan formally declared that a state of war existed with the U.S. and British Empire at 1600 EST on December 7, 1941. That was 4 P.M. Washington time, some three hours after the attack.

```
┌─────────────────────────────────────────────────┐
│ Original        U.  NAVAL AIR STATION, KODIAK ALASKA │
│                     NAVAL COMMUNICATIONS          │
│ Heading  NFU N( 03 F L 2 PSL 07L830 GB4 TARI U B1│
│ From:   CINCPAC                    │ Date 7 DEC 41│
│ To:   ALL SHIPS PRESENT AT HAWAIIN AREA.          │
│ Info:             - U R G L . T -                 │
│ DEFERRED unless otherwise checked │ ROUTINE │ PRIORITY │ AIRMAIL │
│      AIRRAID ON PEARLHARBOR X THIS IS NO DRILL    │
└─────────────────────────────────────────────────┘
```

The above, picked up and transmitted by the Naval Air Station in Kodiak, Alaska, injects yet another version of the historic message. Note the inclusion of "ON" between AIRRAID and PEARLHARBOR.

==

WHY JAPAN HAD TWO AMBASSADORS IN WASHINGTON

On August 4, 1941, Kichisaburo Nomura, the Japanese Ambassador to the U.S., requested that Japan send veteran diplomat Saburo Kurusu to Washington as a special envoy to assist with efforts to secure a "final attempt at peace". Kurusu, who as Japanese Ambassador to Germany signed the Tripartite Pact, was thought of with great respect and confidence in Japanese government circles. In addition, he was married to an American woman and spoke idiomatic English, affording him what the Japanese felt was a guarantee that he would not be misunderstood nor misinterpret anything said to him by the Americans.

An aside to the above: As the product of a mixed race marriage, Kurusu's pilot son strongly resembled the Caucasian features of his American mother rather than his Asian father. After being forced to land his damaged plane in a field during the war he was mistaken for an American and brutally killed by irate Japanese villagers.

47

U.S. CONSIDERED JAPAN A FUTURE ENEMY SINCE 1905

The U.S. code name for Japan prior to hostilities was *Orange*. The designation was widely used in nearly all U.S. communications, codes and tactical planning. The United States began considering Japan to be a potential serious threat and possible future enemy after Japan's strong showing in the 1905 Russian-Japanese war. In the 1930s when Japan was at war with China, and war broke out in Europe, the U.S. developed a top secret plan called "Rainbow 5" which outlined offensive military measures the U.S. should take against Japan (including a declaration of war) if Japan threatened British and Dutch colonial interests in the Pacific but had not yet been attacked by Japan.

★ ★ ★ ★ ★ ★ ★ ★ ★ ★ ★ ★ ★ ★ ★ ★ ★ ★ ★ ★

JAPAN CONSIDERED THE U.S. THE SAME WAY SINCE 1909

The Japanese code name for the United States was *Minami*. From early in 1909, Japan's began considering the United States as a potential serious threat and possible future enemy. In the 1930s, as the U.S. expressed its concern over Japanese expansion in the Pacific and its war with China, the Japanese Navy developed a plan called "Yogeki Saskusen" (literally "ambush operation") to lure the U.S. Pacific Fleet out of its anchorage with enough provocation that the U.S. would fire the first shot against Japan. According to the plan, Japanese submarines would then ambush the more powerful U.S. fleet before it could overwhelm Japanese surface ships.

★ ★ ★ ★ ★ ★ ★ ★ ★ ★ ★ ★ ★ ★ ★ ★ ★ ★ ★ ★

TALK ABOUT THE SUPREME INSULTING REJECTION!

In the days and weeks which followed the Japanese attack on Pearl Harbor, diplomatic exchanges of declarations of war between Allied and Axis powers and various sympathizers were relatively rapid and, obviously, accepted. However, the U.S. refused to accept the Slovakia declaration of war on December 12 and the Croat declaration on December 14, much to these countries' frustration, international embarrassment and chagrin.

COMPARATIVE TIMES

Oahu, Hawaii	Washington, D. C.
0001 12:01 A.M. December 7	0531 5:31 A.M.
0030	0600
0130	0700
0230	0800
0342 Japanese sub sighted	0912
0430	1000
0530	1100
0630 Second sub sighted	1200
0702 Opana radar sighting	1232
0730	1300 Japanese deadline
0755 attack begins	1325
0800	1330 Marshall told of attack
0810	1340 FDR told of attack
0930	1500
1030	1600
1130	1700
1230	1800
1330	1900
1430	2000
1530	2100
1630	2200
1730	2300
1830 6:30 P.M. December 7	2400 December 7, Midnight

FACT: Oahu, Hawaii, Radio station KGMB, which normally did not broadcast all night but did at the request of the military, whenever U.S. aircraft were expected, was doing just that in anticipation of an expected flight of B-17s from the mainland on Dec. 6-7, 1941. The approaching aircraft of the Japanese Kido Butai attack force used the radio signal as a guide to Pearl Harbor.

The light cruiser USS Phoenix (CL-46) was the last ship present at Pearl Harbor on December 7, 1941, which was later sunk by enemy action (41 years later!) In 1951 the U.S. Navy sold CL-46, nicknamed "Lucky Phoenix", to Argentina, which renamed it the General Belgrano. Her luck ran out under the Argentine flag when she was torpedoed and sunk on May 2, 1982 by a British submarine during the Falkland Islands War. Above, the Phoenix, which escaped the Japanese attack unharmed, is seen passing the burning USS Arizona (BB-39). During her life in the U.S. Navy, CL-46 spent 15 months in forward fighting areas and earned nine battle stars in 20 different actions. The Phoenix shot down eight torpedo or kamikaze planes attacking her, as well as a Japanese submarine that had fired two torpedos at her. The only wartime loss of human life aboard the Phoenix occurred when a bomb burst in the water close to her. It killed one man and injured four others.   *---U.S. Navy photo*

FACT: The USS Taney (WPG-37), a 327-foot long endurance cutter, remained in U.S. Navy active service till 1986, longer than any other ship present at Pearl Harbor on Dec. 7, 1941.

★ ★ U.S NAVY SHIPS PRESENT ★ ★ AT PEARL HARBOR, 7 DEC. 1941

Of the 145 ships in Pearl Harbor the morning of the attack, 96 were combat vessels and 26 of these were destroyers, the largest number of any single type ship. At 0755 the USS California (BB-44) was the first battleship in Pearl Harbor to sound the general quarters alarm. This happened the same minute that the attack began.

BATTLESHIPS (BB)

Arizona	(BB-39)
California	(BB-44)
Maryland	(BB-46)
Nevada	(BB-36)
Oklahoma	(BB-37)
Pennsylvania	(BB-38)
Tennessee	(BB-43)
West Virginia	(BB-48)

HEAVY CRUISERS (CA)

New Orleans	(CA-32)
San Francisco	(CA-38)

LIGHT CRUISERS (CL)

Detroit	(CL-8)
Helena	(CL-50
Honolulu	(CL-48)
Phoenix	(CL-46)
Raleigh	(CL-7)
St. Louis	(CL-49)

DESTROYERS (DD)

Allen	(DD-66)
Aylwin	(DD-355)

DESTROYERS (DD) CONTINUED

Bagley	(DD-386)
Blue	(DD-387)
Case	(DD-370)
Cassin	(DD-372)
Chew	(DD-106)
Conyngham	(DD-371)
Cummings	(DD-365)
Dale	(DD-353)
Dewey	(DD-349)
Downes	(DD-375)
Farragut	(DD-348)
Helm	(DD-388)
Henley	(DD-391)
Hull	(DD-350)
Jarvis	(DD-393)
McDonough	(DD-351)
Monaghan	(DD-354)
Mugford	(DD-389)
Patterson	(DD-392)
Phelps	(DD-360)
Ralph Talbot	(DD-390)
Reid	(DD-369)
Shaw	(DD-373)
Schley	(DD-103)

DESTROYERS (DD) CONTINUED

Selfridge	(DD-357)
Tucker	(DD-374)
Ward	(DD-139)
Worden	(DD-352)

DESTROYER MINELAYERS (DM)

Breese	(DM-18)
Gamble	(DM-15)
Montgomery	(DM-17)
Preble	(DM-20)
Pruitt	(DM-22)
Ramsay	(DM-16)
Sicard	(DM-21)
Tracy	(DM-19)

DESTROYER MINESWEEPERS (DMS)

Perry	(DMS-17)
Trever	(DMS-16)
Wasmuth	(DMS-15)
Zane	(DMS-14)

MINESWEEPERS (AM)

Bobolink	(AM-20)
Grebe	(AM-43)
Rail	(AM-26)
Tern	(AM-31)
Turkey	(AM-13)
Vireo	(AM-52)

COASTAL MINESWEEPERS (Amc)

Cockatoo	(Amc-8)
Condor	(Amc-14)
Crossbill	(Amc-9)
Reedbird	(Amc-30)

PATROL GUNBOATS (PG)

Sacramento	(PG-19)

SUBMARINES (SS)

Cachalot	(SS-170)
Dolphin	(SS-169)
Narwhal	(SS-167)
Tautog	(SS-199)

MOTOR TORPEDO BOATS (PT)

PT-20; PT-24; PT-28
PT-21; PT-25; PT-29
PT-22; PT-26; PT-30
PT-23; PT-27; PT-42

SEAPLANE TENDERS (AV)

Advocet	(AVP-4)
Swan	(AVP-7)
Curtiss	(AV-4)
Tangier	(AV-8)
Hulbert	(AVD-6)
Thornton	(AVD-11)

COAST GUARD (CG)

Reliance	(USCG)
CG-8	(USCG)

OTHER SHIPS PRESENT

Solace	(AH-5) hospital
Utah	(AG-16) target
Neosho	(AO-23) oiler
Antares	(AKS-3) supplier
Taney	(PG-37) cutter
Chengho	(IX-52) yacht
Vestal	(AR-4) repair ship

OTHER SHIPS PRESENT CONTINUED

Oglala (CM-4) minelayer	
Argone	(AG-31)
Ash	(YN-2)
Sumner	(AG-32)
Castor	(AKS-1)
Cinchona	(YN-7)
Cockenoe	(YN-47)
Dobbin	(AD-3)
Hoga	(YT-146)
Keosangua	(AT-38)
Manuwai	(YFB-17)
Marin	(YN-53)
Medusa	(AR-1)
Navajo	(AT-64)
Nokomis	(YT-142)
Ontario	(AT-13)
Osceola	(YT-129
Pelias	(AS-14)

Pyro	(AE-1)
Ramapo	(AO-12)
Rigel	(AR-11)
Sotoyomo	(YT-9)
Sunnadin	(AT-28)
Tiger	(PC-152)
Vega	(AK-17)
Wapello	(YN-56)
Whitney	(AD-4)
Widgeon	(ASR-11)

Only hull numbers are given for the following:
YG-21; YMT-5; Yna-17;
YO-21; YO-30; YO-43;
YO-44; YP-108; YP-109;
YT-3; YT-119; YT-130;
YT-152; YT-153; YW-16;
YG-15; YG-17

PACIFIC FLEET SHIPS ABSENT DURING ATTACK:

Task Force Eight (consisting of 13 ships): aircraft carrier USS Enterprise (CV-6); cruisers; Salt Lake City (CA-25); North Hampton (CA-26); Chester (CA-27); destroyers: Balch (DD-363); Gridley (DD-380); Craven (DD-382); Dunlap (DD-384); Fanning (DD-385); Benham (DD-397) Ellet (DD-398); McCall (DD-400); and Maury (DD-401).

Task Force Twelve (9 ships): aircraft carrier USS Lexington (CV-2); heavy cruisers, USS Chicago (CA-29); USS Portland (CA 33); USS Astoria (CA-34); destroyers: USS Porter (DD-356); Mahan (DD-364); Drayton (366); Lamson (DD-367); Flusser (DD-368)

Admiral Husband E. Kimmel, Commander in Chief, U.S. Fleet (CINCUS) and Commander in Chief, U.S. Pacific Fleet (CINCPAC), based at Pearl Harbor, Hawaii on 7 December 1941. The blame for being caught off guard fell on Kimmel, more than any other American, military or civilian, associated with the Japanese attack. Yet a majority of U.S. admirals in the Navy at the time felt he received a raw deal. *—U.S. Navy photo*

54

IT COULD HAVE BEEN GENERAL KIMMEL, NOT ADMIRAL

Admiral Husband E. Kimmel came from a Kentucky family with a West Point military tradition. Upon failing to gain admittance to the Point, he tried and succeeded in being admitted to the Naval Academy, where he graduated thirteenth in a class of sixty-two. His wife was the daughter of an admiral who was the brother of Admiral Thomas C. Kinkaid. Kimmel briefly served as an aide to the then Secretary of the Navy, Franklin D. Roosevelt.

★ ★

THEY CAME TOGETHER, AND LEFT TOGETHER

The Navy and Army commanders at Pearl Harbor, Admiral Husband E. Kimmel and General Walter C. Short, assumed their commands within days of each other in February 1941. Kimmel's tour began on February 1, while Short took over on February 7.

★ ★

FIRST FEMALE TO EARN A PURPLE HEART IN THE WAR

U.S. Army Nurse Ann Fox holds the distinction of receiving the first Purple heart presented to a woman in World War II as a result of injuries she received at Hickam Field on December 7, 1941.

★ ★

"PRAISE THE LORD, AND PASS THE AMMUNITION"

Contrary to popular belief, the above battlecry was not the pious and witty creation of Chaplain Howell Forgy aboard the USS New Orleans during the attack on Pearl Harbor. That the good Chaplain Forgy uttered the remark there is no doubt, and it is Forgy who is credited with popularizing the sentiment to the point that it became one of the music industry's early "wartime" hit records. But the first time someone said Praise the Lord, and pass the ammunition was, according to USMC Major Louis E. Fagen, was by a Reverend Dr. Walker during the defense of Londenderry from the forces of King James II. The year was 1689.

USS Nevada (BB-36) was the only battleship to get underway in Pearl Harbor on December 7, 1941, attempting to escape the harbor. However, to avoid being sunk at the entrance and thereby blocking the harbor, Nevada was deliberately grounded near Hospital Point. The 29,000-ton, 583 ft. long USS Nevada (BB-36) entered service in 1916. *–U.S. Navy photo*

===

FACT: Two leading air officers in the Japanese attack on Pearl Harbor wore red underwear and red shirts in order to conceal any injuries they might sustain during the raid. Flight Leader Mitsuo Fuchida, the overall attack commander, and Lieutenant Commander Shigemaru Murata, leader of the torpedo bombers in the first wave, reasoned that if they were wounded blood wouldn't show up against the red. Their intention was to prevent demoralizing other flying officers.

Log of the USS Nevada (BB-36)

This piece of personal history was provided to the author by Joan Mecteau, daughter of Nevada crewmember Cecil (Mac) Wilburt McCloud. In the interest of presenting the log as a pure historical document, no editorial effort has been made to edit it. Consequently the exact text of the original is reproduced here verbatim as written (sic) the day of the attack, replete with misspellings, grammatical, punctuation and capitalization errors.

SUNDAY, DECEMBER 7th 1941
Aerial attack by Japanese Forces.

Rough Summary of Medical Departments Duties Performed
Befor, During and after Action.

    1. Log Summary of U.S.S. NEVADA.

0801 Condition Zed set
0802 Machine guns opened fire on torpedo planes approaching on
      port beam.
0803 Torpedo struck on bow, port, frame #40.
0806 Several bombs fell close aboard.
0809 ARIZONA afire.
0830   Bomb hit bridge, penetrated to forecastle deck resulting
      severe shock, flareback and water leakage. Fire on bridge and
      below.
0835 Smoke and gas in fire-room.
0840 Underway on various courses at vairious speeds conforming
      to channel.
0850 Concentrated air attack, several hits on forecastle exploding
      below decks- 1 or 2 near crews galley. Fire forward and amid-
      ships.
0900 Grounded bow of ship intentionally between floating dry,
dock and channel Buoy # 24, starboard side to beach. Personnel
casualties transferred to Repair #1.(Crews reception Room).

Log of the USS Nevada (BB-36) --CONTINUED

0907 Bomb hit forecastle killing Chief Boatswain E.J. Hill, USN, (blown overboard) and an unknown number of men.

0920 Tugs fight fire in wardroom country and forward. Casualties transferred to the U.S.S. Solace and Naval Hospital, Pearl Harbor.

1015 No progress in overcoming fires forward. Stern began swinging to middle channel.

1020 Tugs pushed stern towards beach to prevent blocking of channel.

1035 Ship floated off beach and drifted toward Western side of channel. Air attack ceased.

1045 Ship grounded on western side of channel Bouy $9 15 yards off starboard bow.

MAJOR HITS:

(1)   Boat Deck aft of stack.
(2)   Forward of stack thru bridge, thru Captains cabin, signal bridge.
(3)   Forecastle (2) Frame 15.
(4)   Torpedo, port bow, frames 38 to 65.
(5)   Bomb, port bow, frame #25.

FORWARD BATTLE DRESSING STATION:

Central station ordered station secured when smoke filled compartment. Six men or more overcome who were evacuated and revived except one CPO who died from suffocation or better still an acute heart attack as he died with gas mask on, sitting at table.

AMIDSHIPS BATTLE DRESSING STATION:

After lull in battle, about 8 to 10 burn cases treated, several chest wounds and one amputation of foot. One shattered jaw.

AFTER BATTLE DRESSING STATION:

After lull in battle, about 24 cases of burns, fractures, gunshot wounds, etc. were treated.

THE ODDEST U.S. NAVY SHIP AT PEARL HARBOR

The distinction of being considered the oddest and most unlikely ship to be recognized as a commissioned U.S. Navy ship at Pearl Harbor, or anywhere else for that matter, goes to the USS Chengho (IX-52), a Chinese junk motor yacht that the Navy had acquired on July 23, 1941 for use by the 14th Naval District.

★ ★

THE FIRST OF THE ALLIES JOINS IN THE FIGHT

The Dutch passenger liner Jagersfontein, which arrived at the entrance to Honolulu Harbor at 0900 the morning of December 7, 1941, from the U.S. West Coast, became the first representative of America's Allies to engage the enemy when at 0915 she returned fire to Japanese aircraft overhead. The entire crew, and several passengers, later gave badly needed blood at various hospitals.

★ ★

LBJ TRADED HIS HOUSE SEAT FOR NAVY BLUES

The first member of the House of Representatives to enlist in the armed forces (Navy) after the attack on Pearl Harbor was Congressman Lyndon Baines Johnson (D-Texas). After the war he was elected to the United States Senate, became Senate Majority Leader, was elected Vice President in 1960 to John F. Kennedy, and became President on November 22, 1963.

★ ★

SLOW DOWN, BUDDY, THERE'S A WAR ON

The cruiser USS St. Louis (CL-49), which ran at twenty-two knots in an eight-knot zone in order to clear the channel at 10:04 A.M. was the last U.S. ship to sortie in Pearl Harbor on December 7, 1941. She immediately had to take evasive action to avoid two torpedoes fired from a Japanese midget submarine. The fish struck the coral reef near the channel entrance, and St. Louis returned fire at the sub, believing they hit the conning tower.

WHERE SOME PEOPLE WERE ON DEC. 7

Paul W. Tibbets, pilot of the B-29 Enola Gay that would drop the atom bomb on Hiroshima three-and-a-half years later, was piloting a Douglas A-20 bomber heading for Hunter Field near Savannah, Georgia. As Japanese pilots heading for Oahu had done hours earlier, Tibbets honed in on a radio station to get a fix with his radio compass. The Savannah station interrupted Glenn Miller's hit of the day, "Chattanooga Choo Choo", with the news of the attack.

Jackie Robinson, future baseball Hall of Famer. Contrary to a widely held misconception Robinson was *not* in Pearl Harbor at the time. The 22-year-old Robinson had been working in Honolulu on a construction job during the week and playing weekend football with the Honolulu Bears. When the season ended he booked ship passage to California, departing Hawaii on Friday, December 5. That Sunday morning he was playing cards on deck when he noticed crew painting porthole windows black, and learned of the attack.

Daniel Inouye, future U.S. Senator, was a high school student in Hawaii. Seeing red "meatball" on the wings of attacking aircraft he remembered thinking "Those dirty Japs." As soon as he was able Inouye joined the Army. He lost an arm in combat. Upon returning home after the war, and wearing his uniform, he was refused a haircut. (See related item on Inouye elsewhere in this book)

John F. Kennedy, future U.S. President, was a U.S. Navy Ensign. He was among the crowd of 27,000 at Griffith Stadium in Washington, D.C., enjoying a football game between the Redskins and Eagles. As the game progressed newsmen in the press box became aware of the attack. However, no announcement of the attack was ever made over the stadium's speakers because it was "against the policy of the Redskins management to broadcast non-sport news over the stadium's public address system." Redskins owner G.P. Marshall stated.

The 20 Largest Battleships in World War II

Ship and Country	Gross Tonnage	Length (feet)
Yamato, Japan	72,809 (a)	862
Musashi, Japan	72,809 (b)	862
Iowa, U.S. (BB-61)	55,710	887
New Jersey, U.S. (BB-62)	55,710	887
Missouri, U.S. (BB-63)	55,710	887
Wisconsin, U.S. (BB-64)	55,710	887
Bismarck, Germany	50,153	823
Tirpitz, Germany	50,153	823
Richelieu, France	47,500	812
Jean Bart, France	47,500	812
Hood, Great Britain	46,200	860
North Carolina, U.S. (BB-55)	44,800	729
Washington, U.S. (BB-56)	44,800	729
King George V, Great Britain	44,780	754
Prince of Wales, Great Britain	44,780	754
Duke of York, Great Britain	44,780	754
Anson, Great Britain	44,780	754
Howe, Great Britain	44,780	754
Nagato, Japan	42,785	725
Mutsu, Japan	42,785	725

(a) Yamato and Musashi were the same size but Yamato was the only battleship with 18-inch guns. She was sunk after three hours of bombing and torpedo attacks during the Okinawa campaign in April 1945. Despite their size the guns were considerably less accurate than the 16-inch guns of the four American Iowa class battleships.

(b) It took 20 torpedo hits and 17 bombs to sink the Musashi during the Battle of Leyte Gulf.

The USS Tennessee (BB-43) and USS California (BB-44), at 40,500 tons and 624 feet long, would rank 21st and 22nd on the above list.

USS Pennsylvania (BB-38) was absent from Battleship Row during the attack and sustained little damage. She is seen here charging forward in the Philippines in 1945.　*–U.S. Navy photo*

THE EVENTUAL DISPOSITION OF ALL U.S. BATTLESHIPS, 1895-1944

Numbers following a ship's name (-2, -3 etc.) indicate how many other U.S. Navy ships previously carried that name. Asterisks in the "Fate" column note other information at the end of the list.

Hull # and name	Commissioned	Tonnage	Length	Fate
(no#) USS Maine	1895	6.315		sunk
(no#) Texas	1895	6,315		target 1911
BB-1 USS Indiana	1895	10,288	351	scrap 1924
BB-2 USS Massachusetts	1896	10,288	351	target 1925
BB-3 USS Oregon	1896	11,688	351	scrap 1956
BB-4 USS Iowa	1897	11,346	360	scrap 1923
BB-5 USS Kearsarge	1900	11,540	375	scrap 1955
BB-6 USS Kentucky	1900	11,520	375	scrap 1924
BB-7 USS Illinois	1901	11,565	368	scrap 1956
BB-8 USS Alabama	1900	11,565	374	scrap 1924
BB-9 USS Wisconsin	1901	11,564	373	scrap 1922
BB-10 USS Maine-2	1902	12,846	393	scrap 1923
BB-11 USS Missouri-3	1903	13,500	393	scrap 1922
BB-12 USS Ohio-3	1904	12,723	393	scrap 1923
BB-13 USS Virginia-4	1906	14,980	441	target 1923
BB-14 USS Nebraska	1907	16,094	441	scrap 1923
BB-15 USS Georgia	1906	14,948	441	scrap 1923
BB-16 USS New Jersey	1906	14,948	441	target 1923
BB-17 USS Rhode Island	1906	14,948	441	scrap 1923
BB-18 USS Connecticut	1906	16,000	456	scrap 1923
BB-19 USS Louisiana	1906	16,000	456	scrap 1923
BB-20 USS Vermont-2	1907	16,000	456	scrap 1923

FACT: The USS Nevada (BB-36) and USS Oklahoma (BB-37) were the first built to burn fuel oil and the Nevada had the Navy's first geared turbine propulsion system.

U.S. BATTLESHIPS, 1895-1944 continued

Hull # and name	Commissioned	Tonnage	Length	Fate
BB-21 USS Kansas-2	1907	16,000	456	scrap 1923
BB-22 USS Minnesota-2	1907	16,000	456	scrap 1923
BB-23 USS Mississippi-2	1908	13,000	382	sold 1914*
BB-24 USS Idaho-2	1908	13,000	382	sold 1914*
BB-25 USS New Hampshire-2	1908	16,000	456	scrap 1923
BB-26 USS South Carolina-4	1910	16,000	452	scrap 1924
BB-27 USS Michigan-2	1910	16,000	452	scrap 1924
BB-28 USS Delaware-6	1910	20,380	518	scrap 1931
BB-29 USS North Dakota	1910	20,000?	518	scrap 1931
BB-30 USS Florida-5	1911	21,825	521	scrap 1931
BB-31 USS Utah	1911	21,826	521	sunk 1941*
BB-32 USS Wyoming-3	1912	27,243	562	scrap 1947*
BB-33 USS Arkansas-3	1912	27,243	562	sunk 1946*
BB-34 USS New York-5	1914	27,000	573	sunk 1948*
BB-35 USS Texas-2	1914	27,000	573	memorial
BB-36 USS Nevada-2	1916	29,000	583	sunk 1948*
BB-37 USS Oklahoma	1916	29,000	583	sunk 1941
BB-38 USS Pennsylvania	1916	33,400	608	sunk 1948*
BB-39 USS Arizona-2	1916	33,400	608	sunk 1941*
BB-40 USS New Mexico	1918	33,400	624	scrap 1947
BB-41 USS Mississippi-3	1917	33,000	624	scrap 1956
BB-42 USS Idaho-4	1919	33,000	624	scrap 1947
BB-43 USS Tennessee-5	1920	40,500	624	scrap 1959
BB-44 USS California-3	1921	40,500	624	scrap 1959
BB-45 USS Colorado-3	1928	33,590	624	scrap 1969
BB-46 USS Maryland-3	1921	33,590	624	scrap 1959
BB-48 USS West Virginia	1923	33,590	624	scrap 1959
BB-55 USS North Carolina-3	1941	44,800	729	memorial

FACT: The USS West Virginia (BB-48) was the newest U.S. battleship in the Pacific when Pearl Harbor was attacked. She was commissioned in 1923.

U.S. BATTLESHIPS, 1895-1944 continued

Hull # and name	Commissioned	Tonnage	Length	Fate
BB-56 USS Washington-8	1941	44,800	729	scrap 1961
BB-57 USS South Dakota-2	1941	42,000	680	scrap 1962
BB-58 USS Indiana-2	1942	42,000	680	scrap 1964
BB-59 USS Massachusetts	1942	42,000	680	memorial
BB-60 USS Alabama	1942	55,248		memorial
BB-61 USS Iowa	1943	55,248	887	(pending)
BB-62 USS New Jersey	1943	55,248	887	memorial
BB-63 USS Missouri	1944	55,248	887	memorial
BB-64 USS Wisconsin	1944	55,248	887	(pending)
BB-47 (USS Washington)	Cancelled			
BB-65 USS Illinois	Cancelled			
BB-66 USS Kentucky	Cancelled			
BB-67 USS Montana				
BB-68 USS Ohio				
BB-69 USS Maine				
BB-70 USS New Hampshire				
BB-71 USS Louisiana				

Five Montana class ships, from BB-67 through BB-71 were also cancelled. They would have been: 65,000 tons and 903 ft. in length

==

(BB-23) sold to Greece, renamed Lemo, sunk by Germans in 1941
(BB-24) sold to Greece, renamed Kilkis, sunk by Germans in 1941
(BB-31) reclassified target ship (A-16), sunk at Pearl Harbor,
         now a memorial
(BB-32) utilized as a gunnery training ship throughout WWII
(BB-33) sunk in Bikini atom bomb test
(BB-34) survived Bikini atom bomb test, sunk by gunfire in 1948
(BB-36) survived Bikini atom bomb test, sunk by gunfire in 1948
(BB-38) survived Bikini atom bomb test, sunk by gunfire in 1948
(BB-37) sunk at Pearl Harbor
(BB-39) sunk at Pearl Harbor, now a memorial

==

FACT: The USS Pennsylvania (BB-38) and USS Arizona (BB-39) were the first U.S. battleships to exceed 600 ft. in length.

PRESIDENT FRANKLIN D. ROOSEVELT'S DEC. 8

"DATE OF INFAMY"

ADDRESS TO JOINT SESSION OF CONGRESS

The speech was slightly more than six minutes in length.
Congress voted favorably on it in less than an hour.

Yesterday, Dec. 7, 1941 - a date which will live in infamy - the United States of America was suddenly and deliberately attacked by naval and air forces of the Empire of Japan.

The United States was at peace with that nation and, at the solicitation of Japan, was still in conversation with the government and its emperor looking toward the maintenance of peace in the Pacific.

Indeed, one hour after Japanese air squadrons had commenced bombing in Oahu, the Japanese ambassador to the United States and his colleagues delivered to the Secretary of State a formal reply to a recent American message. While this reply stated that it seemed useless to continue the existing diplomatic negotiations, it contained no threat or hint of war or armed attack.

It will be recorded that the distance of Hawaii from Japan makes it obvious that the attack was deliberately planned many days or even weeks ago. During the intervening time, the Japanese government has deliberately sought to deceive the United States by false statements and expressions of hope for continued peace.

The attack yesterday on the Hawaiian islands has caused severe damage to American naval and military forces. Very many American lives have been lost. In addition, American ships have been reported torpedoed on the high seas between San Francisco and Honolulu.

Yesterday, the Japanese government also launched an attack against Malaya.

Last night, Japanese forces attacked Hong Kong.
Last night, Japanese forces attacked Guam.
Last night, Japanese forces attacked the Philippine Islands.
Last night, the Japanese attacked Wake Island.
This morning, the Japanese attacked Midway Island.

Japan has, therefore, undertaken a surprise offensive extending throughout the Pacific area. The facts of yesterday speak for themselves. The people of the United States have already formed their opinions and well understand the implications to the very life and safety of our nation.

As commander in chief of the Army and Navy, I have directed that all measures be taken for our defense.

Always will we remember the character of the onslaught against us. No matter how long it may take us to overcome this premeditated invasion, the American people in their righteous might will win through to absolute victory.

I believe I interpret the will of the Congress and of the people when I assert that we will not only defend ourselves to the uttermost, but will make very certain that this form of treachery shall never endanger us again.

Hostilities exist. There is no blinking at the fact that that our people, our territory and our interests are in grave danger.

With confidence in our armed forces - with the unbounding determination of our people - we will gain the inevitable triumph - so help us God.

I ask that the Congress declare that since the unprovoked and dastardly attack by Japan on Sunday, Dec. 7, a state of war has existed between the United States and the Japanese empire.

At the outbreak of war on December 7, 1941, Japan had more than 3,500 aircraft vs. fewer than 1,300 total Allied aircraft in the war area of the Pacific. The B-17 above was on the ground at Hickham field when it was destroyed. Note photographer's pith helmet and equipment box on tarmac. *–U.S. Navy photo*

==

U.S. HAD LARGEST NAVY IN THE WORLD BY END OF WAR

By the end of the war the United States had the largest navy in the world, numbering 19,000 ships of all types. The combined total of navy ships for all other combatant nations (both Allied and Axis) was just over 5,000 ships. New Zealand, with four ships, was the smallest navy. The U.S. Navy had eight aircraft carriers when it entered the war on December 7, 1941. By the end of the war, less than four years later, the U.S. had 121 flattops (including escort carriers). Japan added 15 aircraft carriers during the war but by the time the atom bomb was dropped on Hiroshima they had two left.

FIRST U.S. SHIPS WERE ATTACKED BY JAPAN IN 1937

On December 12, 1937, while Japan was at war with China but almost two years before war broke out in Europe, the U.S. Navy gunboat Panay (PR-5) and three ships belonging to an American oil company were bombed by aircraft while at anchor in the Yangtze River between Nanking and Wuhu, China. Four British gunboats also came under fire. Two sailors and a civilian were killed and 74 people were injured on the American ships. The clearly marked U.S. gunboat, which had entered service in 1928, came under attack from six Japanese aircraft at 1:38 p.m. The Japanese, who had been at war since invading China in 1931, apologized to both the U.S. and the British for the "mistake" and actually paid the U.S. more than $2.2 million in damages as a settlement of the Panay incident However, less than two months after the attack on Pearl Harbor the Japanese government bestowed the Kinshi Kinsho Medal to Colonel Mngoro Hashimoto, the officer a U.S. Navy court of inquiry determined had given the order for the attack on the Panay.

★ ★

JAPAN BOMBED SECOND U.S. GUNBOAT BEFORE DEC. 7

The first U.S. Navy ship hit by Japanese gunfire in 1941 was the river gunboat USS Tutuila (PG-40), on July 30, more than *four months before Pearl Harbor.* A single bomb from one of 26 Japanese navy planes attacking Chunking, China. hit the vessel. Japan apologized the following day, saying it was an accident.

★ ★

FIRST U.S. SHIP SUNK BEFORE PEARL HARBOR IN 1941

The first U.S. ship sunk by German U-boats in 1941 was the freighter SS Robin Moor on May 21, 1941, *almost seven months before Pearl Harbor.* She was torpedoed in the South Atlantic en route to South America. U.S. President Franklin D. Roosevelt, however, didn't publicly comment on the sinking of the SS Robin Moor until a month later, when on June 20 he termed the attack "the act of an international outlaw."

A HINT THE UNITED STATES WAS PREPARING FOR WAR?

The U.S. placed the largest peacetime naval procurement order of all time on September 9, 1940, when it awarded contracts for 210 ships, including seven battleships and 12 aircraft carriers.

★★★★★★★★★★★★★★★★★★★★★

U.S. WAS IN UNDECLARED WAR SINCE MARCH, 1941

The first U.S. military protection for U.S. merchant ship convoys in the North Atlantic, consisting of aircraft and destroyers, was instituted on March 1, 1941.

★★★★★★★★★★★★★★★★★★★★★

U.S. DEPTH CHARGED U-BOAT 8 MONTHS BEFORE WAR

The first U.S. Navy ship to fire a shot in anger at a German ship was the destroyer USS Niblack (DD-424) on April 10, 1941, *eight months before Pearl Harbor*. The incident occurred just after the Niblack rescued survivors from a torpedoed Dutch merchantman south of Iceland. The Niblack's sonar detected a submarine and the destroyer dropped depth charges. According to the Niblack's log, the captain believed the U-boat managed to leave the area.

★★★★★★★★★★★★★★★★★★★★★

U.S. ANTAGONIZED GERMANY BEFORE PEARL HARBOR

The first U.S. Navy escort protection for British ships leaving U.S. and Canadian North American ports in convoys commenced on September 17, 1941, *less than three months before the Japanese surprise attack on Pearl Harbor and U.S. entry into the war..*

★★★★★★★★★★★★★★★★★★★★★

LAST U.S. SHIP SUNK BY ENEMY BEFORE PEARL HARBOR

The last American ship to be sunk before the United States entered the war was the merchantman SS Sagadahoc, which was torpedoed by a German U-boat in the South Atlantic on December 3, 1941, *four days before Pearl Harbor.*

U.S. SHIP SUNK BY GERMAN MINE BEFORE THE WAR

The first U.S. ship sunk after war began in Europe was the merchantman SS City of Rayville, which struck a mine in the Bass Strait off Cape Otway, Australia. on November 8, 1940. This was *more than a year before Pearl Harbor* and the U.S. entry into World War II. The minefield had been laid by the German raider Penguin one of 10 warships disguised as merchant ships.

The Pinguin became the first German raider sunk when its cargo of 130 mines exploded after being hit by eight-inch shells from the British cruiser Cornwall on May 8, 1941, in the Indian Ocean.

★ ★

115 U.S. SAILORS KILLED BEFORE PEARL HARBOR

The first sinking of a U.S. Navy ship in 1941 occurred on October 31, *38 days before the Japanese attacked Pearl Harbor.* But it wasn't the Japanese this time. The incident occurred when a German U-boat torpedoed the destroyer USS Reuben James (DD-245) off Iceland. One hundred and fifteen men, including the captain and all officers, were lost. Though the sinking fired emotions throughout the U.S., the "Rube", as the destroyer was known, was in clear violation of U.S. neutrality since she was assisting British warships escorting a convoy of merchantmen from Halifax.

★ ★

KIDO BUTAI? WHAT DID THE NAME MEAN?

During a 1989 conversation with this author, Mari Michener, the Japanese-American wife of best-selling author, James Michener, explained Kido Butai (the Japanese attacking group's identification name used for the surprise attack on Pearl Harbor) as meaning "attacking force, or strike force" but added that there is no exact translation to English.

FACT: The only U.S. warship that was present at both Pearl Harbor on December 7, 1941, and at Normandy on D-Day, June 6, 1944, was the battleship USS Nevada (BB-36).

11 U.S. SAILORS KILLED BEFORE PEARL HARBOR

The first U.S. military casualties from hostile action came *nearly two months before Pearl Harbor.* Eleven sailors aboard the USS Kearny (DD-432) were killed when the destroyer, escorting a British convoy off Iceland, was torpedoed by a U-boat,. That same day a U.S. merchantman, the Lehigh, was sunk off the African coast.

★ ★ ★ ★ ★ ★ ★ ★ ★ ★ ★ ★ ★ ★ ★ ★ ★ ★ ★ ★

HEY! THIS SPY BUSINESS ISN'T SO TOUGH AFTER ALL

The Japanese Consul General in Hawaii, Kiichi Gunji, collected details requested by Tokyo about the size, numbers and movements of the U.S. fleet from information which regularly appeared in the news pages of Honolulu newspapers. This included the names and exact arrival and departure times of all U.S. fleet ships. Such data, considered public information in Hawaii, became classified the moment it arrived in Japan. In addition, the Japanese consulate's treasurer, Kohichi Seki, used a copy of Jane's Fighting Ships to scout and identify vessels of the fleet.

★ ★ ★ ★ ★ ★ ★ ★ ★ ★ ★ ★ ★ ★ ★ ★ ★ ★ ★ ★

AT LEAST SHE WAS CONSISTENT IN TWO WARS

The only Member of Congress to vote "no" on December 8, 1941 when President Roosevelt asked the Joint Session of the House and Senate for a declaration of war against Japan was Rep. Janet Rankin (R-Montana). She had also voted "no" against President Woodrow Wilson's request to Congress for a declaration of war with Germany in 1917.

★ ★ ★ ★ ★ ★ ★ ★ ★ ★ ★ ★ ★ ★ ★ ★ ★ ★ ★ ★

EVEN SO, MITSUO, IT DOESN'T MAKE _YOU_ AN ARIAN

Commander Mitsuo Fuchida, the officer whose "Tora! Tora! Tora!" message confirmed to the Japanese that complete surprise had been achieved, admired Adolf Hitler so much that he grew a toothbrush mustache.

MIDGET SUBMARINES? HOW SMALL WERE THEY?

The Japanese two-man midget submarines really were small by any standards. They measured some 45 feet in length and only 12 feet in height from the top of the conning tower to the base of the hull. In tests, underwater speed was officially reported at 19 knots. Each carried two torpedoes and were launched from Japanese I-class fleet submarines between seven and 12 miles from Pearl Harbor starting at 0100 December 7. The submarine in the Navy Department photo above is identified as "a captured 2-man Japanese submarine" yet it appears to be somewhat longer than 45 feet. Japan's first submarine of relatively normal size for the time, was the 215 ft. I-21, which they built from Italian plans. Launched in 1919, she carried a 45 man crew and was armed with five 18 inch torpedo tubes.

===

ONLY ONE OF A KIND, IN THE SILENT SERVICE

The only U.S. Navy submariner wounded in the December 7 attack was Seaman Second Class G. A. Myers, who was hit by Japanese aircraft fire while aboard the USS Cachalot (SS-170). There were four U.S. submarines present in Pearl Harbor on December 7, 1941. In addition to the Cachalot, the others were: Dolphin (SS-169); Narwhal (SS-167); and Tautog (SS-199).

AND THE FIRST JAPANESE PRISONER OF WAR IS . . .

U.S. Army Sergeant David M. Akui captured the commander of a midget submarine that had difficulties and drifted near the Kaneohe-Bellows Field area of Oahu, Hawaii, on December 7, 1941. Unsuccessful in an effort to scuttle the boat, and weakened from exhaustion, Ensign Kazuo Sakamaki passed out in the water and awoke on a beach with Sergeant Akui standing over him. The incident took place late in the evening of the attack, making Sakamaki prisoner of war #1.   *–U.S. Navy photo*

FORTUNATE DECISION BY PRESIDENT ROOSEVELT

During a meeting in The White House with President Franklin Delano Roosevelt on June 9, 1941, Pacific Fleet Commander Admiral Husband E. Kimmel asked his Commander-in-Chief that the battleships USS North Carolina (BB-55) and USS Washington (BB-56) be added to the fleet stationed at Pearl Harbor. Kimmel's reasoning was based, in part, on the fact that Japan at the time had more battleships in the Pacific than the U.S. did. Fortunately, FDR did not comply.

★ ★

YAMAMOTO'S "MARCH INTO WASHINGTON" REMARK

"To make victory certain, we would have to march into Washington and dictate the terms of peace in the White House". Taken out of context, the above statement was made by Admiral Isoroku Yamamoto in a letter to Japanese ultranationalist Ryoichi Sasakawa prior to the Pearl Harbor attack. The excerpt was later used by U.S. nationalists to foster the belief that Yamamoto in- tended to invade the U.S. and capture Washington, D.C. In its entirety, the paragraph was actually a sarcastic cut at Japan's extreme right. Yamamoto was telling them the U.S. was not a hollow giant. It continued: "I wonder if our politicians, among whom armchair arguments about war are being glibly bandied about in the name of state politics, have confidence as to the final outcome and are prepared to make the necessary sacrifices?"

★ ★

NO MONKEY'S UNCLE, THIS JAPANESE ADMIRAL

Rear Admiral Chuichi Hara, commander of the Fifth Carrier Division, which included the aircraft carriers Shokaku and Zuikaku, was nicknamed King Kong by his own sailors. He was one of three carrier division commanders who participated in the attack on Pearl Harbor. On the eve of the Pearl Harbor attack Hara reportedly instructed his pilots to strictly follow the rules of war and only strike military targets.

HOW THE U.S. PACIFIC FLEET CAME TO BE IN HAWAII

The U.S. Navy ships that were in Pearl Harbor left the United States West Coast for maneuvers around Hawaii on April 2, 1940. On May 7, exactly 19 months before the Japanese attack, President Roosevelt sealed its fate by ordering it to remain indefinitely in Hawaii.

★ ★

PEARL HARBOR: A "GOD-DAMNED MOUSETRAP"?

Admiral Husband E. Kimmel's predecessor as U.S. Navy commander in Hawaii was Admiral James O. Richardson, whom Kimmel replaced in February, 1941, ten months before the surprise Japanese attack. Richardson's outspoken opinion of Pearl Harbor's long, narrow channel entrance that required capital ships to enter one at a time was that it amounted to a "God-damned mousetrap." Richardson spent the remainder of his Navy career at a desk job.

★ ★

HISTORIC GOOD LUCK FLAG FOR THE SURPRISE ATTACK

The same flag that had flown in on Admiral Hehachiro Togo's ship in the 1905 Japanese victory over the Russians, was raised on the aircraft carrier Akagi on December 6, 1941 as a good luck omen.

★ ★

MacARTHUR'S UNPREPAREDNESS WAS NOT PUNISHED

Justified or not, General Walter G. Short and Admiral Husband E. Kimmel were both quickly sacked in the aftermath of Pearl Harbor for failing to be prepared. Yet General Douglas MacArthur did not suffer a similar fate after the Japanese attacked U.S. military installations in the Philippines approximately eight hours after Pearl Harbor. As was the case at airfields on Oahu, the Japanese found U.S. military planes parked on the ground to be easy targets.

AUTHOR'S NOTE: *Douglas MacArthur was a sixth cousin of President Franklin D. Roosevelt and an eighth cousin of Prime Minister Winston Churchill. All three had a common ancestor, Sarah Barney Belcher of Taunton, Massachusetts.*

Major General Walter C. Short was promoted to Lt. General and took command of the Hawaii Department Feb. 7, 1941.

100 PERCENT AS AMERICAN AS APPLE PIE

The most decorated World War II veteran ever elected to Congress was Sen. Daniel K. Inouye (D-Hawaii), a third generation American of Japanese ancestry. As a 16-yr. old high school student in Hawaii on Sunday morning Dec. 7, 1941, he was listening to the radio as he dressed to go to church and suddenly heard the news that Pearl Harbor was being attacked. Rushing out of his house he recognized the red Rising Sun identifying aircraft flying overhead as Japanese. "Those dirty Japs," this young American remembered thinking.

★ ★ ★ ★ ★ ★ ★ ★ ★ ★ ★ ★ ★ ★ ★ ★ ★ ★ ★ ★

PICTURES THAT TRULY WERE WORTH 1,000 WORDS

Japan managed to get valuable aerial overhead photography of Pearl Harbor and military installations throughout Oahu via the simple technique of having its agents take private sightseeing plane rides from John Rogers Airport. Their activities were, for the most part, repeated hundreds of times in 1941 by ordinary tourists.

★ ★ ★ ★ ★ ★ ★ ★ ★ ★ ★ ★ ★ ★ ★ ★ ★ ★ ★ ★

WE NEVER CALLED IT A "ZERO"? . . . SURE WE DID!

The famous Mitsubishi A6M3 was nicknamed the Zero by the Japanese, but the U.S. referred to as the Zeke. Japan manufactured more than 10,000 Zeros (or Zekes), including 465 which were modified as kamikazes near the end of the war.

★ ★ ★ ★ ★ ★ ★ ★ ★ ★ ★ ★ ★ ★ ★ ★ ★ ★ ★ ★

AUTHOR OF THE OPERATIONAL PLAN FOR THE ATTACK

If asked who actually created the operational plan for the Japanese attack on Pearl Harbor, most people would say Admiral Isoroku Yamamoto, the commander in chief of the Combined Fleet. A few might venture the name of Commander Minoru Genda, air staff officer of the First Air Fleet (he was the tactical planner). But it was neither. The operational plan was the handiwork of Rear Admiral Ryunosuke Kusaka, the chief of staff of the First Air Fleet.

"BLOOD & GUTS" PATTON WAS THERE IN 1935

Career Army officer George S. Patton had been stationed as the Hawaii Department's Director of Intelligence in 1935. The then 50-year-old future general, who would be the bane of the Germans in the North African and European theaters, created a plan to protect U.S. security from possible local Japanese subversion if the United States and Japan went to war. Patton's plan called for rounding up those of Japanese ancestry and incarcerating them as hostages, not prisoners of war, almost identical to the fate that befell thousands of American citizens of Japanese ancestry on the mainland after the December 7, 1941 attack.

★ ★ ★ ★ ★ ★ ★ ★ ★ ★ ★ ★ ★ ★ ★ ★ ★ ★ ★ ★

HAWAII HAD LARGE JAPANESE POPULATION

Approximately 45% of the population of the Hawaiian Islands, some 160,000 people, were of Japanese ancestry on December 7, 1941. Of these more than 37,500 had not been born in the U.S. or Hawaii.

★ ★ ★ ★ ★ ★ ★ ★ ★ ★ ★ ★ ★ ★ ★ ★ ★ ★ ★ ★

THEY OBVIOUSLY FORGOT THEIR "OLD SCHOOL TIES"

The American opinion of the Japanese prior to, and even after, Pearl Harbor, saw them as a backward, ignorant race. However, it was not commonly known that several leading Japanese officers had attended some of the finest universities and colleges in the U.S. Among the Ivy League participants in the Pearl Harbor attack were: Yamamoto and Nagano (Harvard); Yamaguchi (Princeton); and Arima (Yale). Likewise, in Europe, a number of German generals had studied at Oxford and other English schools.

★ ★ ★ ★ ★ ★ ★ ★ ★ ★ ★ ★ ★ ★ ★ ★ ★ ★ ★ ★

JAPAN'S STRANGE "ALPHA AND OMEGA" COINCIDENCE

After the surprise attack on Pearl Harbor to start the war with the U.S., the victorious Japanese Kido Butai fleet returned home on December 23, 1941. The port they arrived at was Hiroshima.

JAPANESE-AMERICANS WERE MOST DECORATED

The most decorated unit in U.S. military history was the 442nd Regimental Combat Team. It consisted of Japanese-American volunteers who received 4,667 major medals, awards, and citations, including 560 Silver Stars, 28 of which had oak-leaf clusters; 4,000 Bronze Stars; 52 Distinguished Service Crosses; one Congressional Medal of Honor; and 54 other decorations. The 442nd also held the distinction of never having a case of desertion. The majority of soldiers in the 442nd served while their relatives in the U.S. were being held in the infamous detention centers and camps created as a result of the suspicion and panic following Pearl Harbor.

★ ★

MARSHALL WAS OBVIOUSLY AN OPTIMIST

Sometime earlier in 1941, U.S. Army Chief of Staff George C. Marshall is on record stating: "My impression of the Hawaiian [Pearl Harbor] problem has been that if no serious harm is done us during the first six hours of known hostilities, thereafter the existing defenses would discourage an enemy against the hazard of an attack" Marshall obviously never considered that Japan could inflict the kind of harm he feared *in the first six minutes* (author's italics).

★ ★

FRIENDLY FIRE TAKES A HORRIBLE TOLL

Four dive bombers from the aircraft carrier USS Enterprise (CV-6), which had landed safely at Pearl Harbor earlier in the day, were mistaken for enemy planes and shot down the night of Dec. 7, 1941 as they returned after being sent out to search for the Japanese fleet.

★ ★

AGAINST OVERWHELMING JAPANESE AIR SUPERIORITY

By most counts, there were 390 U.S. military aircraft of all types at various bases on Oahu on December. 7, 1941. Thirty-eight got into the sky. Ten of these were shot down.

BUT NONE WERE PRESENT TO SINK AT PEARL HARBOR

During the surprise attack on Pearl Harbor Japan effectively employed 144 Nakajima B5N2 torpedo bombers (which the U.S. nicknamed/code-named Kate). In the original planning, their primary targets were to be U.S. aircraft carriers. Nonetheless, Kates had success against Battleship Row and other ships present. As the war went on Kates were credited with sinking the U.S. aircraft carriers Lexington (CV-2); Yorktown (CV-5); and Hornet (CV-8).

★ ★

SAFE HAVEN FOR USS PENNSYLVANIA (BB-38)

The minelayer USS Oglala (CM-4) was at Dock 1010 on Battleship Row instead of the Pennsylvania (BB-38), which was in dry dock across the harbor. Oglala was outboard the cruiser USS Helena (CL-50). Oglala was the flagship of Rear Admiral William Rhea Furlong, commander, Battle Forces Pacific (service vessels). It was Furlong who gave the order to the fleet, "All ships in harbor sortie."

★ ★

HOW DOCTORS AND NURSES KNEW WHO WAS "SHOT"

To avoid the serious mistake of administering double injections of morphine to the injured, the medical personnel at hospitals and impromptu emergency care facilities throughout Pearl Harbor indicated which of the injured had already received a shot by painting Mercurochrome marks on their foreheads. More than 300 casualties arrived at the medical facilities of Patrol Wing Two within the first half hour of the attack.

★ ★

JAPANESE PLANE HAD WAR DEBUT AT PEARL HARBOR

Japan's Aichi E13A1 seaplane, code-named Jake, made its offensive combat debut on December 7, 1941. Catapulted from ships, its primary function was reconnaissance. More than 1,400 were eventually produced.

A considerable number of U.S. military personnel killed during the attack on Pearl Harbor were laid to rest together on Oahu. Nearly half of the 2,403 American servicemen who died were aboard the battleship USS Arizona (BB-39).   *–U.S. Navy photo*

===

FACT: None of the Japanese airmen involved in the attack on Pearl Harbor wore parachutes.

In terms of human life, Japanese losses in the Pearl Harbor attack, were remarkable small, considering the scope of the operation and the American losses. Japan lost 55 fliers, nine midget submariners, plus an unknown number of submariners aboard an I-class submarine. Of the 432 Japanese aircraft that participated in the Sunday morning raid, twenty-nine were shot down. In this photo, Lieutenant Fusata Iida, a pilot who crashed at Kaneohe Bay, is buried with honor by U.S. personnel on Hawaii.   *--U.S. Navy photo*

"BOMBS AWAY"....ON SOMETHING, MAYBE

Prior to their extensive training in preparation for the Pearl Harbor attack, Japan's horizontal bombers were considered a poor risk, or at best, a minimally effective force, with regard to the impending attack. The opinion was largely based on the fact that the Japanese used a modified version of the German Boyco bombsight, which was critically inferior to the Norden bombsight used by the U.S. bombers. Accuracy of the Japanese-Boyco depended greatly upon the expertise of the bombardier and pilot working as a team.

★ ★

FAIR OR NOT, HE KNEW HOW THE GAME WAS PLAYED

"If I were in charge in Washington I would relieve Kimmel at once. It doesn't make any difference why a man fails in the Navy, he has failed". That sobering, fatalistic conclusion was uttered by Admiral Husband E. Kimmel, speaking about himself and his expected fate, to two staff members shortly after the Pearl Harbor attack.

★ ★

IT SOUNDS AS IF JAPAN DIDN'T BELIEVE NOMURA

On May 20, 1941, more than six months before hostilities began, Japan's Ambassador in Washington, Admiral Kichisaburo Nomura, advised Tokyo that the U.S. was reading the Japanese diplomatic code (a low-grade "J" code). Incredibly, Tokyo responded by telling its Washington embassy to have all sensitive material handled by only one person. One might conclude that the inference was that Tokyo thought it more likely there was a security leak or a spy in the embassy, rather than that the U.S. was reading the diplomatic code.

★ ★

JAPANESE "LOOK ALIKE" ISLAND USED FOR TRAINING

The island that the Japanese used as the training center for the attack on Pearl Harbor was Kyushu, the southernmost of the four main Japanese islands. Ariake Bay, frequently the home of the fleet, is said to have a rather strong resemblance to Pearl Harbor.

FROM FDR TO FORMER NAVAL PERSON

On December 8, 1941, shortly after the U.S. Congress had acknowledged, as President Roosevelt had asked, that "a state of war existed" between the United States and Japan, FDR wrote to British Prime Minister Winston S. Churchill, "Today all of us are in the same boat with you and the people of the Empire and it is a ship which will not and cannot be sunk". As their wartime correspondence increased the sometimes impish Churchill, who had been First Lord of the Admiralty early in his career, often signed his letters to Roosevelt as "Former Naval Person".

★ ★ ★ ★ ★ ★ ★ ★ ★ ★ ★ ★ ★ ★ ★ ★ ★ ★ ★ ★

THE SO-CALLED JAPANESE "BOMB PLOT" MESSAGE

On September 24, 1941. Tokyo sent a coded message to its agents on Oahu requesting that in all future communications they divide the area of Pearl Harbor into a grid when referring to locations. The message was immediately intercepted by U.S. intelligence codebreakers when it was sent, but not translated until October 9. At the time it was considered by most U.S. military personnel involved as an example of the extreme detail the Japanese were famous for, and not as a grid pattern for an attack. After the December 7 attack it was looked at differently and became known as the "Bomb Plot" message. Some historians, Gordon Prange among others, question why more significance was given at the time to the "East wind, rain" message rather than the implications of this more obvious one.

★ ★ ★ ★ ★ ★ ★ ★ ★ ★ ★ ★ ★ ★ ★ ★ ★ ★ ★ ★

MORSE CODE HELPED OVERCOME THE 100 MILE LIMIT

Prior to 1941, Japan had never had a Navy fighter plane involved in action more than 100 miles from its home base or aircraft carrier because their radiotelephone communications system was unable to function beyond that distance. Throughout the summer of 1941, Japanese Navy pilots and communications personnel had to become proficient in Morse Code in order to sustain communications during the planned Pearl Harbor attack.

JAPANESE PLANES WERE SEEN ON RADAR

The Opana Mobile Radar Station, located on the northern end of Oahu at Kahuku Point, was one of five mobile radar stations on Oahu. The other four were: Kaaawa; Kawailoa; Koko Head; and Fort Shafter (actually a backup station). The five had only gone into operational service in November, 1941. The military considered Opana to be the best of the five and equipped with a then state-of-the-art 270-B radar system which could be transported on two trucks, hence the inclusion of "mobile" in their names. Opana was staffed since Saturday afternoon, Dec. 6, by U.S. Army privates Joseph L. Lockard and George E. Elliott who were due to go off duty at 7 A.M. Sunday morning but remained later to watch an unusual blip which had appeared some 136 miles off the coast, coming in from the north, just as their shift was about to end. The sighting was reported to the Army's Information Center. However, Lieutenant Kermit Tyler, the pursuit officer who had the authority to "intercept enemy planes," was convinced that the blip was the flight of U.S. B-17s expected from the mainland.

★ ★

A FINE PLACE TO WATCH A JAPANESE-AMERICAN WAR?

Sometime during 1941, Takeo Yoshikawa, a trained Japanese intelligence agent who functioned at the consulate in Hawaii under the name of Tadashi Morimura, commented that "Hawaii would be a fine place from which to watch a Japanese-American war". The casual remark was made to Kohichi Seki, the Japanese consulate's treasurer and the man who had reported the movements of the U.S. fleet prior to Yoshikawa's arrival there. Neither man had any advance knowledge about the planned attack on Pearl Harbor.

★ ★

BASED ON EVENTS, I THINK YOU COULD SAY THAT

"So sorry, we sank your fleet this morning. Supposing we are at war?" Comment reportedly made by a Japanese newsman to C. L. Sulzberger of the *New York Times,* at the Grand Hotel in Moscow.

MADE IN JAPAN...BUT DESIGNED IN GERMANY

Though they were unquestionably built and made in Japan, the original concept and design for the interesting but ineffective Japanese midget submarines came from Germany.

★ ★

SAILOR'S WIFE HAD A PREMONITION

When the USS Oklahoma (BB-37) departed from San Francisco for Pearl Harbor in October, the wife of Gunner's Mate Edgar Beck told the sailor she had a premonition that something bad would happen to the ship in Hawaii.

★ ★

ENSIGN WAS RIGHT ON THE MONEY

During a casual group discussion ON December 6 about the tense situation with Japan in the wardroom of the USS Vestal (AR-4) Ensign Fred Hall commented to fellow officers that the Japanese "will attack right here." However, nobody bothered to ask him when or why the attack would take place. The following morning Hall was the officer of the deck and pulled the general quarters signal at 7:55 A.M. as the Japanese attack began.

★ ★

ASTUTE CONCLUSION ON EVE OF ATTACK

On December 6, Cleveland Davis, a sailor aboard the USS Ralph Talbot (DD-390) blurted out to Lt. R.A. Newton "I think Pearl is very vulnerable and a sneak attack could be very devastating. Davis gave no specific reason for the statement, claiming that it was just an impression that popped into his thoughts.

★ ★

SOME FOUND BETTER THINGS TO SHOOT AT THAT DAY

A Sunday morning, December 7, rifle shooting competition, with a fifty-cents entry fee and winner-take-all pot, was scheduled at Hickam Field, pitting officers against non-commissioned officers.

UPI SAT ON THE "SCOOP" OF THE CENTURY ⇨

The first unofficial word of the Pearl Harbor attack was transmitted on the only commercial cable line linking Hawaii to the mainland by United Press International's Honolulu Bureau Chief Frank Tremaine at 10:30 A.M. PST, on December 7, 1941. It was received at UPI's San Francisco office by the Weekend Bureau Chief James Sullivan who flagged the cable "FLASH" (highest priority) and transcribed it to the news agency's main office in New York. Tremaine watched the attack from his house overlooking the harbor. He shouted what he was witnessing to his wife Kay who repeated his words verbatim over the phone. In what must be regarded as a remarkable display of journalistic restraint, in deference to The White House, UPI did not report this information until President Roosevelt confirmed Tremaine's report. *The photo on the adjoining page is an actual UPI teletype newswire page, reduced in size to fit this book.*

---Author's collection

★ ★

THEY REJOINED THEIR SHIPMATES AT PEARL HARBOR

As of December 7, 2000, 59 years after the attack on Pearl Harbor, 16 former USS Arizona (BB-39) crewmen who survived the attack have had their ashes interred on the sunken hull of the ship. Of the 337 Arizona crewmen who survived the carnage that Sunday morning, only 50 were believed to still be alive and to have seen the millennium. Over the years, the ashes of more than 40 other survivors have been scattered on the waters of Pearl Harbor. Only personnel who were part of the Arizona crew on December 7, 1941 are entitled to have their ashes entombed in the ship by divers. Lewis P. Robinson who died at age 78 in 1997, was the most recent Arizona crewmember to rejoin his mates. When the attack commenced Robinson was among dozens of sailors waiting at the dock for a boat ride back to their ships after spending shore leave on Oahu. Of the 1,177 Arizona crewmembers killed, 945 are entombed in the hull.

```
F L A S H


    WASHINGTON--WHITE HOUSE SAYS JAPS ATTACK PEARL HARBOR.


                                              222PES




B U L L E T I N


    WASHINGTON, DEC. 7 (AP)-PRESIDENT ROOSEVELT SAID IN A
STATEMENT TODAY THAT THE JAPANESE HAD ATTACKED PEARL HARBOR, HAWAII,
FROM THE AIR.
    THE ATTACK OF THE JAPANESE ALSO WAS MADE ON ALL NAVAL AND MILITARY
"ACTIVITIES" ON THE ISLAND OF OAHU.
    THE PRESIDENT'S BRIEF STATEMENT WAS READ TO REPORTERS BY STEPHEN
EARLY, PRESIDENTIAL SECRETARY.  NO FURTHER DETAILS WERE GIVEN
IMMEDIATELY.
    AT THE TIME OF THE WHITE HOUSE ANNOUNCEMENT, THE JAPANESE AMBASSADY
KIURISABORO NOMURA AND SABURO KURUSU, WERE AT THE STATE DEPARTMENT.


F L A S H
       WASHINGTON--SECOND AIR ATTACK REPORTED ON ARMY AND NAVY BASES
IN MANILA.
```

===

EXTRA, EXTRA, READ ALL ABOUT IT!
In an amazing fete of instant journalism, *The Honolulu Star
Bulletin's* hit the streets with the blazing headline written by Editor
Riley Allen: **WAR! OAHU BOMBED BY JAPANESE PLANES**
at 0930 A.M., while the attack was still going on.

BLACK HERO RECEIVED NAVY CROSS, SHIP NAMESAKE

The first Black American to receive the Navy Cross in World War II was Doris (Dorie) Miller, a mess attendant on the USS West Virginia (BB-48) for courageous action beyond the call of duty. Miller, from Waco, Texas, was cited for braving enemy strafing to assist in removing the ship's mortally wounded captain to a place of greater safety. He was also cited for his initiative in manning a machine gun on the battleship's deck and is credited with shooting down a Japanese plane. As a mess attendant he had not been trained in firing such weapons. In recognition of Miller's heroism and valor he was presented the Navy Cross by Admiral Chester W. Nimitz. On June 30, 1973 the U.S. Navy commissioned a destroyer escort in his honor, the USS Miller (DE-1091).

★ ★ ★ ★ ★ ★ ★ ★ ★ ★ ★ ★ ★ ★ ★ ★ ★ ★ ★

DON'T BLAME THE MESSENGER!

Tadao Fuchikami was the RCA motorcycle messenger in Honolulu who delivered the Western Union telegram from Washington advising General Short and Admiral Kimmel that the Japanese were issuing an ultimatum at "1 P.M. Eastern Standard Time today..." (7:30 A.M. in Honolulu). It was received by Honolulu RCA twenty-two minutes *before* the attack but not delivered until four hours later and then took another three hours to decode.

★ ★ ★ ★ ★ ★ ★ ★ ★ ★ ★ ★ ★ ★ ★ ★ ★ ★ ★

LAST GATHERING OF BATTLESHIPS HAD BEEN JULY 4

Prior to the weekend of Dec. 6-7, 1941, the last time all eight of the battleships in the Pacific Fleet were together in Pearl Harbor had been during the July 4 holiday.

★ ★ ★ ★ ★ ★ ★ ★ ★ ★ ★ ★ ★ ★ ★ ★ ★ ★ ★

CHAMPIONSHIP NET MATCH PERMANENTLY POSTPONED

The baseball teams from the USS Arizona (BB-39) and the USS Enterprise (CV-6) were slated to play for the Pacific Fleet Championship on December 7.

HOW WAS YOUR FIRST DAY IN COMMAND, LIEUTENANT?

Lt. William W. Outerbridge's first day of his first patrol in his first command, was as the C.O. of the destroyer USS Ward (DD-139). The Ward was a four-pipe destroyer from the World War I era with a flank speed of 30 knots. Outerbridge became the first American to sink a Japanese warship in 1941. It was nearly an hour before the enemy air attack began at Pearl Harbor when the Ward sank a Japanese midget sub.

★ ★

MAYBE THE DOG WAS PSYCHIC. WHAT DID HE KNOW?

In the morning hours of 7 December just prior to the attack, the howling and whining of Honolulu Police Chief William A. Gabrielson's dog was so intense and prolonged that it woke everyone in the house. In a December 1956 story published in the *Idaho Sunday Statesman*, to mark the 15th anniversary of the attack, Gabrielson stated that the animal had never previously acted like that, nor did it ever do it again.

★ ★

DO YOU THINK ANYONE REMEMBERS WHO WON?

On December 6 the Annual Shrine Football game was played at Honolulu Stadium. Approximately 24,000 people watched the local favorite University of Hawaii Rainbows fight it out with Oregon's Willamette University's Bearcats in this pigskin classic.

★ ★

FEELING WAS ONE DAY TOO EARLY

Rear Admiral Milo F. Draemel, the commander of the Battle Fleet's destroyer division, remained aboard his flagship the light cruiser USS Detroit (CL-8) well into Saturday evening, Dec. 6, because he had a feeling the Japanese would attack Pearl Harbor that day.

FACT: Admiral Kimmel declined an invitation to a December 6 evening cocktail reception at the Japanese Consulate in Honolulu.

KIMMEL JUMPED 32 SENIOR ADMIRALS FOR HAWAII POST

Prior to assuming command as CINCUS (Commander-in-Chief, United States Fleet) in February, 1941, Admiral Husband E. Kimmel had been Commander of Cruisers, Battle Force. Kimmel was personally known to President Roosevelt from FDR's tenure as Assistant Secretary of the Navy more than two decades earlier. It was Roosevelt who personally picked Kimmel and bumped him ahead of 32 senior admirals.

★ ★ ★ ★ ★ ★ ★ ★ ★ ★ ★ ★ ★ ★ ★ ★ ★ ★ ★ ★

COMMERCIAL TELEGRAMS WERE SAFE WAY TO TALK

While it was permissible for the intelligence sections of the U.S. Navy and U.S. Army to intercept and break coded messages of Japan (or any country for that matter) it was illegal to "read" what were considered private communications sent or transmitted by commercial carriers. Such intrusions were prohibited by the 1934 Federal Communications Act. Consequently, the opportunity to know the contents of commercially sent messages between Tokyo and its diplomats remained sacrosanct! Not until less than a week before the Pearl Harbor attack did the Navy convince RCA (Radio Corporation of America) to permit the Navy's intelligence people to see file copies of telegrams between the Japanese Consulate in Hawaii and Tokyo.

★ ★ ★ ★ ★ ★ ★ ★ ★ ★ ★ ★ ★ ★ ★ ★ ★ ★ ★ ★

CRUISESHIP CHECKED COURSE DATA AND SPIED ON U.S.

In a brilliant example of using available resources to improve spying capabilities, the Taiyo Maru, a Japanese passenger liner set course from Japan to Hawaii on October 22, 1941. On board were Naval officers whose purpose for being on the trip was to check, verify, and confirm various weather conditions, distance, and sea conditions which the Kido Butai might encounter en route to Pearl Harbor. In a classic ending to the trip, the Taiyo Maru made port and docked in Honolulu Harbor (about seven miles from Pearl Harbor) at 0830 on a Saturday morning. The next morning the officers were able to observe what conditions would be like on a Sunday morning.

"BATTLE OF THE BANDS" PICKED BEST IN THE FLEET
A "Battle of the Bands" competition was held ashore in Pearl Harbor, on December 6 and won by the talented music makers from the USS Pennsylvania (BB-38). All members of the USS Arizona (BB-39) band were among those killed the following day.

★ ★ ★ ★ ★ ★ ★ ★ ★ ★ ★ ★ ★ ★ ★ ★ ★ ★ ★ ★

PEARL HARBOR'S ORIGINAL HAWAIIAN NAME
In 1887, during the Administration of President Grover Cleveland, the United States and the Kingdom of Hawaii signed a treaty that gave the U.S. exclusive use of a harbor to repair, fuel, and maintain ships. In U.S. Navy circles at the time, it was thought the greatest benefit from such a harbor would be as a coal supply, and later fuel supply base, commonly called a "cooling station". The Navy had decided that the new base would be known and called Pearl Harbor Naval Station instead of by its actual name, Puuloa.

★ ★ ★ ★ ★ ★ ★ ★ ★ ★ ★ ★ ★ ★ ★ ★ ★ ★ ★ ★

WHY NO TORPEDO NETS WERE INSIDE PEARL HARBOR
Kimmel was aware of the outspoken sentiments of his predecessor, Admiral Richardson, who felt Pearl Harbor was a dangerous trap. And, considering the so-called "bottleneck" entrance and relatively close quarters and space available for ships to sortie in Pearl Harbor, Kimmel felt the introduction of torpedo nets would risk congestion and slow down the process of escaping the harbor in an emergency.

★ ★ ★ ★ ★ ★ ★ ★ ★ ★ ★ ★ ★ ★ ★ ★ ★ ★ ★ ★

U.S. TROOPS IN HARMS WAY
There were approximately 25,000 U.S. military personnel stationed in the Hawaiian Islands, mainly Oahu, on December 7, 1941.

★ ★ ★ ★ ★ ★ ★ ★ ★ ★ ★ ★ ★ ★ ★ ★ ★ ★ ★ ★

INCREDIBLE AS IT MAY SEEM, IT'S TRUE!
Prior to World War II, the intelligence sections of the U.S. Navy and U.S. Army only shared or compared information in rare instances.

93

Trio of Army reservists were among several hundred people who paused on Times Square in New York City to read the latest update on the moving lights bulletin board the evening of the attack. At least this soldier's newspaper suggested where Pearl Harbor was. Most Americans did not know it was a U.S. Navy base, nor had they ever heard of it. But for the rest of their lives they would remember Pearl Harbor.   ---*U.S. Army photo*

THE UNSANITIZED VERSION OF WHAT HULL SAID

Books and movies have captured the somber, historic moment when U.S. Secretary of State Cordell Hull reads Tokyo's 14-part message presented by Ambassador Kichisaburo Nomrua and Special Envoy Saburo Kurusu who then silently as he read it. President Roosevelt had called and told Hull about the attack on Pearl Harbor. He suggested Hull receive the Japanese for the scheduled meeting but to treat them coolly. The official version says that after reading only a few pages Hull looks up and says the following to the emissaries:

"I must say that in all my conversations with you during the last nine months, I have never uttered one word of untruth. This is borne out absolutely by the record. In all my fifty years of public service I have never seen a document that was more crowded with infamous falsehoods and distortions—infamous falsehoods and distortions on a scale so huge that I never imagined until today that any government on this planet was capable of uttering them."

Hull then reportedly raised his hand to stifle any response from the two Japanese and pointed to the office door. However, in his book *Washington Goes To War* longtime newsman and broadcast journalist David Brinkley says Hull's actual remarks were much more to the point. He called them "bastards" and "pissants".

★ ★ ★ ★ ★ ★ ★ ★ ★ ★ ★ ★ ★ ★ ★ ★ ★ ★ ★ ★

J. EDGAR HOOVER DISLIKED SPY'S HANKY-PANKY!

On August 11, 1941, Dusko Popov, a British double-agent who functioned as a trusted German spy, and who was known to the FBI as "Tricycle", told the U.S. Federal Bureau of Investigation that he had been ordered by his German masters to travel to Hawaii for the purpose of collecting information about airfields, Pearl Harbor, and ammunition dumps on Oahu. When this astonishing information reached the desk of J. Edgar Hoover, the director dismissed it. Hoover did not like Popov's promiscuous morals, or scandalous behavior. According to FBI reports, the double agent was known to engage in sexual acts with two women at a time, which reportedly earned him the sarcastic Hoover codename.

At shipyards and kindred plants on both coasts civilian volunteers came forward for the salvage operation. Group shown was at the Brooklyn Navy Yard.   *---U.S. Navy photo*

===

HUMAN AND MATERIAL COST OF PEARL HARBOR TO U.S.

In terms of human lives lost, the attack on Pearl Harbor and military installations on Oahu was a horrible tragedy. But as a military operation it produced considerably less damage to the U.S. war effort than the Japanese had hoped for, or thought they had achieved immediately after the attack. Of the eight battleships in the harbor five were sunk but only the USS Arizona (BB-39) and USS Oklahoma (BB-00) were totally lost. In all some 21 ships were sunk, but around the clock salvage operations returned most of them to active duty.

CBS NEWSMAN WARNED OF PEARL HARBOR ATTACK

CBS Radio newsman Eric Sevaried (who in 1940 had been the first to report that France was about to capitulate to the Germans and ask for an armistice) was told in October 1941 by trusted Korean confidants that Japan was planning to attack the U.S. Naval base at Pearl Harbor, Oahu, Hawaii, before that Christmas.

★ ★

JAPANESE DIDN'T TRUST THEIR GERMAN SPY IN HAWAII

In an arrangement with the German Navy, Japan had a German Naval officer positioned as a "sleeper agent" (spy) in Honolulu from 1935 onward. Using the front of operating a furniture business, Bernard Keuhn, passed along various intelligence to Tokyo. Despite his Caucasian features, which distinguished him from the large Oriental population and were believed to give him easier access, Keuhn was not highly valued and in most instances the information he turned in was considered low-grade or of questionable value. Meanwhile, Keuhn was apparently not as inconspicuous as he, Tokyo or Berlin thought he would be. U.S. Navy intelligence had flagged Keuhn as a possible Axis spy by 1939.

★ ★

THE COMPLEX WORLD OF CODES & CRYPTANALYSTS

The U.S. considered the so-called "J" codes to be a series of lower-grade coded transmissions between the Foreign Ministry in Tokyo and several of its consulates, including Honolulu. The U.S. had broken and was reading them from the summer of 1940. The "J" codes are not to be confused with the higher level, and more difficult, Purple Code, which the U.S. had been reading since early in 1939. The significance of the "J" codes, particularly one known as J-19, is that the U.S. was fully aware of Tokyo's interest in the position and/or movement of the U.S. fleet based in Hawaii. In early December 1941, the Japanese consulate in Hawaii changed from a J code to the PA-K2 code. {Note: As late as 1944 the Japanese reported ship movements in a special code known as the "Doll Woman", broken by noted cryptanalyst Elizabeth Friedman"}.

The USS Arizona (BB-39), in her death throe and starting to settle in the muddy bottom of Pearl Harbor, exactly where she remains today. This photo was taken shortly after she was hit and only minutes before the more frequently seen photograph of the mortally wounded ship with her mast crumpled.

--U.S. Navy photo

FDR USED AL CAPONE'S CAR AFTER PEARL HARBOR

On the morning after the Pearl Harbor attack the Secret Service determined that a bulletproof car was needed immediately to protect President Roosevelt from possible assassins sympathetic to Japan or Germany. But federal law prohibited purchasing any automobile that cost more than $750. Agent Mike Reilly, head of the White House detail, discovered that after the income tax evasion case against Al Capone the Treasury Dept. seized the gangster's bulletproof limousine. Roosevelt used the car until the Ford Motor Co. built a presidential limousine for White House use. They got around the cost restriction by leasing it to the government for $500 annually.

★ ★

THEY CORRECTLY CONCLUDED MESSAGE MEANT WAR

In Washington, D.C. on the morning of December 7, 1941, more than five hours before the attack on Pearl Harbor began, three U.S. military intelligence officers correctly guessed that the unusual wording of the 14-part Japanese message breaking diplomatic relations at 1 P.M. Washington time (0730 in Pearl Harbor) indicated that hostilities against Pearl Harbor were nearly certain. The fourteenth part of the message had been intercepted by the U.S. Navy's Bainbridge Island station before 0300, Dec. 7. It was sent to Washington, D.C., and immediately seen by Lieutenant Commander A. D. Kramer when he arrived at his office at 0730 and shortly after by Commander Arthur H. McCollum (both of Naval Intelligence) and Colonel Rufus S. Bratton of Army Intelligence.

FACT: The 14-part message the Japanese ambassadors delivered to Sec. Of State Cordell Hull was not a declaration of war, nor did it break off negotiations. Reading it in context, it amounts to a rehashing of Japanese grievances against the United States, United Kingdom and the Netherlands. In fact, the Japanese government did not prepare a declaration of war against the United States until it was prepared at a meeting which convened at 1244, Dec. 7th, Pearl Harbor time, well after the attack was over.

General Hideki Tojo became Japan's prime minister in October, 1941 after his predecessor as PM, Prince Konoye, resigned when President Franklin D. Roosevelt rejected his plea for a summit. Konoye and Emperor Hirohito were anxious to avert war with the U.S., but Tojo and the Supreme War Council believed war was the only solution to. Tojo is seen here awaiting the Tokyo War Crimes trials. *--Exclusive photo by George Schroth*

YOU'LL NEVER GUESS WHO "56" TAKANO WAS

His first name was spelled with the ideographs of the number 56, which was the age of his natural father when Isoroku Takano was born on April 4, 1884. It indicated his father's pride in having produced a son at that age. However, in observance of a Japanese custom to prevent a family name from dying if there were no male heirs, Isoroku was adopted into another family when he was 32 years old. He then took the name of his new family and, in so doing, guaranteed it a place in Japanese and world history. As Isoroku Yamamoto, "56" Takano will always be remembered as one of Japan's greatest admirals.

★ ★

LESSONS LEARNED FROM WAR GAMES DIDN'T HELP

On May 12, 1941, seven months before the Japanese attack on Pearl Harbor, the U.S. Army and Navy held what were described as "the greatest war drills ever staged" in Hawaii. Army bombers "attacked" enemy aircraft carriers several hundred miles at sea just as one carrier was preparing to launch planes against the islands. In an ironic note, a formation of twenty-one B-17s landed on Oahu from the mainland during the "attack". The games contained many phases and options and continued for two weeks, with the U.S. forces gaining the upper hand. The Navy had held similar games involving a Pearl Harbor attack by aircraft carriers in 1933 and in 1939. In the 1939 exercise, aircraft from the carrier USS Saratoga (CV-3) launched a Sunday morning surprise attack "sinking" ships Pearl in Harbor and attacked Hickam, Wheeler and Ford Island air fields.

★ ★

BATTLESHIP "X" WAS ALSO KNOWN AS "BIG BASTARD"

After Pearl Harbor attack, and for some time thereafter, the USS South Dakota (BB-57) was frequently identified in government press releases as "Battleship X". To the fleet she was often called "Sodak" but to her crew the 42,000-ton, 680 ft. long battleship was affectionately called the "Big Bastard".

WHEN YOU DON'T KNOW THE FACTS...IMPROVISE!

Popular network radio newsman H.V. Kaltenborn felt obliged to say something more than just report the attack. Without a shred of evidence or information, he proceeded to speculate on the number of days and hours (even considering the wind and sea currents!) that it would take the U.S. fleet to sail across the Pacific to "devastate the home islands of Japan."

★ ★ ★ ★ ★ ★ ★ ★ ★ ★ ★ ★ ★ ★ ★ ★ ★ ★ ★ ★

ROOSEVELT CALLED IT "A DATE" ... *not* "A DAY"

Perhaps the most frequently misquoted utterance from the war years is the seven word phrase *"a date which will live in infamy"* in the opening lines of President Franklin D. Roosevelt's historic address to Congress on December 8, 1941. It has been misquoted in a number of otherwise excellent books, magazine stories and in the annual newspaper stories that mark the attack on Pearl Harbor. The culprit behind the misquote is most likely the live broadcast at the time and the recordings of it which millions of people have heard since then. In the audio it is easy to hear "day" instead of "date". The full text of FDR's address appears elsewhere in these pages. The opening paragraph is reproduced here in toto"

"Yesterday, Dec. 7, 1941 - a date which will live in infamy - the United States of America was suddenly and deliberately attacked by naval and air forces of the Empire of Japan."

Most recently the misquote has turned up on some Internet websites, with yet a second error in those seven words! Besides the incorrect substitution of "day" for "date", these versions have also replaced "will live" with "shall live".

FACT: By the time of the Pearl Harbor attack, the British had been using radar to their advantage for more than a year. The radar stations on Oahu were experimental even though the first U.S. Navy ships to have radar were the battleships USS Texas and USS New York, in 1939. By 1943 more than 200 U.S. ships had radar.

Forward magazine of USS Shaw (DD-373) explodes at 0930, during the second wave, after Shaw is hit by three bombs and the exact moment is captured on film. The destroyer, being overhauled in Floating Drydock #2 (which took five bomb hits) had all ammunition stored below decks. The explosion blew away the ship's bow. This was one of the single most memorable events during the attack and one of the most remarkable photos taken during World War II.   *–U.S. Navy Photo*

FATE OF THE JAPANESE OFFICERS INVOLVED IN THE ATTACK ON PEARL HARBOR

Most of the key Japanese officers involved in the planning and execution of the Pearl Harbor attack on December 7 lost their lives during the war. With the exception of Minoru Genda, who was the tactical planner, and Flight Leader Mitsuo Fuchida, whose "Tora! Tora! Tora!" initiated hostilities (both survived the war), here is the fate of some of the others:

- Admiral Isoroku Yamamoto, who insisted that war with the U.S. begin with the destruction of the U.S. fleet at Pearl Harbor, was ambushed by U.S. fighters over Bougainville, April 18, 1943.

- Vice Admiral Chuichi Nagumo, commander-in-chief, 1st Air Fleet (the senior officer present in the attack fleet), was killed in action at Saipan.

- Rear Admiral Tamon Yamaguchi, commander-in-chief, 2nd Carrier Division, died aboard his aircraft carrier during the Battle of Midway, June, 1942.

- Lieutenant Commander Kakuiche Takahashi, leader of the dive-bombers in the first wave, was killed in May, 1942, in the Battle of the Coral Sea (actually fought in the Solomon Sea).

- Lieutenant Commander Shigemaru Murata, leader of the torpedo bombers in the first wave, was killed in battle at Santa Cruz, October 26-27, 1942.

- Lieutenant Commander Takashige Egusa, leader of the dive-bombers in the second wave, was killed over Saipan.

- Lieutenant Commander Shigeru Itaya, leader of the first wave of fighter planes, was shot down by mistake by Japanese Army planes over the Kuriles.

- Rear Admiral Matome Ugaki, chief of staff to Yamamoto and the man who wrote the historic "Climb Mount Niitaka" message signaling the irrevocable order to attack Pearl Harbor, died piloting a kamikaze plane on the last day of the war.

- Lieutenant Commander Shigekazu Shimazaki, commander of the second-wave attack force, was killed on January 9, 1945, off the Philippines.

- Of the two major participants who survived, Genda became an Army lieutenant general and later served in the upper house of the Diet (the Japanese equivalent of the U.S. Senate). Fuchida, as noted elsewhere in this volume, converted to Christianity and toured overseas extensively as a nondenominational evangelist.

★ ★ ★ ★ ★ ★ ★ ★ ★ ★ ★ ★ ★ ★ ★ ★ ★ ★ ★ ★

JAPANESE GENERAL STAFF WAS "IFFY" ON ATTACK

The Imperial Japanese Navy General Staff, under Admiral Osami Nagano, so strongly opposed Admiral Yamamoto's plan to attack Pearl Harbor as being too risky that they continued to question Yamamoto up to the very last minute as to whether the admiral could be sure the United States fleet would be there. It was the powerful and confident personage of Yamamoto himself that conquered any fears and managed to get the IJN General Staff to permit him from going ahead and executing the attack. However, this was all predicated upon the fact that Japan continued to get assurances from its consulate in Oahu that the fleet remained stationed there. When the U.S. government ordered all twenty-four German consulates in the U.S. closed, plus all Italian consulates, during June 1941, Japan feared that as a member of the Tripartite Pact it would also face similar closures. It is believed that under such conditions (the lack of espionage revealing the presence of the U.S. fleet) the IJN General Staff may well have canceled Yamamoto's plan to attack Pearl Harbor. However, for several political reasons, the U.S. government did not close the Japanese consulates.

Commander Minoru Genda came up with the idea of fitting wooden stabilizers to torpedo fins so they wouldn't hit the 45 foot bottom of Pearl Harbor. It was a widely held belief that a minimum 70 foot depth was needed.   *-- author's collection*

KIDO BUTAI: THE JAPANESE NAVY PEARL HARBOR STRIKE FORCE

The Japanese fleet that left home waters in November 1941 for its infamous rendezvous with the U.S., included 22 surface warships, eight oiler and supply ships, and 30 submarines, 60 ships total. *All but three of them would be sunk during the course of the war.* The trio of survivors included the destroyer Ushio and submarine I-21, which both surrendered, and the oiler Kyokuto Maru.

Warships		Subsequent Fate	Date of Action
CV	Akagi	Sunk, Midway	5 June 1942
CV	Kago	Sunk, Midway	4 June 1942
CVL	Hiryu	Sunk, Midway	5 June 1942
CVL	Soryu	Sunk, Midway	4 June 1942
CV	Shokaku	Sunk, Philippines	19 June 1944
CV	Zuikaku	Sunk, Leyte Gulf	25 Oct. 1944
BB	Hiei	Sunk, Guadalcanal	13 Nov. 1942
BB	Kirishima	Sunk, Guadalcanal	15 Nov. 1942
CA	Chikuma	Sunk, Leyte Gulf	25 Oct. 1944
CA	Tone	Sunk, Kure	24 July 1945
CL	Abukuma	Sunk, Leyte Gulf	26 Oct. 1944
DD	Akigumo	Sunk, Philippines	11 Apr. 1944
DD	Arare	Sunk, Aleutians	5 July 1942
DD	Asakaze	Sunk, Philippines	23 Aug. 1944
DD	Homakaze	Sunk, Okinawa	7 Apr. 1945
DD	Kagero	Sunk, Solomons	8 May 1943
DD	Kasumi	Sunk, Okinawa	7 Apr. 1945
DD	Shiranumi	Sunk, Leyte Gulf	27 Oct. 1944
DD	Tonikoze	Sunk, Philippines	9 June 1944
DD	Urokoze	Sunk, Formosa	21 Nov. 1944
DD	Sozonami	Sunk, Yap	14 Jan. 1944
DD	Ushio	Surrendered	

Warships		Subsequent Fate	Date of Action
SS	I-1	Sunk, Guadalcanal	29 Jan. 1943
SS	I-2	Sunk, Bismarck Sea	7 July 1944
SS	I-3	Sunk, Guadalcanal	10 Dec. 1942
SS	I-4	Sunk, Guadalcanal	20 Dec. 1942
SS	I-5	Sunk, Guam	19 July 1944
SS	I-6	Sunk, unknown	June 1944
SS	I-7	Sunk, Aleutians	5 July 19431
SS	I-8	Sunk, Okinawa	31 Mar. 1945
SS	I-9	Sunk, Aleutians	11 June 1943
SS	I-10	Sunk, Saipan	4 July 1944
SS	I-15	Sunk, Guadalcanal	2 Nov. 1942
SS	I-16	Sunk, Solomons	19 May 1944
SS	I-17	Sunk, Noum6a	19 Aug. 1943
SS	I-18	Sunk, Guadalcanal	11 Feb. 1943
SS	I-19	Sunk, unknown	Oct. 1943
SS	I-20	Sunk, New Hebrides	16 Sept. 1943
SS	I-21	Surrendered	
SS	I-22	Sunk, unknown	Oct. 1942
SS	I-23	Sunk, Guadalcanal	29 Aug. 1942
SS	I-24	Sunk, Aleutians	11 June 1943
SS	I-25	Sunk, New Hebrides	3 Sept. 1943
SS	I-26	Sunk, Philippines	Oct. 1944
SS	I-68	Sunk, Bismarck Sea	27 July 1943
SS	I-69	Sunk, Truk	4 Apr. 1944
SS	I-70	Sunk, Pearl Harbor	10 Dec. 1941
SS	I-71	Sunk, Solomons	1 Feb. 1944
SS	I-72	Sunk, Guadalcanal	11 Nov. 1942
SS	I-73	Sunk, Midway	27 Jan. 1942
SS	I-74	Sunk, unknown	Apr. 1944
SS	I-75	Sunk, Marshalls	1 Feb. 1944

The eight oilers and supply ships: Only *Kyokuto Maru* survived.

Kyokuto Maru	Kyokuyo Maru	Kenya Maru	Kokuyo
Shinkoku Maru	Toho Maru	Toei Maru	Nippon Maru

USS California (BB-44), at 0755, was the first battleship in Pearl Harbor to sound general quarters, the same minute the attack began. California commenced firing at 0825. The flagship of Vice Admiral William S. Pye, second highest ranking Naval officer in Pearl Harbor, the California had several manholes open (removed or loosened) in preparation for inspection the following day. As a result, the California nearly capsized after being hit by two torpedoes at 0805, and a bomb shortly thereafter. Water poured into the fuel system and cut off fight and power, causing a serious list by 0829. However, Ensign Edgar M. Fain initiated immediate counterflooding measures, an effort which is considered to have saved the ship from capsizing as the USS Oklahoma (BB-37) had done. California settled on the bottom three days later. The 40,500-ton, 624 ft. long USS California entered service in 1919. *—U.S. Navy photo*

The wartime President of The United States Franklin Delano Roosevelt, and the only president elected to The White House more than twice, is seen here during his first term (1932-36) when he was focused on domestic issues rather than war.

BIOGRAPHIES

HISTORIC U.S. AND JAPANESE MILITARY AND POLITICAL FIGURES RELATED TO EVENTS LEADING UP TO AND THROUGH THE ATTACK ON PEARL HARBOR..

ROOSEVELT, Franklin Delano (1882-1945)
President of the United States, 1933-45

Franklin D. Roosevelt is among the five most written about U.S. presidents. His 12 years in the White House remain the longest tenure of any American chief executive. He remains the only U.S. President elected to more than two terms (he won four terms). But without a doubt the turbulent World War II years account for most of what has been written about him, and continues to be written about him. He has been praised and vilified, adored by many as almost a saint and accused by others of having had advance knowledge of the Japanese attack on Pearl Harbor. Prior to the war his presidency had been spent leading America out of the bad economic situation brought on by the Depression. Roosevelt's life and political career before World War II are well known. Therefore we will only cover that briefly here. It is worth noting that even if the war had never occurred, Franklin D. Roosevelt would still have earned a place as one of America's greatest presidents. He was born into one of America's most aristocratic families, educated by private tutors and at an exclusive preparatory school before going on to Harvard and Columbia University Law School. He entered politics at the age of 29, ran, and won, as a Democratic Party candidate the New York State Senate. In 1913 President Woodrow Wilson appointed him Assistant Secretary of the Navy. He lost in the 1914 elections to the United States Senate and remained in his navy post. In 1921, at age 39, he was stricken with polio and was barely able to stand for the rest of his life. His next political office was election as Governor of New York state. Roosevelt was elected to the first two of his four terms as President of the United States in 1932 and in 1936 His far reaching and radical "New Deal" legislation began lifting the United States out of the Depression (the industrial buildup of World War II completed the job). In 1935 Congress passed the Neutrality Act banning the provision of arms to all nations at war, which Roosevelt publicly opposed. As tensions in Europe rose and war finally broke out, FDR knew the extent and intensity of American unwillingness to become involved in the European war. Nonetheless, he believed it was in America's best interest to aide Britain and her allies. To this end he circumvented the Neutrality Act and offered the Lend-Lease Act in March, 1941. It made supplies of war material available without cash payment up front. He and British Prime Minister Winston Churchill were old acquaintances and were in agreement about war aims, formalized in August 1941, as the Atlantic Charter. The Japanese surprise attack on Pearl Harbor found America far less prepared for war than the civilian population realized. Since Roosevelt and Churchill both knew that Germany was working on an atomic bomb, and both believed the Nazis were far ahead of where they actually were in the project, it was determined that Germany had to be defeated first. Another reason was that of the Axis powers, only Germany had the industrial and technical capability to win the war single-handed. The United States became the "arsenal of democracy." With ultimate Allied victory dependent on American material and manpower, it could hardly have been otherwise. Churchill once observed, that he was only his country's political chief while Roosevelt was also the head of state. He compare it to being equivalent to that of Churchill and King George VI combined. When a growing number of ships carrying Lend-Lease supplies across the Atlantic were sunk it strengthened isolationist support for the "America First" movement. By September, 1941, the United States moved closer to war when Roosevelt asked Congress for amendments to the Neutrality Act so American ships in the Atlantic and elsewhere could "shoot on sight". In October two more attacks on U.S. ships outraged Americans. Congress agreed with FDR and passed the changes on 14 November. Most historians have avoided looking too closely at this period of American hostility without an actual declaration of war, and promote the position that the Japanese attack on Pearl Harbor in December 1941, was the beginning of the American involvement. Splitting hairs, that is accurate, but Roosevelt's policy of having merchant ships armed, and German U-boats sinking American destroyers, it is very likely that a declaration of war by the United States against Nazi Germany would have come in 1942. Roosevelt actually wanted to avoid war with Japan and actually was carrying on involved and delicate negotiations with them. As he realized that war with Japan looked more and more likely, he fostered the position that the first shots must be fired by the Japanese. That way, America could respond with a defensive declaration of war. He also realized that if he declared war on Japan he could expect her Axis allies, Germany and Italy, to come to her aid. When this scenario played out, then, the U.S. could finally drop the cloak of "neutrality" and join Britain in the fight. But because of the unfolding events, numerous warnings and intelligence information the U.S. had all through 1941, Roosevelt's detractors and conspiracy theorists say the President had to know that Japanese intentions were to attack the U.S. fleet at Pearl Harbor. Roosevelt let it happen, they say, so his wish that they would be firing the first shot could be fulfilled. That he expected war with Japan can not be denied, nor can any fault be found in his wish that, if and when war came, that the enemy fire the first shot. He did not want the U.S. to be remembered in history as the aggressor. Much of the material which raises suspicions about what he knew and when he know it, has been included in this book. This author recommends further reading on the subject include Gordon Prange's *At Dawn We Slept* and John Toland's *Infamy*. Both take opposite sides of the issue. On 12 April 1945, Franklin Roosevelt was at his retreat in Warm Springs, Georgia, having his portrait painted. He suddenly slumped over in his chair, and whispered: "I have a terrific headache." He died a few hours later of a cerebral hemorrhage. Roosevelt had won an unprecedented third term as President in 1940 and a fourth in 1944. When he died, on 12 April 1945, he was mourned throughout the Allied and neutral nations, foremost in Britain.

CHURCHILL, Winston S. (1874-1965)
Wartime Prime Minister of Great Britain 1940-45

The feisty and articulate wartime Prime Minister of Great Britain brought to the stage of world affairs a felicity of the English language rarely, if ever, seen in politicians before him, and certainly not since. His passionate and poetic oratory did more for Allied morale than can easily be measured. Winston Spencer Churchill, a Member of Parliament, was the First Lord of the Admiralty in the Conservative government of Neville Chamberlain on 1 September 1939 when Nazi Germany invaded Poland the world war began in earnest. He had previously served as First Lord of the Admiralty during World War I. After British setbacks against the Nazis in the Norwegian Campaign Chamberlain resigned as Prime Minister and, as is British custom, King George V summoned Churchill on 11 May 1940 to form a National Government. Churchill took on the dual duties of Prime Minister and Minister of Defense. Winston Churchill's vigorous leadership of Britain and total support of the Allied effort during World War II are legendary. The genuine trust and friendship shared by Churchill and President Franklin D. Roosevelt of the United States resulted in an hitherto unprecedented exchange between two sovereign nations of wartime essentials and arms while the U.S. was officially neutral. The live-saving Lend-Lease Act of March 1941 permitted Britain to order and "borrow" war goods on credit with ownership while such items were technically still owned by the U.S. Churchill and Roosevelt had what amounted to daily telephone and mail contact though major decisions regarding war strategy which involved other Allied nations were discussed at a series of widely publicized international conferences. In some instances other leaders were conspicuously obvious by their absence, i.e.: Soviet dictator Josef Stalin; Charles DeGaulle or other representatives of France; and China's Chiang Kai-shek. The first such wartime attended by Churchill and Roosevelt was at Argentina Bay in August 1941. It resulted in the signing of the Atlantic Charter. The following December (after Pearl Harbor) the Washington Conference announced a "Germany First" policy, meaning the Allied powers would concentrate their greatest efforts to defeating Germany (the more immediate world threat) before turning their full resources against Japan. This was much to the chagrin of the United States Navy, which wanted to quickly settle its score with Japan. Allies and friends they certainly were, but Churchill and Roosevelt nonetheless had several disagreements regarding strategy. In retrospect, nearly all of these were the result of each leader having to support provincial concerns of their top military and political advisers. Churchill was also not pleased with the trust Roosevelt had that Stalin would be a team player. Churchill's vigorous anti-Communism stance caused him to be suspicious of Stalin. Roosevelt, however, erroneously felt he understood Stalin and could find an agreement with him over Eastern Europe. Churchill's dealings with Stalin in February 1945 at the Yalta Conference left the British Prime Minister convinced that Stalin wanted to take over Eastern Europe. The Americans were annoyed by Churchill's frequent postponements of the planned invasion of Europe (Operation Overlord) in lieu of intervention in the Mediterranean and the Balkans. Churchill did get complete support from the U.S. for Operation Torch, the Allied invasion of North Africa, and the subsequent invasions of Sicily and Italy. When the actual planning for Operation Overlord and the D-Day invasion began Churchill and Roosevelt were of a common mind. Churchill, like Roosevelt, were without a doubt superb politicians, but their abilities as a military commanders were far less conspicuous. Overall, Churchill's wartime policies were accepted by Parliament and the British population. He survived two "no confidence" votes in Parliament. His many radio broadcasts greatly helped the morale of his countrymen and the free world in general. After the war against the Nazis ended in May 1945, those same British citizens who had clung to his every word and leadership, voted him out of office in the July 1945 elections. Apparently the British considered Churchill the perfect wartime Prime Minister but preferred a different leadership for reconstruction of Britain. Winston S. Churchill remains to most English speaking people the ultimate British hero in the Twentieth Century.

Hirohito (1901-1989)
Wartime Emperor of Japan

Hirohito, the Imperial Son of Heaven of Great Japan, was emperor from 1926 until his death in 1989. He was the last Japanese ruler to uphold the divinity of the Japanese emperor. His reign lasted longer than that of any other monarch in Japanese history. Many Westerners believe he was responsible for expanding the war into a global conflict. However, he was the emperor of his country by birth right, not because of any political machinations. Hirohito was more interested in marine biology and other pursuits than in politics and war. The role of emperor, in the Japanese constitution, was far less powerful than the title suggests. He presided at cabinet meetings but never participated in discussions. He simply gave his assent to decisions. As was also true with the king of England, the emperor was not part of a political party Hirohito was aware that General and Prime Minister Hideki Tojo had put Japan into a war mode and that Tojo's actions would lead to war. He tried to caution Tojo to be more cautious. However when war broke out it was in his name and all proclamations and orders were issued in his name. The Japanese people loved and respected the emperor as a living God. Most fought the war with a fanatical devotion to the death for him. Hirohito disapproved of the increasing belligerence in Japanese foreign policy and was personally against the pact with Germany and Italy. However his advisers had always urged him not to become entangled in politics in order to avoid compromising the imperial family. Admiral Isoroku Yamamoto, among others, kept Hirohito informed of the war's progress, but he continued to remain silent in the background. When the Japanese home islands were on the brink of being invaded, Hirohito finally became personally involved and sent Prince Konoye on a peace mission to the USSR. However, before tangible results could be obtained Hirohito personally witnessed the relentless U.S. B-29 bombing of Tokyo. After the war he confided that the destruction caused by the dropping of the two atomic bombs on Hiroshima and Nagasaki stunned him completely. On 9 August 1945, the day the second

116

Emperor Hirohito of Japan seen in formal uniform in this post World War II picture.   *--U.S. Government photo*

bomb was dropped, the cabinet was deadlocked on whether to accept the Potsdam Declaration. The great concern was about the emperor's status after the war, even though Hirohito was willing to risk his position to achieve peace. Tojo was gone as Prime Minister and Hirohito found his new Prime Minister, Kantaro Suzuki much more agreeable. On 14 August Japan surrendered. Hirohito recorded a speech, broadcast the following day, telling his people why. It was the first time a Japanese Emperor had ever spoken to his people, and the first time they heard his voice. Among the most memorable quotes was that Japan had to "'accept the unacceptable, endure the unendurable." During the U.S. occupation after the war Hirohito remained on the throne because it was widely believed that to remove him would create anti-American feelings and make occupation dangerous and difficult for U.S. troops. In January 1946 Hirohito announced to his people that he was not devine. That, like them, he was just a man. He received a friendly welcome on a visit to the United States in 1975. However, questions about his responsibility for Japan's role in World War II remained strong for many Americans.

TOJO, Hideki (1884-1948)
General and Wartime Prime Minister of Japan

Tojo war virtually the military dictator of Japan. Born in Tokyo his family tree contained a line of samurai warriors. He began his lifelong military career in 1915. By 1936 he had risen to chief of staff to the Kwantung army in Manchuria and saw combat in China. In 1938 he was appointed vice-minister for war, and rose to minister of war in 1940. He had been given a special Imperial dispensation to hold a military and a cabinet post simultaneously. He was responsible for building Japan's military strength to be able to fight a possible two-front war with China and Russia and undertook a policy of southward expansion. When the Roosevelt Administration imposed its embargo on exports to Japan, Tojo vigorously endorsed a war with the U.S. Unable to cope or control Tojo and not wanting a war with the U.S., Prime Minister Konoye resigned in October 1941 and Tojo became prime minister. (It is noted here, to avoid confusion with similar sounding names that during the 1930s and 40s Japan's ambassador to Berlin was Shigenori Togo (1882-1950) who also served as foreign minister in Tojo's cabinet). Emperor Hirohito wanted the new prime minister to start fresh and resolve all problems peacefully. However, Tojo had assumed for himself the three posts of prime minister, war minister and chief of army staff and was totally responsible for the conduct of the war and was determined that only war could bring Japan what it rightfully deserved. With Japan's successes in the first six months after the attack on Pearl Harbor Tojo gained increasing power. The unbelievable defeat at the Battle of Midway, and frequent, successive losses thereafter reduced his influence. When by 1944 American B-29 bombers were regularly bombing Tokyo, the other government ministers and several military leaders forced him to resign on 9 July. On 11 September 1945, less than a month after Japan surrendered and 10 days after the official document was signed, U.S. General Douglas MacArthur ordered Tojo arrested as a war criminal. But, like German Field Marshal Hermann Goering had done months earlier when he faced the gallows after the Nuremberg War Crimes Trials, Tojo tried to kill himself. shot himself in the chest. Goering succeeded. Tojo did not. He was revived and went to trial. The Tokyo War Crimes Trials were larger and had more defendants than the German trials, though not as well publicized. Tojo was found guilty of war crimes and hanged on 23 December 1948. Shigenori Togo was found guilty of a criminal role in the war and was sentenced to 20 years in jail, where he died.

Yamamoto, Admiral Isoroku (1884-1943)
Mastermind of the Pearl Harbor attack

Considered Japan's greatest military strategist and naval officer, he was minister of the navy from 1938 onward and from 1939 till his death he was commander in chief of the 1st Fleet from 1939. Like Tojo, his family had a samurai history. During this period his role in Japan was similar to that of U.S. Admiral Harold R. Stark in building both countries navies to be ready for the war most ranking military leaders expected. Yamamoto was responsible for the great pre-war build up and updating of the Japanese Navy and naval air power. Yamamoto was personally against a war with the United States. He had studied at Harvard and been a naval attaché in Washington and his exposure to America had very much impressed him. He was outspoken in his belief that Japan would inevitably lose a protracted war against the powerful U.S. with its astonishing amount of natural and industrial resources. But when ordered to plan for war with the U.S., Yamamoto eventually determined that Japan's only chance would be a preemptive strike against the U.S. fleet to cripple to cripple it at the outset. He considered the U.S. a sleeping giant that should not be roused, but believed that if enough damage was done to the U.S. fleet to keep it from offensive action for at least the first six months of war then Japan would be in a much stronger position to negotiate peace. His planning for the 7 December 1941 Pearl Harbor attack got underway in early 1940. It was codenamed Operation Z. Working in his cabin on his flagship, the 725-ft, 42,785-ton Nagato, (the only Japanese battleship still floating at the time of the surrender in 1945) Yamamoto did the detailed planning for the air strike, gathering intelligence about Pearl Harbor, and putting his pilots through a special training in mock attacks against a Japanese bay south of Hyushu which closely resembled Pearl Harbor. By March 1941 Operation Z was nearly complete and Rear Admiral Chuichi Nagumo, was selected as the Kido Butai attack force commander. The plan was approved on 3 November 1941. On 17 November, after a ceremony aboard Nagumo's flagship, the aircraft carrier Akagi, Yamamoto gave a brief and confident pep-talk. From the shore he watched Kido Butai slip out into the late night sea for their appointment with history. Though the Pearl Harbor attack was considered a great success, Yamamoto was distressed that the U.S. aircraft carriers had been absent and remained operational. The Doolittle raid on Tokyo in April 1941, only four months after Pearl Harbor, and launched from the deck of an aircraft carrier, shocked and stunned Yamamoto and the Japanese in general. Yamamoto knew he had to wipe out what was left of the US Pacific Fleet in a single, decisive battle. Plans were made to do just that at Midway in June 1942. Midway was crucial. If the Japanese navy could wipe out the U.S. Pacific fleet, Japan would be free to go anywhere they wanted in the Pacific. But if they failed, the American industrial machine would restore American control of the ocean within two years. In early 1942 arguments had raged in Japan about the strategic moves to be followed when the early phase of expansion came to an end. Finally, at the beginning of April, Yamamoto sent a message to the naval general staff: "In the last analysis the success of our strategy in the Pacific will be determined by whether or not we succeed in destroying the United States fleet, particularly its carrier task force.... We believe that by launching the proposed operation against Midway, we can succeed in drawing out the enemy's carrier strength and destroying it in decisive battle. If, on the other hand, the enemy should avoid our challenge, we shall still realize an important gain by advancing our defensive perimeter to Midway and the Western Aleutians without obstruction." Yamamoto created a far reaching plan involving the movement of eight separate task forces. One was to be a diversionary attack on the Aleutian Islands off Alaska. Armed with the benefit of having broken the Japanese Naval code, the U.S. knew a major attack was planned against Midway on 4 June and was able to prepare an ambush. The result was a devastating defeat for Japan, its first naval defeat ever, and included the loss of four aircraft carriers. The stunning U.S. victory at Midway came six months after Pearl Harbor. The battle of Midway left the United States in control of the air over the Pacific, and therefore proved a turning point in the war. Yamamoto's own words about crippling the U.S. fleet for six months came back to haunt him. Japan was never able to regroup or fully recover from the losses at Midway and never won a major sea battle against the U.S. in the rest of the war, though many were close and costly to both sides. In April 1943 the U.S. intercepted reports that Yamamoto would do an inspection tour of Japanese installations in the Western Solomons. Details and timing of his route were immediately dispatched to fighter control at Henderson Field, Guadalcanal, with orders: "Squadron 339 P38 must at all cost reach and destroy Yamamoto and staff... President attaches extreme importance this operation." Shortly after 7 in the morning of 18 April, 1943, sixteen Lockheed Lightnings from the island of Bougainville surprised Yamamoto's camouflaged bomber, his staff in a second plane, and their six plane fighter escort, and shot the admiral's aircraft out of the sky.

FUCHIDA, Commander Mitsuo (1902-76)
Leader of Japanese air attack on Pearl Harbor

Because of the extensive amount of information throughout this book about Fuchida, the biographical information here is brief.

Fuchida was an experienced veteran airman with combat time in Japan's war against China. His widely acknowledged superb tactics and planning skills resulted in his selection to lead the Japanese air attack on Pearl Harbor on December 7, 1941. Fuchida personally coordinated all the preparations and led the first wave. It was considered extraordinary and unprecedented to have a single Flight Commander for a major mission. His appointment was a tribute to Fuchida's skill and courage. Fuchida was scheduled to lead the flying operations at the June, 1942 Battle of Midway but was unexpectedly sidelined by appendicitis. Ironically, U.S. Admiral William F. Halsey, who would have been the overall commander of U.S. Naval forces, was also out of the action and in the hospital at the time because of illness. Fuchida's close friend, Commander Minoru Genda, replaced Fuchida.

FRIEDMAN, William Frederic (1891-1969)
"The Man Who Broke the Japanese Purple Code"

Probably the most famous military codebreaker in the 20th Century, Friedman was born in Russia in 1891, but at age five his family emigrated to the United States in 1896. A natural born mathematician, his enthusiasm and expertise for military code-breaking first took place in 1917 for the U.S. Army in France during World War I while he was stationed at the U.S. Expeditionary Force

Headquarters. Between the two world wars Friedman remained in government service and was joined in his pursuits by his very able and equally talented wife Elizabeth. In 1940 Friedman succeeded in breaking the secret Japanese diplomatic code commonly called "Purple" by the U.S. intelligence community. To many, the information garnered from Purple intercepts should have been sufficient to alert the U.S. in advance that the Japanese were planning to attack U.S. military installations in Hawaii. The fact that this information was not favorably acted on in time to prevent the Pearl Harbor attack, is frequently pointed to by conspiracy theorists as proof that America sacrificed its fleet in order to get into the world war without firing the first shot. The mental stress and physical exhaustion associated with Friedman work breaking the Purple Code caused him to have a nervous breakdown. Nothing he ever did professionally thereafter even came close to the heights he reached breaking the Purple Code.

FORRESTAL, James Vincent (1892-1949)
Secretary of the Navy, 1944-47

American administrator who served as first undersecretary of the navy during the second world war, and played a key role in building up United States naval strength. After a varied but extremely successful early career as a cub reporter, banker, and financial speculator, Forrestal entered political life in 1940 in a form of public service, as a low-paid assistant to President Roosevelt. Six weeks later he was given the new post as first undersecretary of the navy and for the next four years was instrumental in the production and procurement of naval supplies. He did not avoid friction with senior naval officers, consistently maintaining that a civilian could carry out the task of building up the navy as well as a professional seaman. By the late stages of the war he had turned the United States navy into a larger organization than the combined fleets of the rest of the world. In 1944 Secretary of the Navy Knox died and Forrestal took his place. He expressed forceful political opinions from then on, having developed a passionate hatred of Communism and a determination to see his country contain it through strength. He was also against measures which would destroy the strength of Germany and Japan, and opposed proposals to share atomic knowledge. He fought to maintain budget spending on defense as a means of containing the Soviet threat and preserving world peace, but President Truman whose views later came more into line with Forrestal's, initially reduced Forrestal's budget proposals. His career was crowned by the appointment as first secretary of defense, but he resigned after only a few months through ill health, and in 1949 entered Bethesda Naval Hospital for psychiatric care. Forrestal's self-esteem deteriorated by what he believed was his failure to impress President Truman with his experience and performance. On 21 May 1949 he jumped from a sixth-floor window and was killed. (In one of the more bizarre events associated with him is his alleged role in the cover-up of the so-called UFO crash at Roswell, New Mexico in 1947. In this story Forrestal killed himself because he was unable to cope with the realization that alien life visited earth.)

GENDA, Commander Minoru (1904-1989)
Tactical planner of the Pearl Harbor attack

Outside of Japan, very little biographical information has been previously published about Genda in the West. He is most frequently remembered and mentioned for his participation in both the Pearl Harbor attack and the Battle of Midway as an exceptionally talented Japanese fighter commander. Genda was appointed by Rear Admiral Takijiro Onishi to plan a feasibility study for Admiral Isoroku Yamamoto's proposed Pearl Harbor attack. He worked with Commander Mitsuo Fuchida doing this. Genda was considered a valuable member of Admiral Chuichi Nagumo's aircraft carrier fleet and was greatly depended upon for advice on the tactical use of air power. Genda led the first attack in the Battle of Midway. As previously noted in these pages, he crossed services and became a Japanese Army general. After the war he served in the upper house of the Diet (similar to the U.S. Senate).

William F. Halsey, the tenacious American admiral the Japanese feared the most, is seen here at a Hawaiian Luau honoring repatriated U.S. servicemen who had been Japanese POW's. With him is Major General Clark L. Ruffner.

–U.S. Army photo

GREW, Joseph (1880-1965)
U.S. Ambassador to Japan, 1932-41

Grew, a longtime personal friend of President Roosevelt, served as Ambassador to Japan from 1932-41. Considered an expert on Japanese government, military and social affairs, Grew recognized that the Japanese Cabinet had little power, authority or control of the hawkish militarists in the Japanese Army. Ambassador Grew worked to the best of his abilities to prevent war in the Far East. Nonetheless, in September 1940 he sent the so-called 'Green Light' telegram to Washington which recommended that "a show of force together with a determination to employ it if need be' (could) alone contribute effectively" to maintaining peace in the area. President Roosevelt, with the advice of Secretary of State Cordell Hull, trusted Grew's insight and the result was a U.S. oil embargo against Japan. Grew was arrested in Tokyo after the Japanese attacked Pearl Harbor. He, and other Allied diplomats were returned to their home countries in the summer of 1942 as a result of an Allied-Axis exchange for Japanese diplomats being held. Upon returning to the U.S., Grew remained with the State Department throughout the war as an expert adviser on Japanese affairs.

HALSEY, William Frederick (1882-1959)
U.S. Navy admiral

The first thing that should be mentioned in any biographical sketch about Halsey is that he was never called "Bull" by anyone who knew him in the U.S. Navy. That nickname had been given to his father many years earlier because of the Stentorian tones the elder Halsey employed addressing midshipmen. Early in World War II a reporter either mistakenly, or for some other reason, associated the father's nickname to the son. And it stuck, much to Halsey's dismay. Among the many things Halsey is remembered for is the blunt remark he made upon returning to Pearl Harbor the evening of December 7, 1941 and seeing the devastation: "Before we're through with them, the Japanese language will only be spoken in hell!" Aboard his flagship USS Enterprise (CV6), Halsey had delivered aircraft to Wake Island. His caustic remark at the sight of seeing the fleet in Pearl Harbor struck the appropriate chord in expressing the feelings of most Americans. Halsey was a career military officer and, as is true with many of the others in these pages, much of what is preserved and remembered about him is his military accomplishments. In Halsey's case they are legion. He commanded several victorious actions against the Japanese in the Pacific. Two months after Pearl Harbor he led offensive actions against the Japanese in the Gilbert and Marshall Islands and Wake Island. In April 1942 he led Task Force 16 the small, two aircraft carrier force consisting of his flagship the USS Enterprise and the USS Hornet (CV-8) which launched the United State's first raid against Japan itself. The bombers in Lt. Col. Jimmy Doolittle's famous "Thirty Seconds Over Tokyo" raid took off from the Hornet. By October 1942 Halsey had overall command of the South Pacific area. Halsey defeated the Japanese at Guadalcanal, sinking twenty-three Japanese ships. In June 1944 he became commander of the Third Fleet in the Pacific, as well as commander of Western Pacific task forces. It was Halsey who suggested the "island hopping" tactics of bypassing certain islands, known to have fortified Japanese positions, in favor of capturing others closer to the homeland. Halsey's most celebrated engagement was in the great Battle of Leyte Gulf from 23-25 October 1944. His forces sank four carriers and a battleship, contributing to total losses for the Japanese that were greater than any other naval battle in history. The only major naval engagement Halsey missed in the Pacific was the Battle of Midway because he was hospitalized with a bad skin disorder.

Hopkins, Harry (1890-1946)
FDR's closest adviser during the WWII years

A close friend, aide and trusted adviser to President Roosevelt Hopkins also served as Secretary of Commerce, Chairman of the Munitions Assignment Board, member of the Pacific War Council, the War Production Board and the War Resources Board. His 1941 talks with Churchill led to implementation of the Lend-Lease program which let the United States get around the Neutrality Act and supply Britain. Hopkins was recognized as FDR's official spokesman by foreign leaders as well as to the Combined Joint Chiefs of Staff. Because of his closeness to FDR, Hopkins was regarded by many friends and foes alike as the second most powerful man in the U.S. Though known to have been in poor health throughout the war, Harry Hopkins' imprint, opinions, and advice were said to have been present in every major decision the U.S. and Roosevelt made during the war years. His last important mission was after Roosevelt's death when President Truman asked him to serve as special envoy to Soviet dictator Josef Stalin in Moscow for talks about post-war Europe. Hopkins died within a year of his friend FDR.

Hull, Cordell (1871-1955)
U.S. Secretary of State, 1933-44

Widely considered a refined gentleman and man of peace, Hull often appeared out of place in the rough and tumble world of wartime politics. An internationalist, he and played a major role in the creation of the United Nations. Prior to the attack on Pearl Harbor, Hull had been at the center of negotiations with the Japanese, which had begun in earnest in July 1941. Because of U.S. codebreaking, Hull was privy to all Japanese diplomatic messages from Tokyo to Washington, making the U.S. aware that the Japanese were preparing for war. In September 1941 Hull persuaded President Roosevelt not to have a face-to-face meeting with Japanese Prime Minister Konoye. Hull believed such a meeting could only be held if a diplomatic protocol and agreement was in place first. The final stage of negotiations to avoid a wider expansion of Japanese military conquests in Asia began on 22 November 1941 when the both sides considered proposals for a timetable setting Japanese withdrawal from Indo-China and China itself. In retrospect, had this succeeded, it might very well have prevented the attack on Pearl harbor. However, the Chinese did not like the proposal, fearing that they were being abandoned by the US. Instead, Hull, with the advice and consent of Roosevelt, submitted a final demand that Japan withdraw from all of mainland Asia. This was unacceptable to the Japanese and they handed Hull the Declaration of War two hours after the attack on Pearl Harbor had begun. During the war Roosevelt conducted much of US foreign affairs himself through his special envoys such as Harry Hopkins. Hull had no more than weekly meetings with the President. Nonetheless, his plate was full and he played a major role in numerous diplomatic events and situations throughout the war. He was in poor health when he led the US delegation to the Foreign Ministers' Conference at Moscow in 1943 which addressed and solved many postwar problems. Hull was also a driving force for the Dumbarton Oaks Conference that laid the groundwork for the proposed United Nations. His efforts in helping create the U.N. earned him the 1945 Nobel Peace Prize.

KIMMEL, Admiral Husband E. (1882-1968)
U.S. Navy commander at Pearl Harbor

Because of the extensive amount of information throughout this book about the U.S. Navy and U.S. Army commanders, Admiral Kimmel and General Short, the biographical information here has deliberately been kept brief.

Handpicked by President Franklin D. Roosevelt, Admiral Husband E. Kimmel had been jumped ahead of 32 senior admirals when he was unexpectedly appointed Commander in Chief of the U.S. Fleet (CINCUS) on 1 February 1941. Kimmel was personally known to Roosevelt from FDR's tenure as Assistant Secretary of the Navy more than two decades earlier. Prior to assuming command as CINCUS Kimmel had been Commander of Cruisers, Battle Force. Kimmel's predecessor as U.S. Navy commander in Hawaii was Admiral James O. Richardson, who had lost favor with Roosevelt because of frequent outspoken comments that Pearl Harbor's long, narrow channel entrance (requiring capital ships to enter one at a time) amounted to a "God-damned mousetrap." Kimmel was relieved of command on December 17, ten days after the Japanese attack. On February 19, 1942, less than two months after Pearl Harbor, Kimmel's request for retirement was granted. He was reduced in rank on charges of dereliction of duty and for "making errors in judgment," though neither of these were officially lodged against him. In 1946 a Congressional Investigating Committee concluded that Kimmel was guilty of errors of judgment and not dereliction of duty.

KNOX, Frank (1874-1944)
Secretary of the Navy, 1940-1944

Frank Knox's introduction to politics came via an early career as a successful journalist and newspaperman. Knox failed to win the Republican Party's vice-presidential nomination in the 1936 national elections against the Democratic ticket headed by incumbent Franklin D. Roosevelt. Initially, Knox declined Roosevelt's 1939 invitation to serve as Secretary of the Navy in a bipartisan government, but he accepted the post when FDR repeated the invitation in July of the following year. Knox totally supported Roosevelt's wartime policies and traveled thousands of miles throughout the world to inspect and visit U.S. Naval bases and ships wherever they operated. He was the first and most senior Administration official to visit Pearl Harbor after the Japanese attack. He died in office of a heart attack on 28 April 1944.

KING, Admiral Ernest (1878-1956)
Chief of U.S. Naval Operations, 1942-45

Ernest King had graduated fourth in his class from the United States Naval Academy at Annapolis, Maryland, in 1901. A veteran of the Spanish-American war, King was promoted rear admiral in 1933 and admiral in 1941. On February 1, 1941 he was named commander of the newly formed United States Atlantic Fleet (the same day Admiral Husband E. Kimmel assumed command of the U.S. Pacific Fleet based in Hawaii). When the United States entered World War II in December, 1941, King was named Commander in

Chief of the U.S. Navy. Three months later, in March 1942, King replaced Admiral Harold R. Stark as Chief of Naval Operations, making King the highest ranking and most important officer in the U.S. Navy. He was the first officer to hold both posts at the same time. King was a member of both the U.S. Joint Chiefs of Staff and the Allied Combined Chiefs of Staff (U.S. and British). He was convinced that the U.S. Navy could defeat the Japanese in the Pacific if it were given a greater share of resources. He was unwilling to accept the necessity of defeating Germany before concentrating on the defeat of Japan. Roosevelt's insistence on sticking to the 'Germany first' policy overcame King's objections, although King never moderated his view. This position often put him at odds conflict with the British. King's xenophobia also resulted in British commanders having difficulty securing intelligence from American sources about the war in the Far East. King reportedly said: 'What operations are or are not conducted in the Pacific is no affair of the combined chiefs of staff since this theatre is exclusively American.' As Chief of Naval Operations King fully supported Admiral Chester Nimitz conduct of operations in the Pacific and helped make Nimitz's "fleet train" system work. This system helped to keep carriers and battle cruisers at sea without needing to return to base for repairs or servicing. King spent most of the war in Washington, D.C. In 1944 King was promoted to the newly created rank of fleet admiral. After the war, he served as adviser to the secretary of defense and secretary of the navy.

LEAHY, William Daniel (1875-1959)
United States admiral and diplomat

Leahy's 42-year military career began at the turn of the century with the Spanish-American war. By 1937 he had risen to the highest post in the U.S. Navy, of chief of naval operations. He retired from active service in 1939 but was almost immediately appointed by President Franklin D. Roosevelt as governor of Puerto Rico. Then, in 1940 with war raging in Europe, Roosevelt appointed him ambassador to Vichy France, with the two main responsibilities of keeping the

Vichy government independent of Germany, and to prevent French colonies and the French fleet from being absorbed or allied with the Germans. His results were less than was expected. Roosevelt called Leahy back to the U.S. and appointed him White House Chief of Staff in 1942 and here he served with distinction and became a trusted and close adviser to Roosevelt. After FDR's death President Truman relied heavily on Leahy at the Potsdam Conference. Leahy continued as White House Chief of staff until March 1949.

MARSHALL, George Catlett (1880-1959)
General and United States Army Chief of Staff

It was Marshall's confidence on the morning of 7 December 1941 that he could get the warning of Japanese intentions from Washington to Pearl Harbor quicker than Admiral Harold Stark which permitted the attack to truly be a surprise. Marshall's warning, sent over commercial wires, reached the U.S. Fleet commander, Admiral Husband E. Kimmel, hours after the attack was over. Though he was initially widely criticized in private for this failure, he was never seriously chastised or reprimanded openly. George Marshall graduated from the prestigious Virginia Military Institute (VMI) in 1901 and began a colorful and active military career as a second lieutenant in 1902. He became a general in 1939 thereafter appointed by President Franklin D. Roosevelt to the ultimate job for every soldier, Army Chief of Staff. He served in that position throughout World War II. He is regarded by many historians as the greatest master of logistics in the history of warfare. Under Marshall the United States Army grew from a small, poorly equipped force of under 400,000 men into the largest, fully equipped, combat-ready army the world had ever seen. By the time World War II ended, Marshall had mustered approximately 9-million troops into service. Marshall was a member of the U.S. and British Combined Chiefs of Staff, the Allied body responsible for setting and implementing military strategy and tactics against Nazi Germany and her allies. Next to Roosevelt and Churchill, Marshall was often the most dominant figure at all wartime gatherings of world leaders. Because of his desk job in Washington, and the fact that he was not a combat field commander, Marshall remains a relatively obscure general. George Marshall is not remembered by the dashing exploits of a Patton, Rommel, Bradley, or Gavin, but his vast contribution to the Allied success in the war is undeniable. He retired as chief of staff in 1945, and was appointed Ambassador to China by President Truman, whom he thereafter served Secretary of State in 1947-8. It was during this period when he authored the famous post-war recovery program for Europe that carries his name: the Marshall Plan. Marshall also served Truman as Secretary of Defense in 1950-1, and received the Nobel Peace Prize in 1953.

Nagumo, Vice-Admiral Chuichi
Commander of the Pearl Harbor strike force

Nagumo was the senior officer present (SOP) with the Kido Butai fleet that attacked Pearl Harbor on 7 December 1941. Nagumo was a qualified ordnance officer, not an aviator like U.S. Admiral William F. Halsey, nor was he pleased with command of the aircraft carrier attack force. Considered overly cautious in many instances, even by his colleagues, Nagumo failed to order a third wave attack for fear that the missing American aircraft carriers might suddenly appear. As the Japanese commander during the Battle of Midway, six months after Pearl Harbor, he suffered Japan's first major Naval defeat ever, loosing four aircraft carriers. He also came up short twice against the U.S. Navy in battles off Guadalcanal in 1942. By this time the Japanese fleet he commanded had little resemblance to the one he led against Pearl Harbor less than a year earlier and he was relieved of command. His final military posting was as commander of the defense of Saipan, where. Nagumo committed suicide on 6 July 1944 upon finally admitting Japan was doomed to loose the war. Had he been more aggressive at Pearl Harbor and sent a third wave to destroy the oil tank farm and also sent his formidable air fleet to find and sink the American aircraft carriers, then there would have been no Japanese defeat at Midway. And the course of the war in the Pacific could have turned out quite differently.

NIMITZ, Chester William (1885-1966)
U.S. Pacific Fleet commander, replacing Kimmel

Less than two weeks after the Japanese attack on Pearl Harbor, President Franklin D. Roosevelt, jumped Admiral Chester W. Nimitz over 28 other career officers more senior in time as the replacement for Admiral Husband E. Kimmel as commander of the United States Pacific Fleet. In 1942 he was named commander of all Allied forces in the Central Pacific, while General Douglas MacArthur had equal authority in the Southwest Pacific. Nimitz is remembered for his ability to survive and succeed in the difficult job of rebuilding the devastated fleet while taking offensive action against the Japanese. But his greatest operational accomplishment was the American victory over the Japanese in the Battle of Midway. The fact that the U.S. was able to break the Japanese navy code permitted Nimitz to ambush the enemy with aircraft carrier borne planes and land-based aircraft from Midway and Hawaii. The U.S. victory, six months after Pearl Harbor, was the turning point in the Pacific war. It ended any hope Japan had for domination of the Pacific.

STARK, Admiral Harold Raynsford (1880-1972)
Chief of U.S. Naval Operations, 1939-42

Admiral Stark was appointed Chief of Naval Operations (CNO) in 1939 and was responsible for the tremendous expansion of the United States Navy immediately prior to the start of World War II. Stark went before the U.S. Congress in June 1940, when German domination of Europe was imminent, and requested $4-billion dollars above the U.S. Navy's normal appropriation. He explained that the funding was necessary to build a 'two-ocean navy'. He pointed out that it would take two years to repair the deficiencies arising from the United States' pre-war neutrality policy. At this time he also took part in secret discussions with the British regarding the coming war. In an effort to contain the threat of further German expansion as much as possible, Stark introduced convoys for merchant shipping supplying American bases overseas as well as ships carrying Lend-Lease supplies across the Atlantic. He organized naval patrols to protect US shipping from German submarine and surface ships. Towards the end of 1941 as Japanese-American negotiations reached a critical point, Stark put the Navy on war alert and it was able to move into action immediately after Pearl Harbor. However he failed to give Admiral Husband E. Kimmel in Pearl Harbor sufficient warning and was criticized in the government inquiries which followed. In March 1942 Stark was named Commander of all U.S. Naval Forces in the European Theater of Operations. His duties were mostly administrative and diplomatic with respect to all Allied conferences and planning sessions throughout the rest of the war. Stark was from the start one of the principal advocates of giving the war against the Germans top priority. During the planing and preparations for Operation Overlord, the D-Day, June 6. 1944 Allied invasion of Europe, Stark played the sometimes very difficult role in keeping Anglo-American relations smooth and cooperative. Harold R. Stark was known throughout his career by a strange nickname "Betty", which he had acquired while a young midshipman at the U.S. Naval Academy at Annapolis, Maryland.

STIMSON, Henry Lewis (1867-1950)
U.S. Secretary of War, 1940-45

Stimson, a graduate of Yale and of Harvard, was a lawyer and active in Republican politics in New York City by the turn of the century. In 1910 he ran for governor of New York on the Republican ticket and lost. He was Secretary of War for President Taft between 1911 and 1913, served as a U.S. Army colonel in the First World War, and was Secretary of State (1929-33) in Republican President Herbert Hoover's administration. Despite his Republican credentials Stimson was named to Democratic President Franklin D. Roosevelt's wartime cabinet as Secretary of War in July 1940. Already over seventy when World War II began, Stimson was nevertheless an energetic forward thinking, and productive administrator. Stimson was strongly against America's isolationist position and vigorously supported Roosevelt's Lend-Lease program along with increasing aid to Britain. Part of his policy was to provide the maximum possible help to Britain in the Atlantic battle and was one of the most outspoken members of the Roosevelt Administration who fought for the repeal of the Neutrality Act, so that American merchant ships could be armed. He introduced America's first compulsory military service, the "Draft," in peacetime in 1940. Secretary Stimson, along with Roosevelt and a handful of other American leaders, was aware that Germany had been working on an atomic bomb since 1938. Consequently, was an ardent advocate of defeating Germany before Japan. Stimson was very active in organizing scientific research in all areas of weaponry during the war. Very early on he was involved in exploring the possibilities of atomic warfare and was personally responsible for overseeing the development program for the atomic bomb, codenamed the Manhattan Project. Stimson was especially vocal in advocating the initiation of a 'second front' in northwest Europe as soon as possible. This was something that Soviet dictator Joseph Stalin was also repeatedly asking the Allies for. Stimson urged British Prime Minister Winston Churchill to plan for a cross-channel European invasion in 1943. Churchill, and Army Chief of Staff General George C. Marshall and General Dwight D. Eisenhower, Supreme Allied Commander in Europe, eventually managed to convince the Secretary of War that in order to launch a successful invasion, it would be impossible to collect sufficient material and manpower for an invasion before the spring of 1944 at the very earliest. After the defeat of Nazi Germany Stimson, who believed using the atomic bomb could save thousands of American lives, was outspoken in his support and recommendation for dropping the atom bomb on Japan to end the war. After President Roosevelt's sudden death in April 1945, it was Stimson, while at the Potsdam Conference, told the new President, Harry S Truman, about the bomb and that the device was ready for use. After Japan signed the surrender document in September 1945, Stimson, then 77, resigned and retired from public life.

WORLD WAR II STILL IN THE NEWS

Though it may seem like "ancient history" to some readers of this book, the following items, and numerous others like them, were in news as the author was working on this book.

Remains of U.S. Pilot Who Survived Pearl Harbor Only to be Shot Down in Europe Discovered in France in February, 2001

An American pilot who survived the Japanese attack on Pearl Harbor and later shot down three Japanese planes during the June, 1942 Battle of Midway, was discovered in France in February, 2001. Lieutenant William Patton was reported missing in action in January 1945 when his P-51 Mustang fighter became separated from bombers it was escorting from England on a raid on Germany. He was last seen over Roubaix, France, near the Belgian border. His plane's wreckage was discovered in that area by a farmer digging a drain. Military "dog tags" identified Patton as the pilot.

Japan's Top Fighter Ace, 84, Died After Dinner At U.S. Military Base in September 2000

Saburo Sakai, Japan's top fighter ace in World War II with 64 enemy planes to his credit, died in September, 2000 after suffering a heart attack at the U.S. Naval base in Atsugi, Japan. Sakai had been attending a dinner with U.S. military officers. In the decades following the war Sakai had been an outspoken opponent of war and a leading spokesman for reconciliation with the U.S. and other Allied powers. He had frequently called for Japan to acknowledge its war guilt. As recently as a month before his death he is quoted as saying ``Who gave the orders for that stupid war? Glorifying death was a mistake. Because I survived, I was able to move on and make friends in the U.S. and other countries." Sakai had been wounded four times and lost an eye.

137

Remains of 18 Marines Killed on Makin Atoll In Gilberts, Discovered in 58 Years Later

Mason Yarbrough, and 18 other U.S. Marine Raiders, listed as missing in action for 58 years, died on 17 August 1942 on Makin Atoll, now known as Butaritari, in the Gilbert Islands. They were reported as MIA even though other Marines paid an islander to bury the bodies in temporary graves on the beach. Recovery efforts in the decades that followed were unsuccessful. The case was finally looked at by the U.S. Army Central Identification Laboratory. In 1999 the now old man who had buried the Marines led an identification team to the site. The discovery of 20 bodies was the single largest recovery that the Central Identification Laboratory has ever made: the 19 Marine Raiders and a local resident. As this book goes to press, the CIL continues to work on identifying the remains of the other Marine Raiders.

Five C-46 Crewmen Missing Since 1944 Found Virtually Intact in 1993; First is Buried in 1997

The virtually intact remains of Pfc. Bartholomew Peter Giacalone and four crewmates aboard a U.S. Army C-46 cargo plane were found in 1993 where they crashed on a Tibetan glacier in 1944. Giacalone was positively identified by DNA provided by his family. Giacalone's body was returned to his family and interred at St. James Cemetery in Woodbridge, N.J. in December 1997, replete with a military honor guard from Fort Monmouth, N.J. Giacalone's sisters, 86 year old sister Angeline Brigiani, 80 year old Gertrude Costello were presented with the American Flag that had draped his casket. According to the U.S. Army Central Identification Laboratory at Hickam Field on Oahu, Hawaii, the long delay between the 1993 discovery and the return of remains was due to extensive efforts at positive identification. There was no flight record of the mission and no tail number remained on the plane. *(This information was provided to the author by a relative of Pfc. Giacalone, Mrs. Joan Nemick of Mountainside, N.J.)*

The two-year-old USS Arizona (BB-39) in New York Harbor in 1918, with the Brooklyn Bridge and skyline behind it. She wouldn't be modernized until 1932.

. . .And as she looked entering Pearl Harbor, her final home port, in July, 1941.   *–U.S. Navy photos*

USS Arizona (BB-39)
Casualty List

Military personnel killed on the battleship Arizona, December 7, 1941. U.S. Navy Reservists and United States Marines are so designated following rank. All others are regular Navy personnel.

NAME	RANK	HOME
AARON, Hubert Charles Titus	F2c	Arkansas
ABERCROMBIE, Samuel Adolphus	S1c	Texas
ADAMS, Robert Franklin	S1c	Alabama
ADKISON, James Dillion	S1c	Texas
AGUIRRE, Reyner Aceves	S2c	
AGUON, Gregorio San N.	MATT1c	Guam
AHERN, Richard James	F1c	California
ALBEROVSKY, Francis Severin	BMKR1c	California
ALBRIGHT, Galen Winston	S1c	Indiana
ALEXANDER, Elvis Author	S2c	Arkansas
ALLEN, Robert Lee	SF3c	Texas
ALLEN, William Clayborn	EM1c	California

===

ALL RANKS PRESENT IN USS ARIZONA (BB-39) DEAD

Every rank in the U.S. Navy of 1941, including admiral, is represented among those who died aboard the USS Arizona (BB-39) on December 7, 1941. Rear Admiral Isaac C. Kidd was killed manning a machine gun. The Arizona was his flagship.

<u>USS Arizona (BB-39) Casualty List</u> --continued

ALLEN, William Lewis	SK2c,USNR	Texas
ALLEY, Jay Edgar	GM1c	
ALLISON, Andrew K.	F1c	Missouri
ALLISON, J. T.	F1c	
ALTEN, Ernest Mathew	S2c	California
AMON, Frederick Purdy	S1c	
AMUNDSON, Leo DeVere	PVT,USMC	
ANDERSON, Charles Titus	CM2c	California
ANDERSON, Delbert Jake	BM2c	Minnesota
ANDERSON, Donald William	SM3c	
ANDERSON, Harry	S1c	California
ANDERSON, Howard Taisey	F1c	Maryland
ANDERSON, Irwin Corinthis	MATT1c	
ANDERSON, James Pickins Jr.	S1c	
ANDERSON, Lawrence Donald	ENS,USNR	
ANDERSON, Robert Adair	GM3c	Missouri
ANDREWS, Brainerd Wells	CCMP	Vermont
ANGLE, Earnest Hersea	F2c	West Virginia
ANTHONY, Glenn Samuel	S1c	California
APLIN, James Raymond	CWTP	California
APPLE, Robert William	F1c	Illinois
APREA, Frank Anthony	COX	
ARLEDGE, Eston	SM2c	Louisiana
ARNAUD, Achilles	F3c	Louisiana
ARNEBERG, William Robert	F2c	
ARNOLD, Claude Duran Jr.	F3c	Louisiana
ARNOLD, Thell	SC1c	Arkansas
ARRANT, John Anderson	MM1c	Florida
ARVIDSON, Carl Harry	CMMP	Washington
ASHMORE, Wilburn James	S2c	Louisiana
ATCHISON, John Calvin	PVT,USMC	Missouri
ATKINS, Gerald Arthur	HA1c	Nebraska
AUSTIN, Laverne Alfred	S1c	New York

<u>USS Arizona (BB-39) Casualty List</u>   --continued

AUTRY, Eligah T. Jr.	COX	Arkansas
AVES, Willard Charles	F2c	
AYDELL, Miller Xavier	WT2c	Louisiana
AYERS, Dee Cumpie	S2c	
BADILLA, Manuel Domonic	F1c	
BAILEY, George Richmond	PFC, USMC	California
BAIRD, Billy Bryon	S1c	Indiana
BAJORIMS, Joseph	S1c	Illinois
BAKER, Robert Dewey	CMM	
BALL, William V.	S1c	
BANDY, Wayne Lynn	MUS2c	Missouri
BANGERT, John Henry	FC1c	
BARAGA, Joseph	SGT,USMC	Michigan
BARDON, Charles Thomas	S2c	Oklahoma
BARKER, Loren Joe	COX	Iowa
BARNER, Walter Ray	S2c	Texas
BARNES, Charles Edward	Y3c	Missouri
BARNES, Delmar Hayes	LTJG,USNR	California
BARNETT, William Thermon	S2c	Arkansas
BARTLETT, David William	CPL,USMC	California
BARTLETT, Paul Clement	MM1c	Texas
BATES, Edward Munroe Jr.	ENS,USNR	New York
BATES, Tobert Alvin	PHM3c	Texas
BATOR, Edward	F1c	New York
BAUER, Harold Walter	RM3c	Kansas

==

HE ISSUED THE "ABANDON SHIP" ORDER

After the deaths of Admiral Kidd and the USS Arizona's (BB-39) commanding officer, Captain Van Valkenburgh the order to abandon ship was given by Lt. Commander Samuel G. Fuqua, one of 16 Pearl Harbor survivors awarded the Medal of Honor.

USS Arizona (BB-39) Casualty List --continued

BEATON, Freddie	PVT,USMC	California
BEAUMONT, James Ammon	S2c	Texas
BECK, George Richard	S1c	California
BECKER, Marvin Otto	GM3c	Kansas
BECKER, Wesley Paulson	S1c	Kansas
BEDFORD, Purdy Renaker	F1c	Kentucky
BEERMAN, Henry Carl	CM3c	Washington
BEGGS, Harold Eugene	F1c	Missouri
BELL, Hershel Homer	FC2c	Illinois
BELL, Richard Leroy	S2c	California
BELLAMY, James Curtis	OS3c	California
BELT, Everett Ray Jr.	PFC,USMC	Missouri
BENFORD, Sam Austin	BKR2c	Minnesota
BENNETT, William Edmond Jr.	Y3c	Illinois
BENSON, James Thomas	S1c	Alabama
BERGIN, Roger Joseph	F2c	Canada
BERKANSKI, Albert Charles	COX	Pennsylvania
BERNARD, Frank Peter	F2c	
BERRY, Gordon Eugene	F2c	Colorado
BERRY, James Winford	F2c	California
BERSCH, Arthur Anthony	S1c	Iowa
BERTIE, George Allan Jr.	S2c	Arizona
BIBBY, Charles Henry	F2c	Alabama
BICKEL, Kenneth Robert	F1c	Nebraska
BICKNELL, Dale Deen	S1c	Washington
BIRCHER, Frederick Robert	RM3c	Pennsylvania
BIRDSELL, Rayon Delois	F2c	Missouri
BIRGE, George Albert	S1c	New York
BISHOP, Grover Barron	MM1c	Texas
BISHOP, Millard Charles	F3c	Alabama
BISHOP, Wesley Horner Jr.	RM3c,USNR	New York
BLACK, James Theron	PVT,USMC	Alabama
BLAIS, Albert Edward	RM3c,USNR	New York

USS Arizona (BB-39) Casualty List --continued

BLAKE, James Monroe	F2c	Missouri
BLANCHARD, Albert Richard	COX	Minnesota
BLANKENSHIP, Theron A.	S1c	Alabama
BLANTON, Atticus Lee	SF3c	Florida
BLIEFFERT, Richmond Frederick	S1c	Washington
BLOCK, Ivan Lee	PHM2c	New Mexico
BLOUNT, Wayman Boney	S1c	Texas
BOGGESS, Roy Eugene	SF2c	California
BOHLENDER, Sam	GM2c	Colorado
BOLLING, Gerald Revese	S1c	Arkansas
BOLLING, Walter Karr	F3c	Kentucky
BOND, Burnis Leroy	CPL,USMC	Missouri
BONEBRAKE, Buford Earl	F2c	Kansas
BONFIGLIO, William John	EM1c	New York
BOOTH, Robert Sinclair Jr.	ENS,USNR	
BOOZE, Asbury Legare	BM1c	Georgia
BORGER, Richard	CMMA	California
BOROVICH, Joseph John	S1c	California
BORUSKY, Edwin Charles	CPL,USMC	North Dakota
BOSLEY, Kenneth Leroy	EM3c	Missouri
BOVIALL, Walter Robert	AMM2c	Wisconsin
BOWMAN, Howard Alton	S2c	Iowa
BOYD, Charles Andrew	CM3c	Alabama
BOYDSTUN, Don Jasper	S2c	Texas
BOYDSTUN, R. L.	S2c	Texas

===

CRUSHED WATER MAIN LINES HINDERED FIREFIGHTING

The efforts of the Ford Island Fire Brigade to contain or control the numerous fires were seriously hindered when the USS Arizona (BB-39) sank. The battleship settled on the island's main water lines, resulting in a complete loss of pressure.

USS Arizona (BB-39) Casualty List --continued

BRABBZSON, Oran Merrill	MUS2c	New York
BRADLEY, Bruce Dean	S2c	Illinois
BRAKKE, Kenneth Gay	F3c	Washington
BRICKLEY, Eugene	PVT,USMC	Indiana
BRIDGES, James Leon	S1c	Tennessee
BRIDGES, Paul Hyatt	S1c	Arkansas
BRIDIE, Robert Maurice	F1c	
BRIGNOLE, Erminio Joseph	S2c	California
BRITTAN, Charles Edward	S2c	California
BROADHEAD, Johnnie Cecil	F2c	Alabama
BROCK, Walter Pershing	S1c	Kentucky
BROMLEY, George Edward	SM3c	Washington
BROMLEY, Jimmie	S1c	
BROOKS, Robert Neal	ENS,USNR	Washington
BROOME, Loy Raymond	SM3c	Oklahoma
BROONER, Allen Ottis	S1c	Indiana
BROPHY, Myron Alonzo	F2c	Vermont
BROWN, Charles Martin	S2c	California
BROWN, Elwyn Leroy	EM3c	Kansas
BROWN, Frank George	QM3c	Oregon
BROWN, Richard Corbett	S1c	California
BROWN, William Howard	S2c	Oregon
BROWNE, Harry Lamont	CMMA	California
BROWNING, Tilmon David	S1c	West Virginia
BRUNE, James William	RM3c	Missouri
BRYAN, Leland Howard	S1c	Texas
BRYANT, Lloyd Glenn	BM2c	California
BUCKLEY, Jack C.	FC3c	Kentucky
BUDD, Robert Emile	F2c	Michigan
BUHR, Clarence Edward	S1c	New Mexico
BURDEN, Ralph Leon	RM3c	Ohio
BURDETTE, Ralph Warren	MUS2c	New Jersey
BURKE, Frank Edmond Jr.	SK2c	Tennessee

USS Arizona (BB-39) Casualty List --continued

BURNETT, Charlie Leroy	S2c	
BURNS, John Edward	F1c	Pennsylvania
BUSICK, Dewey Olney	F3c	Ohio
BUTCHER, David Adrian	F2c	Washington
BUTLER, John Dabney	F1c	Texas
BYRD, Charles Dewitt	S1c	Tennessee
CABAY, Louis Clarence	S1c	Illinois
CADE, Richard Esh	S2c	Washington
CALDWELL, Charles Jr.	F3c	Missouri
CALLAGHAN, James Thomas	BM2c	Colorado
CAMDEN, Raymond Edward	S2c	Oklahoma
CAMM, William Fielden	Y2c	Arkansas
CAMPA, Ralph	S1c	California
CAMPBELL, Burdette Charles	S1c	California
CAPLINGER, Donald William	SC3c	Ohio
CAREY, Francis Lloyd	SK3c	New York
CARLISLE, Robert Wayne	S1c,USNR	Texas
CARLSON, Harry Ludwig	SK3c	Connecticut
CARMACK, Harold Milton	F2c	Colorado
CARPENTER, Robert Nelson	MATT1c	Virginia
CARROLL, Robert Lewis	S1c	
CARTER, Burton Lowell	S2c	California
CARTER, Paxton Turner	WO	California
CASEY, James Warren	S1c	

===

THE USS ARIZONA (BB-39) IN HAPPIER DAYS

The USS Arizona (BB-39), considered America's most famous battleship and now a permanent memorial to the U.S. personnel who died during the December 7, 1941, attack on Pearl Harbor, was seen in a 1934 Hollywood movie, *Here Comes The Navy*, starring Jimmy Cagney and Pat O'Brien.

<u>USS Arizona (BB-39) Casualty List</u> --continued

CASILAN, Epifanio Miranda	OS3c	New York
CASKEY, Clarence Merton	S1c	Washington
CASTLEBERRY, Claude W. Jr.	S1c	Texas
CATSOS, George	F1c	California
CHACE, Raymond Vincent	CSKP	California
CHADWICK, Charles Bruce	MM2c	Mississippi
CHADWICK, Harold	MATT1c	California
CHANDLER, Donald Ross	PVT,USMC	Alabama
CHAPMAN, Naaman N.	S1c	Nebraska
CHARLTON, Charles Nicholas	WT1c,USNR	California
CHERNUCHA, Harry Gregory	MUS2c	New York
CHESTER, Edward	S1c	Kansas
CHRISTENSEN, Elmer Emil	MM2c	Wyoming
CHRISTENSEN, Lloyd Raymond	F1c	Nebraska
CHRISTIANSEN, Edward Lee	BKR3c	Wyoming
CIHLAR, Lawrence John	PHM3c	Minnesota
CLARK, George Francis	GM3c	Illinois
CLARK, John Crawford Todd	F3c	California
CLARK, Malcolm	BKR3c	Louisiana
CLARK, Robert William Jr.	FC3c	Pennsylvania
CLARKE, Robert Eugene	S1c	Kansas
CLASH, Donald	F2c	Michigan
CLAYTON, Robert Roland	COX	Missouri
CLEMMENS, Claude Albert	S1c	Oklahoma
CLIFT, Ray Emerson	COX	Missouri
CLOUES, Edward Blanchard	ENS	New Hampshire
CLOUGH, Edward Hay	GM1c	Nebraska
COBB, Ballard Burgher	S1c	Texas
COBURN, Walter Overton	S1c	Oklahoma
COCKRUM, Kenneth Earl	MM1c	Indiana
COFFIN, Robert	SF3c	Washington
COFFMAN, Marshall Herman	GMec	Indiana
COLE, Charles Warren	SGT,USMC	Washington

USS Arizona (BB-39) Casualty List   --continued

COLE, David Lester	ENS,USNR	California
COLEGROVE, Willett S. Jr.	S2c	Washington
COLLIER, John	F2c	Oregon
COLLIER, Linald Long Jr.	BKR3c	Texas
COLLINS, Austin	SF3c	
COLLINS, Billy Murl	S1c	California
CONLIN, Bernard Eugene	S2c	Illinois
CONLIN, James Leo	F2c	Illinois
CONNELLY, Richard Earl	CQMA	California
CONRAD, Homer Milton Jr.	S1c	Ohio
CONRAD, Robert Frank	S2c	California
CONRAD, Walter Ralph	QM2c	
COOPER, Clarence Eugene	F2c	
COOPER, Kenneth Erven	F2c	
CORCORAN, Gerard John	S1c	New York
COREY, Ernest Eugene	PHM3c	Washington
CORNELIUS, P. W.	SC3c	
CORNING, Russell Dale	RM3c	
COULTER, Arthur Lee	S1c	Oklahoma
COWAN, William	COX	Missouri

===

IS THIS THE MAN WHO SANK THE USS ARIZONA (BB-39)?

Contrary to facts, Japan initially reported (and continued to report through the spring of 1942) that the Arizona (BB-39) was sunk by one of its midget submarines. However, Japanese Petty Officer Noboru Kanai, considered the top horizontal bombardier in the Imperial Navy at the time, is believed to have dropped the bomb that sank the USS Arizona (BB-39) at Pearl Harbor. Experts, however, disagree as to whether the bomb actually went down the smokestack or struck the ship in a vulnerable position. Kanai lost his life during the battle for Wake Island.

USS Arizona (BB-39) Casualty List --continued

COWDEN, Joel Beman	S2c	Oregon
COX, Gerald Blinton	MUS2c	Illinois
COX, William Milford	S1c	Kentucky
CRAFT, Harley Wade	CM3c	Oregon
CRAWLEY, Wallace Dewight	COX	Indiana
CREMEENS, Louis Edward	S1c	Arizona
CRISCUOLO, Michael	Y2c	California
CRISWELL, Wilfred John	S1c	Indiana
CROWE, Cecil Thomas	GM2c	Kentucky
CROWLEY, Thomas Ewing	LCDR (DC)	California
CURRY, William Joseph	WT2c	Oregon
CURTIS, Lloyd B.	S1c	Missouri
CURTIS, Lyle Carl	RM2c	Wisconsin
CYBULSKI, Harold Bernard	S1c	
CYCHOSZ, Francis Anton	S1c	Michigan
CZARNECKI, Stanley	F1c	Michigan
CZEKAJSKI, Theophil	SM3c,USNR	Michigan
DAHLHEIMER, Richard Norbert	S1c	Minnesota
DANIEL, Lloyd Naxton	Y1c	Montana
DANIK, Andrew Joseph	S2c	Ohio
DARCH, Phillip Zane	S1c	Massachusetts
DAUGHERTY, Paul Eugene	Em3c	Ohio
DAVIS, John Quitman	S1c	Louisiana
DAVIS, Milton Henry	S1c	Kansas
DAVIS, Murle Melvin	RM2c	Ohio
DAVIS, Myrle Clarence	F3c,USNR	Iowa
DAVIS, Thomas Ray	SF1c	California
DAVIS, Virgil Denton	PVT,USMC	Missouri
DAVIS, Walter Mindred	F2c	Missouri
DAWSON, James Berkley	PVT,USMC	Kentucky
DAY, William John	S2c	Washington
DE ARMOUN, Donald Edwin	GM3c	California
DE CASTRO, Vicente	OS3c	
DEAN, Lyle Bernard	COX	

USS Arizona (BB-39) Casualty List   **--continued**

DELONG, Frederick Eugene	CPL,USMC	Ohio
DERITIS, Russell Edwin	S1c	
DEWITT, John James	COX	
DIAL, John Buchanan	S1c	
DICK, Ralph R.	GM1c	California
DINE, John George	F2c	California
DINEEN, Robert Joseph	S1c	Pennsylvania
DOBEY, Milton Paul Jr.	S1c	Texas
DOHERTY, George Walter	S2c	California
DOHERTY, John Albert	MM2c	California
DONOHUE, Ned Burton	F1c	
DORITY, John Monroe	S1c	California
DOUGHERTY, Ralph Mc Clearn	FC1c	Massachusetts
DOYLE, Wand B.	COX	Kentucky
DREESBACH, Herbert Allen	PFC	Illinois
DRIVER, Bill Lester	RM3c	California
DUCREST, Louis Felix	S1c	Louisiana
DUKE, Robert Edward	CCSTDA	California

===

BROTHERS CAN STILL SERVE ABOARD SAME SHIP

Several misconceptions, common during World War II and after, continue to circulate about the death of the five Sullivan brothers aboard the USS Juneau (CL-52) and the assignment of family members to U.S. Navy ships. Reference to a "Sullivan Act" in connection with family members serving in the same ship/unit is a popular misconception. The Sullivan Law of 25 May 1911 is a New York City ordinance dealing with firearms. Although proposed after the death of the five Sullivan Brothers, no "Sullivan Act" was ever enacted by Congress related to family members serving together. Similarly, to this day, no American President has ever issued any executive order forbidding assignment of family members to the same ship/unit.

<u>*USS Arizona (BB-39) Casualty List*</u> --continued

DULLUM, Jerald Fraser	EM3c	Montana
DUNAWAY, Kenneth Leroy	EM3c	Oklahoma
DUNHAM, Elmer Marvin	S1c	
DUNNAM, Robert Wesley	PVT,USMCR	Texas
DUPREE, Arthur Joseph	F2c	Missouri
DURHAM, William Teasdale	S1c	North Carolina
DURIO, Russell	PFC,USMC	Louisiana
DUVEENE, John	1SGT,USMC	California
DVORAK, Alvin Albert	BM2c	Minnesota
EATON, Emory Lowell	F3c	Oklahoma
EBEL, Walter Charles	CTCP	California
EBERHART, Vincent Henry	COX	Minnesota
ECHOLS, Charles Louis Jr.	EM3c	Tennessee
ECHTERNKAMP, Henry Clarence	S1c	Michigan
EDMUNDS, Bruce Roosevelt	Y2c	New Hampshire
EERNISSE, William Frederick	PTR1c	California
EGNEW, Robert Ross	S1c	Illinois
EHLERT, Casper	SM3c	Wisconsin
EHRMANTRAUT, Frank Jr.	S1c	Indiana
ELLIS, Francis Arnold Jr.	EM3c	Canada
ELLIS, Richard Everrett	S2c	Nebraska
ELLIS, Wilbur Danner	RM2c	California
ELWELL, Royal	S1c	Texas
EMBREY, Bill Eugene	F3c	California
EMERY, Jack Marvin	ENS	California
EMERY, John Marvin	GM3c	North Dakota
EMERY, Wesley Vernon	SK2c	Indiana
ENGER, Stanley Gordon	GM3c	Minnesota
ERICKSON, Robert	S1c	
ERSKINE, Robert Charles	PFC,USMC	Illinois
ERWIN, Stanley Joe	MM1c	Texas
ERWIN, Walton Aluard	S1c	Texas
ESTEP, Carl James	S1c	Texas

USS Arizona (BB-39) Casualty List   --continued

ESTES, Carl Edwen	S1c	Texas
ESTES, Forrest Jesse	F1c	California
ETCHASON, Leslie Edgar	S1c	Illinois
EULBERG, Richard Henry	FC2c	Iowa
EVANS, David Delton	PVT,USMC	Louisiana
EVANS, Evan Frederick	ENS,USNR	California
EVANS, Mickey Edward	S1c	Missouri
EVANS, Paul Anthony	S1c	Illinois
EVANS, William Orville	S2c	Idaho
EWELL, Alfred Adam	WT1c	
EYED, George	SK3c	Indiana
FALLIS, Alvin E.	PHM2c	California
FANSLER, Edgar Arthur	S1c	Oklahoma
FARMER, John Wilson	COX	Tennessee
FEGURGUR, Nicolas San Nicolas	MATT2c	Guam
FESS, John Junior	F1c	California
FIELDS, Bernard	RM3c,USNR	
FIELDS, Reliford	MATT2c	Florida
FIFE, Ralph Elmer	S1c	California
FILKINS, George Arthur	COX	Minnesota
FINCHER, Allen Brady	ACK,USMC	Texas
FINCHER, Dexter Wilson	SGT,USMC	Oregon
FINLEY, Woodrow Wilson	PFC,USMC	Tennessee
FIRTH, Henry Amis	F3c	
FISCHER, Leslie Henry	S1c	Washington

==

LAST TO CARRY THE NAME USS ARIZONA

The third ship to carry the name USS Arizona (BB-39) was placed in commission in 1916. Her original cage masts were replaced by tripod masts during modernization in the 1930s She was considered the mightiest ship in the U.S. fleet in the 1920s. No other U.S. Navy ship will ever carry the name Arizona.

USS Arizona (BB-39) Casualty List --continued

FISHER, Delbert Ray	S1c	Wyoming
FISHER, James Anderson	MATT1c	Virginia
FISHER, Robert Ray	S2c	California
FISK, Charles Porter III	Y1c	California
FITCH, Simon	MATT1c	Texas
FIRZGERALD, Kent Blake	PVT,USMC	Utah
FITZSIMMONS, Eugene James	F3c	Illinois
FLANNERY, James Lowell	SK3c	Ohio
FLEETWOOD, Donald Eugene	PFC,USMC	Iowa
FLOEGE, Frank Norman	MUS2c	Illinois
FLORY, Max Edward	S2c	Indiana
FONES, George Everett	FC3c	Washington
FORD, Jack C.	S1c	California
FORD, William Walker	EM3c	Kentucky
FOREMAN, Elmer Lee	F2c	Indiana
FORTENBERRY, Alvie Charles	COX	Mississippi
FOWLER, George Parten	S2c	Texas
FOX, Daniel Russell	LTCOL,USMC	California
FRANK, Leroy George	S1c	Arkansas
FREDERICK, Charles Donald	EM2c	Louisiana
FREE, Thomas Augusta	MM1c	Texas
FREE, William Thomas	S2c	Texas
FRENCH, John Edmund	LCDR	Wash., D.C.
FRIZZELL, Robert Niven	S2c	Alabama
FULTON, Robert Wilson	AMSMTH1c	Missouri
FUNK, Frank Francis	BM2c	Missouri
FUNK, Lawrence Henry	S1c	Wisconsin
GAGER, Roy Arthur	S2c	Kansas
GARGARO, Ernest Russell	S2c	
GARLINGTON, Raymond Wesley	S1c	California
GARRETT, Orville Wilmer	SF2c	Missouri
GARTIN, Gerald Ernest	S1c	California
GAUDETTE, William Frank	S1c	Washington

USS Arizona (BB-39) Casualty List   --continued

GAULTNEY, Ralph Martin	Em3c	Illinois
GAZECKI, Philip Robert	ENS, USNR	Wisconsin
GEBHARDT, Kenneth Edward	S1c	North Dakota
GEER, Kenneth Floyd	S2c	California
GEISE, Marvin Frederick	S1c	Wisconsin
GEMIENHARDT, Samuel Henry Jr.	MM2c	Ohio
GHOLSTON, Roscoe	Y2c	Texas
GIBSON, Billy Edwin	S1c	West Virginia
GIESEN, Karl Anthony	Y2c	Iowa
GILL, Richard Eugene	S1c	Nevada
GIOVENAZZO, Michael James	WT2c	Illinois
GIVENS, Harold Reuben	Y3c	
GOBBIN, Angelo	SC1c	California
GOFF, Wiley Coy	S2c	Oklahoma
GOMEZ, Edward Jr.	S1c	Colorado
GOOD, Leland	S2c	Illinois
GOODWIN, William Arthur	S2c	Colorado
GORDON, Peter Charles Jr.	F1c	Colorado
GOSSELIN, Edward Webb	ENS, USNR	Illinois
GOSSELIN, Joseph Adjutor	RM1c	Massachusetts
GOULD, Harry Lee	S1c	Illinois
GOVE, Rupert Clair	S1c	California
GRANGER, Raymond Edward	F3c	Iowa
GRANT, Lawrence Everett	Y3c	Missouri
GRAY, Albert James	S1c	Washington
GRAY, Lawrence Moore	F1c	Missouri
GRAY, William James Jr.	S1c	California

===

THEY WERE THE LONGEST BATTLESHIPS WHEN NEW

At 608 feet in length, the USS Arizona (BB-39) and her sister ship the USS Pennsylvania (BB-38) were the first U.S. battleships to exceed 600 feet.

USS Arizona (BB-39) Casualty List   --continued

GREEN, Glen Hubert	S1c	Mississippi
GREENFIELD, Carroll Gale	S1c	Oregon
GRIFFIN, Lawrence J.	PFC, USMC	Louisiana
GRIFFIN, Reese Olin	EM3c	Texas
GRIFFITHS, Robert Alfred	EM3c	California
GRISSINGER, Robert Beryle	S2c	Illinois
GROSNICKLE, Warren Wilbert	EM2c	Iowa
GROSS, Milton Henry	CSKA	California
GRUNDSTROM, Richard Gunner	S2c	Iowa
GURLEY, Jesse Herbert	SK3c	Illinois
HAAS, Curtis Junior	MUS2c	Missouri
HADEN, Samuel William	COX	Kansas
HAFFNER, Floyd Bates	F1c	Illinois
HAINES, Robert Wesley	S2c	California
HALL, John Rudolph	CBMP	Arkansas
HALLORAN, William Ignatius	ENS,USNR	Ohio
HAMEL, Don Edgar	FLDMUS,USMCR	Illinois
HAMILTON, Clarence James	MM1c	Washington
HAMILTON, Edwin Carrell	S1c	
HAMILTON, William Holman	GM3c	Oklahoma
HAMMERUD, George Winston	S1c	North Dakota
HAMPTON, "J" "D"	F1c	Kansas
HAMPTON, Ted "W" Jr.	S1c	Oklahoma
HAMPTON, Walter Lewis	BM2c	Pennsylvania
HANNA, David Darling	EM3c	Texas
HANSEN, Carlyle B.	MM2c	
HANSEN, Harvey Ralph	S1c	Wisconsin
HANZEL, Edward Joseph	WT1c	Michigan
HARDIN, Charles Eugene	S1c	Missouri
HARGRAVES, Kenneth William	S2c	Washington
HARMON, William D.	PFC,USMC	Oregon
HARRINGTON, Keith Homer	S1c	Missouri
HARRIS, George Ellsworth	MM1c	Illinois

USS Arizona (BB-39) Casualty List --continued

HARRIS, Hiram Dennis	S1c	Georgia
HARRIS, James William	F1c	Michigan
HARRIS, Noble Burnice	COX	Missouri
HARRIS, Peter John	COX	Nebraska
HARTLEY, Alvin	GM3c	Oklahoma
HARTSOE, Max June	GM3c	Missouri
HARTSON, Lonnie Moss	SM3c	Texas
HASL, James Thomas	F1c	Nebraska
HAVERFIELD, James Wallace	ENS,USNR	Ohio
HAVINS, Harvey Linfille	S1c	
HAWKINS, Russell Dean	SM3c	Illinois
HAYES, John Doran	BM1c	California
HAYES, Kenneth Merle	F1c	California
HAYNES, Curtis James	QM2c	Idaho
HAYS, William Henry	SK3c	Kansas
HAZDOVAC, Jack Claudius	S1c	California
HEAD, Frank Bernard	CYA	California
HEATER, Verrell Roy	S1c	Oregon
HEATH, Alfred Grant	S1c	Wisconsin
HEBEL, Robert Lee	SM3c,USNR	Illinois
HECKENDORN, Warren Guy	S1c	
HEDGER, Jess Laxton	S1c	California
HEDRICK, Paul Henry	BM1c	California
HEELY, Leo Shinn	S2c	Colorado
HEIDT, Edward Joseph	F1c	California
HEIDT, Wesley John	MM2c	California
HELM, Merritt Cameron	S1c	Minnesota
HENDERSON, William Walter	S2c	
HENDRICKSEN, Frank	F2c	Michigan
HERRICK, Paul Edward	PVT,USMC	Wisconsin
HERRING, James Jumior	SM3c	Iowa
HERRIOTT, Robert Asher Jr.	S1c	Texas
HESS, Darrel Miller	FC1c	Utah
HESSDORFER, Anthony Joseph	MM2c	Washington

USS Arizona (BB-39) Casualty List --continued

HIBBARD, Robert Arnold	BKR2c	
HICKMAN, Arthur Lee	SM3c	
HICKS, Elmer Orville	GM3c	Washington
HICKS, Ralph Dueard	PTR2c,USNR	Missouri
HILL, Bartley Talor	AOM3c	California
HILTON, Wilson Woodrow	GM1c	
HINDMAN, Frank Weaver	S1c	Alabama
HODGES, Garris Vada	F2c	Texas
HOELSCHER, Lester John	HA1c	Nebraska
HOLLAND, Claude Herbert Jr.	S2c	Alabama
HOLLENBACH, Paul Zepp	S1c	New York
HOLLIS, Ralph	LTJG,USNR	California
HOLLOWELL, George Sanford	COX	Arizona
HOLMES, Lowell D.	F3c	Alabama
HOLZWORTH, Walter	MGYSGT,USMC	New Jersey
HOMER, Henry Vernon	S1c	Michigan
HOPE, Harold W.	PVT,USMC	Illinois
HOPKINS, Homer David	S1c	Michigan
HORN, Melvin Freeland	F3c	Ohio
HORRELL, Harvey Howard	SM1c	
HORROCKS, James William	CGMP	Arizona
HOSLER, John Emmet	S1c	Ohio
HOUSE, Clem Raymond	CWTP	California
HOUSEL, John James	SK1c	Missouri
HOWARD, Elmo	S1c	Kentucky
HOWARD, Rolan George	GM3c	Minnesota
HOWE, Darrell Robert	S2c	Oregon
HOWELL, Leroy	COX	Indiana
HUBBARD, Haywood Jr.	MATT2c	Virginia
HUDNALL, Robert Chilton	PFC,USMC	Texas
HUFF, Robert Glenn	PVT,USMC	Texas
HUFFMAN, Clyde Franklin	F1c	Ohio
HUGHES, Bernard Thomas	MUS2c	Pennsylvania

157

<u>USS Arizona (BB-39) Casualty List</u> --continued

HUGHES, Lewis Burton Jr.	1c	Alabama
HUGHES, Marvin Austin	PVT,USMCR	Texas
HUGHEY, James Clynton	S1c	
HUIE, Doyne Conley	HA1c	Missouri
HULTMAN, Donald Standly	PFC,USMC	Minnesota
HUNTER, Robert Fredrick	S1c	Ohio
HUNTINGTON, Henry Louis	S2c	California
HURD, Willard Hardy	MATT2c	Tennessee
HURLEY, Wendell Ray	MUS2c	Indiana
HUVAL, Ivan Joseph	S1c	Louisiana
HUX, Leslie Creade	PFC,USMC	Louisiana
HUYS, Arthur Albert	S1c	Indiana
HYDE, William Hughes	COX	Missouri
IAK, Joseph Claude	Y3c	
IBBOTSON, Howard Burt	F1c	California
INGALLS, Richard Fitch	SC3c	New York
INGALLS, Theodore "A"	SC3c	New York
INGRAHAM, David Archie	FC3c	
ISHAM, Orville Adalbert	CGMA	Hawaii
ISOM, Luther James	S1c	Alabama
IVERSEN, Earl Henry	S2c	California
IVERSEN, Norman Kenneth	S2c	California
IVEY, Charles Andrew Jr.	2c	California
JACKSON, David Paul Jr.	S1c	Texas
JACKSON, Robert Woods	Y3c	Iowa
JAMES, John Burditt	S1c	Texas
JANTE, Edwin Earl	Y3c	
JANZ, Clifford Thurston	T	California
JASTRZEMSKI, Edwin Charles	1c	Michigan
JEANS, Victor Lawrence	WT2c	Oregon
JEFFRIES, Keith	COX	Pennsylvania
JENKINS, Robert Henry Dawson	S2c	Texas
JENSEN, Keith Marlow	EM3c	Utah

USS Arizona (BB-39) Casualty List --continued

JERRISON, Donald D.	CPL,USMC	California
JOHANN, Paul Frederick	GM3c	Iowa
JOHNSON, David Andrew Jr.	OC2c	Virginia
JOHNSON, Edmund Russell	MM1c	California
JOHNSON, John Russell	RM3c	Massachusetts
JOHNSON, Samuel Earle	CDR(MC)	Alabama
JOHNSON, Sterling Conrad	COX	Washington
JOLLEY, Berry Stanley	S2c,USNR	Idaho
JONES, Daniel Pugh	S2c	Alabama
JONES, Edmon Ethmer	S1c	Colorado
JONES, Floyd Baxter	MATT2c	
JONES, Harry Cecil	S1c	Kansas
JONES, Henry Jr.	MATT1c	California
JONES, Homer Lloyd	S1c	Colorado
JONES, Hugh Junior	S2c	California
JONES, Leland	S1c	Tennessee
JONES, Quincy Eugene	PFC,USMC	Texas
JONES, Thomas Raymond	ENS,USNR	Louisiana
JONES, Warren Allen	Y3c	Nebraska
JONES, Willard Worth	S1c	Tennessee
JONES, Woodrow Wilson	S2c	Alabama
JOYCE, Calvin Wilbur	F2c	Ohio
JUDD, Albert John	COX	Michigan
KAGARICE, Harold Lee	CSKA	California
KAISER, Robert Oscar	F1c	Missouri
KALINOWSKI, Henry	PVT,USMCR	Texas
KATT, Eugene Louis	S2c	California
KEEN, Billy Mack	PVT,USMC	Texas
KELLER, Paul Daniel	MLDR2c	Michigan
KELLEY, James Dennis	SF3c	Oklahoma
KELLOGG, Wilbur Leroy	F1c	Iowa
KELLY, Robert Lee	CEMA	California
KENISTON, Donald Lee	S2c	Ohio

USS Arizona (BB-39) Casualty List --continued

KENISTON, Kenneth Howard	F3c	Ohio
KENNARD, Kenneth Frank	GM3c	Idaho
KENNINGTON, Charles Cecil	S1c	Tennessee
KENNINGTON, Milton Homer	S1c	Tennessee
KENT, Texas Thomas Jr.	S2c	Arkansas
KIDD, Isaac Campbell	RADM	
KIEHN, Ronald William	MM2c	California
KIESELBACH, Charles Ermin	MM1c	California
KING, Gordon Blane	S1c	Tennessee
KING, Leander Cleaveland	S1c	Texas
KING, Lewis Meyer	F1c	
KING, Robert Nicholas Jr.	ENS,USNR	New York
KINNEY, Frederick William	MUS1c	Washington
KINNEY, Gilbert Livingston	QM2c	California
KIRCHHOFF, Wilbur Albert	S1c	Missouri
KIRKPATRICK, Thomas Larcy	CAPT(CHC)	Missouri
KLANN, Edward	SC1c	Michigan
KLINE, Robert Edwin	GM2c	New York
KLOPP, Francis Lawrence	GM3c	Ohio
KNIGHT, Robert Wagner	EM3c	Ohio
KNUBEL, William Jr.	S1c	Missouri
KOCH, Walter Ernest	S1c	Minnesota
KOENEKAMP, Clarence D.	F1c	Washington
KOEPPE, Herman Oliver	SC3c	Illinois
KOLAJAJCK, Brosig	S1c	Texas
KONNICK, Albert Joseph	CM3c	Pennsylvania
KOSEC, John Anthony	BM2c	California
KOVAR, Robert	S1c	Illinois
KRAHN, James Albert	PFC,USMC	North Dakota
KRAMB, James Henry	S1c	New York
KRAMB, John david	MSMTH1c	New York
KRAMER, Robert Rudolph	GM2c	Indiana
KRAUSE, Fred Joseph	S1c	Minnesota

USS Arizona (BB-39) Casualty List   --continued

KRISSMAN, Max Sam	S2c	California
KRUGER, Richard Warren	QM2c	California
KRUPPA, Adolph Louis	S1c	Texas
KUKUK, Howard Helgi	S1c	New York
KULA, Stanley	SC3c	Nebraska
KUSIE, Donald Joseph	RM3c	New York
LA FRANCEA, William Richard	S1c	Michigan
LA MAR, Ralph B.	FC3c	California
LA SALLE, Willard Dale	S1c	Washington
LADERACH, Robert Paul	FC2c	West Virginia
LAKE, John Ervin Jr.	WO	California
LAKIN, Donald Lapier	S1c	California
LAKIN, Joseph Jordan	S1c	California
LAMB, George Samuel	CSFA	California
LANDMAN, Henry	AM2c	Michigan
LANDRY, James Joseph Jr.	BKR2c	Massachusetts
LANE, Edward Wallace	COX	
LANE, Mancel Curtis	S1c	Oklahoma
LANGE, Richard Charles	S1c	California
LANGENWALTER, Orville J.	SK2c	Iowa
LANOUETTE, Henry John	COX	Connecticut
LARSON, Leonard Carl	F3c	Washington
LATTIN, Bleecker	RM3c	
LEE, Carroll Volney Jr.	S1c	Texas
LEE, Henry Lloyd	S1c	South Carolina
LEEDY, David Alonzo	FC2c	Iowa
LEGGETT, John Goldie	BM2c	Washington
LEGROS, Joseph McNeil	S1c	Louisiana
LEIGH, Malcolm Hedrick	GM3c	North Carolina
LEIGHT, James Webster	S2c	California
LEOPOLD, Robert Lawrence	ENS,USNR	Kentucky
LESMEISTER, Steve Louie	EM3c	North Dakota
LEVAR, Frank	CWTP,USNR	Washington

USS Arizona (BB-39) Casualty List   --continued

LEWIS, Wayne Alman	CM3c	South Carolina
LEWISON, Neil Stanley	FC3c	Wisconsin
LIGHTFOOT, Worth Ross	GM3c	
LINBO, Gordon Ellsworth	GM1c	Washington
LINCOLN, John William	F1c	Iowa
LINDSAY, James E.	PFC,USMC	California
LINDSAY, James Mitchell	SF2c	Colorado
LINTON, George Edward	F2c	
LIPKE, Clarence William	F2c	Michigan
LIPPLE, John Anthony	SF1c	Iowa
LISENBY, Daniel Edward	S1c	
LIVERS, Raymond Edward	S1c	New Mexico
LIVERS, Wayne Nicholas	F1c	New Mexico
LOCK, Douglas A.	S1c	New York
LOHMAN, Earl Wynne	S1c	
LOMAX, Frank Stuart	ENS	Nebraska
LOMIBAO, Marciano	OS1c	Philippines
LONG, Benjamin Franklin	CYP	California
LOUNSBURY, Thomas William	S2c	Illinois
LOUSTANAU, Charles Bernard	S1c	Iowa
LOVELAND, Frank Crook	S2c	Idaho
LOVSHIN, William Joseph	PFC,USMC	Minnesota
LUCEY, Neil Jermiah	S1c	New Jersey
LUNA, James Edward	S2c	Oklahoma
LUZIER, Ernest Burton	MM2c	
LYNCH, Emmett Isaac	MUS2c	Washington
LYNCH, James Robert Jr.	GM3c	Texas
LYNCH, William Joseph Jr.	S1c	Texas
MADDOX, Raymond Dudley	CEMP	California
MADRID, Arthur John	S2c	California
MAFNAS, Francisco Reyes	MATT2c	Guam
MAGEE, Gerald James	SK3c	New York
MALECKI, Frank Edward	CYP	California

<u>USS Arizona (BB-39) Casualty List</u> --continued

MALINOWSKI, John Stanley	SM3c,USNR	Michigan
MALSON, Harry Lynn	SK3c	Indiana
MANION, Edward Paul	S2c	Illinois
MANLOVE, Arthur Cleon	WO	California
MANN, William Edward	GM3c	Washington
MANNING, Leroy	S2c	Kentucky
MANSKE, Robert Francis	Y2c	Iowa
MARINICH, Steve Matt	COX	Utah
MARIS, Elwood Henry	S1c	
MARLING, Joseph Henry	S2c	Montana
MARLOW, Urban Herschel	COX	Missouri
MARSH, Benjamin Raymond Jr.	ENS,USNR	Michigan
MARSH, William Arthur	S1c	
MARSHALL, Thomas Donald	S2c	California
MARTIN, Hugh Lee	Y3c	Utah
MARTIN, James Albert	BM1c	Texas
MARTIN, James Orrwell	S2c	California
MARTIN, Luster Lee	F3c	Arkansas
MASON, Byron Dalley	S2c	Idaho
MASTEL, Clyde Harold	S2c	California
MASTERS, Dayton Monroe	GM3c	Texas
MASTERSON, Cleburne E. Carl	PHM1c	California
MATHEIN, Harold Richard	BMKR2c	Illinois
MATHISON, Charles Harris	S1c	Wisconsin
MATNEY, Vernon Merferd	F1c	Wisconsin
MATTOX, James Durant	AM3c	Florida
MAY, Louis Eugene	SC2c	Kansas
MAYBEE, George Frederick	RM2c,USNR	California
MAYFIELD, Lester Ellsworth	F1c	Colorado
MAYO, Rex Haywood	EM2c	Florida
MEANS, Louis	MATT1c	Texas
MEARES, John Morgan	S2c	South Carolina
MENEFEE, James Austin	S1c	Mississippi

USS Arizona (BB-39) Casualty List   --continued

MENO, Vicente Gogue	MATT2c	
MENZENSKI, Stanley Paul	COX	
MERRILL, Howard Deal	ENS	Utah
MILES, Oscar Wright	S1c	Arkansas
MILLER, Chester John	F2c	Michigan
MILLER, Doyle Allen	COX	Arkansas
MILLER, Forrest Newton	CEMP	California
MILLER, George Stanley	S1c	Ohio
MILLER, Jessie Zimmer	S1c	Ohio
MILLER, John David	S1c	
MILLER, William Oscar	SM3c	Illinois
MILLIGAN, Weldon Hawvey	S1c	Texas
MIMS, Robert Lang	S1c	Georgia
MINEAR, Richard J. Jr.	PFC,USMC	
MLINAR, Joseph	COX	Pennsylvania
MOLPUS, Richard Preston	CMSMTHP	California
MONROE, Donald	MATT2c	Missouri
MONTGOMERY, Robert E.	S2c	California
MOODY, Robert Edward	S1c	Mississippi
MOORE, Douglas Carlton	S1c	South Carolina
MOORE, Fred Kenneth	S1c	Texas
MOORE, James Carlton	SF3c	South Carolina
MOORHOUSE, William Starks	MUS2c	Kansas
MOORMAN, Russell Lee	S2c	California
MORGAN, Wayne	S1c	California
MORGAREIDGE, James Orries	F2c	Wyoming
MORLEY, Eugene Elvis	F2c	Illinois
MORRIS, Owen Newton	S1c	Alabama
MORRISON, Earl Leroy	S1c	Montana
MORSE, Edward Charles	S2c	Michigan
MORSE, Francis Jerome	BM1c	California
MORSE, George Robert	S2c	Montana
MORSE, Norman Roi	WT2c	Virginia

USS Arizona (BB-39) Casualty List   --continued

MOSS, Tommy Lee	MATT2c	Kentucky
MOSTEK, Francis Clayton	PFC,USMC	Idaho
MOULTON, Gordon Eddy	F1c	California
MUNCY, Claude	MM2c	California
MURDOCK, Charles Luther	WT1c	Alabama
MURDOCK, Melvin Elijah	WT2c	Alabama
MURPHY, James Joseph	S1c	Arizona
MURPHY, James Palmer	F3c	Ohio
MURPHY, Jessie Huell	S1c	Louisiana
MURPHY, Thomas J. Jr.	SK1c	Virginia
MYERS, James Gernie	SK1c	Missouri
McCARRENS, James Francis	CPL,USMC	Illinois
McCARY, William Moore	S2c	Alabama
McCLAFFERTY, John Charles	BM2c	Ohio
McCLUNG, Harvey Manford	ENS,USNR	Pennsylvania
McFADDIN, Lawrence James	Y2c	California
McGLASSON, Joe Otis	GM3c	Illinois
McGRADY, Samme Willie Genes	MATT1c	Alabama
McGUIRE, Francis Raymond	SK2c	Michigan
McHUGHES, John Breckenridge	CWTA	Washington
McINTOSH, Harry George	S1c	Virginia
McKINNIE, Russell	MATT2c	
McKOSKY, Michael Martin	S1c	Oklahoma
McPHERSON, John Blair	S1c	Tennessee
NAASZ, Erwin H.	SF2c	Kansas
NADEL, Alexander Joseph	MUS2c	New York
NATIONS, James Garland	FC2c	South Carolina
NAYLOR, "J" "D"	SM2c	Louisiana
NEAL, Tom Dick	S1c	Texas
NECESSARY, Charles Raymond	S1c	Missouri
NFIPP, Paul	S2c	California
MELSEN, George	SC2c	Washington
NELSON, Harl Coplin	S1c	Arkansas

165

USS Arizona (BB-39) Casualty List   --continued

NELSON, Henry Clarence	BM1c	Minnesota
NELSON, Lawrence Adolphus	CTCP	California
NELSON, Richard Eugene	F3c	North Dakota
NICHOLS, Alfred Rose	S1c	Alabama
NICHOLS, Bethel Allan	S1c	Washington
NICHOLS, Clifford Leroy	TC1c	
NICHOLS, Louis Duffie	S2c	Alabama
NICHOLSON, Glen Eldon	EM3c	North Dakota
NICHOLSON, Hancel Grant	S1c	
NIDES, Thomas James	EM1c	California
NIELSEN, Floyd Theadore	CM3c	Utah
NOLATUBBY, Henry Ellis	PFC,USMC	California
NOONAN, Robert Harold	S1c	Michigan
NOWOSACKI, Theodore Lucian	NS	New York
NUSSER, Raymond Alfred	GM3c	
NYE, Frank Erskine	S1c	California
O'BRIEN, Joseph Bernard	PFC,USMC	Illinois
O'BRYAN, George David	FC3c	Massachusetts
O'BRYAN, Joseph Benjamin	FC3c	Massachusetts
O'NEALL, Rex Eugene	S1c	Colorado
O'NEILL, William Thomas Jr.	ENS,USNR	Connecticut
OCHOSKI, Henry Francis	GM2c	Washington
OFF, Virgil Simon	S1c	Colorado
OGLE, Victor Willard	S2c	Oklahoma
OGLESBY, Lonnie Harris	S2c	Mississippi
OLIVER, Raymond Brown	S1c	California
OLSEN, Edward Kern	ENS,USNR	Kansas
OLSON, Glen Martin	S2c	Washington
ORR, Dwight Jerome	S1c	California
ORZECH, Stanislaus Joseph	2c	Connecticut
OSBORNE, Mervin Eugene	F1c	Kentucky
OSTRANDER, Leland Grimstead	PHM3c	Minnesota
OTT, Peter Dean	S1c	Ohio

USS Arizona (BB-39) Casualty List   --continued

OWEN, Fredrick Halden	S2c	Texas
OWENS, Richard Allen	SK2c	Colorado
OWSLEY, Thomas Lea	SC2c	Idaho
PACE, Amos Paul	BM1c	California
PARKES, Harry Edward	BM1c	California
PAROLI, Peter John	BKR3c	California
PATTERSON, Clarence Rankin	PFC,USMC	
PATTERSON, Harold Lemuel	S1c	Texas
PATTERSON, Richard Jr.	SF3c	Connecticut
PAULMAND, Hilery	OS2c	Philippines
PAVINI, Bruno	S1c	California
PAWLOWSKI, Raymond Paul	S1c	New York
PEARCE, Alonzo Jr.	S1c	
PEARSON, Norman Cecil	S2c	California
PEARSON, Robert Stanley	F3c	Montana
PEAVEY, William Howard	QM2c	Iowa
PECKHAM, Howard William	F2c	Missouri
PEDROTTI, Francis James	PVT,USMC	Missouri
PEERY, Max Valdyne	S2c	California
PELESCHAK, Michael	S1c	Alabama
PELTIER, John Arthur	EM3c	Ohio
PENTON, Howard Lee	S1c	Alabama
PERKINS, George Ernest	F1c	Rhode Island
PETERSON, Albert H. Jr.	FC3c	New Jersey
PETERSON, Elroy Vernon	FC2c	California
PETERSON, Hardy Wilbur	FC3c	Washington
PETERSON, Roscoe Earl	S2c	California
PETTIT, Charles Ross	CRMP	California
PETYAK, John Joseph	S1c	Tennessee
PHELPS, George Edward	S1c	New York
PHILBIN, James Richard	S1c	Colorado
PIASECKI, Alexander Louis	CPL,USMC	
PIKE, Harvey Lee	EM3c	Georgia

USS Arizona (BB-39) Casualty List --continued

PIKE, Lewis Jackson	S1c	Georgia
PINKHAM, Albert Wesley	S2c	North Carolina
PITCHER, Walter Giles	GM1c	California
POOL, Elmer Leo	S1c	Indiana
POOLE, Ralph Ernest	S1c	Ohio
POST, Darrell Albert	CMMA	California
POVESKO, George	S1c	Connecticut
POWELL, Jack Speed	PFC,USMC	California
POWELL, Thomas George	S1c	Illinois
POWER, Abner Franklin	PVT,USMC	
PRESSON, Wayne Harold	S1c	Ohio
PRICE, Arland Earl	RM2c	Oregon
PRITCHETT, Robert Leo Jr.	S1c	Louisiana
PUCKETT, Edwin Lester	SK3c	Kentucky
PUGH, John Jr.	SF3c	California
PUTNAM, Avis Boyd	SC3c	Alabama
PUZIO, Edward	S1c	Pennsylvania
QUARTO, Mike Joseph	S1c	Connecticut
QUINATA, Jose Sanchez	MATT2c	Guam
RADFORD, Neal Jason	MUS2c	Nebraska
RASMUSSEN, Arthur Severin	CM1c	California
RASMUSSON, George Vernon	F3c	Minnesota
RATKOVICH, William	WT1c	California
RAWHOUSER, Glen Donald	F3c	Oregon
RAWSON, Clyde Jackson	BM1c	Maryland
RAY, Harry Joseph	BM2c	California
REAVES, Casbie	S1c	Arkansas
RECTOR, Clay Cooper	SK3c	Kentucky
REECE, John Jeffris	S2c	Oklahoma
REED, James Buchanan Jr.	SK1c	California
REED, Ray Ellison	S2c	Oklahoma
REGISTER, Paul James	LCDR	North Dakota
REINHOLD, Rudolph Herbert	PVT,USMC	Utah

USS Arizona (BB-39) Casualty List   --continued

RESTIVO, Jack Martin	Y2c	Maryland
REYNOLDS, Earl Arthur	S2c	Colorado
REYNOLDS, Jack Franklyn	S1c	
RHODES, Birb Richard	F2c	Tennessee
RHODES, Mark Alexander	S1c	North Carolina
RICE, William Albert	S2c	Washington
RICH, Claude Edward	S1c	Florida
RICHAR, Raymond Lyle	S1c	
RICHARDSON, Warren John	COX	Pennsylvania
RICHISON, Fred Louis	GM3c	California
RICHTER, Albert Wallace	COX	
RICO, Guadalupe Augustine	S1c	California
RIDDEL, Eugene Edward	S1c	Michigan
RIGANTI, Fred	SF3c	California
RIGGINS, Gerald Herald	S1c	California
RIVERA, Francisco Unpingoo	MATT2c	Guam
ROBERTS, Dwight Fisk	F1c	Kansas
ROBERTS, Kenneth Franklin	BM2c	
ROBERTS, McClellan Taylor	CPHMP	California
ROBERTS, Walter Scott Jr.	RM1c	Missouri
ROBERTS, Wilburn Carle	BKR3c	Louisiana
ROBERTS, William Francis	S2c	
ROBERTSON, Edgar Jr.	MATT3c	Virginia
ROBERTSON, James Milton	MM1c	Tennessee
ROBINSON, Harold Thomas	S2c	California
ROBINSON, James William	S2c	California
ROBINSON, John James	EM1c	Oregon
ROBINSON, Robert Warren	PHM3c	West Virginia
ROBY, Raymond Arthur	S1c	California
RODGERS, John Dayton	S1c	Pennsylvania
ROEHM, Harry Turner	MM2c	Illinois
ROGERS, Thomas Sprugeon	CWTP	Alabama
ROMANO, Simon	OC1c	Virginia

<u>USS Arizona (BB-39) Casualty List</u>   --continued

ROMBALSKI, Donald Roger	S2c	Washington
ROMERO, Vladimir M.	S1c	Virginia
ROOT, Melvin Leonard	S1c	Ohio
ROSE, Chester Clay	BM1c	Kentucky
ROSENBERY, Orville Robert	SF2c	Illinois
ROSS, Deane Lundy	S2c	New York
SANDALL, Merrill Deith	SF3c	Illinois
SANDERS, Eugene Thomas	ENS	New York
SANDERSON, James Harvey	MUS2c	California
SANFORD, Thomas Steger	F3c	
SANTOS, Filomeno	OC2c	California
SATHER, William Ford	PMKR1c	California
SAVAGE, Walter Samuel Jr.	ENS	Louisiana
SAVIN, Tom	RM2c	Nebraska
SAVINSKI, Michael	S1c	Pennsylvania
SCHDOWSKI, Joseph	S1c	
SCHEUERLEIN, George Albert	GM3c	Pennsylvania
SCHILLER, Ernest	S2c	Texas
SCHLUND, Elmer Pershing	MM1c	Nebraska
SCHMIDT Vernon Joseph	S1c	Minnesota
ROSS, William Fraser	GM3c	New York
ROWE, Eugene Joseph	S1c	New Jersey
ROWELL, Frank Malcolm	S2c	Texas
ROYALS, William Nicholas	S1c	Virginia
ROYER, Howard Dale	GM3c	Ohio
ROZAR, John Frank	WT2c	California
ROZMUS, Joseph Stanley	S1c	New Hampshire
RUDDOCK, Cecil Roy	S1c	
RUGGERIO, William	FC3c	
RUNCKEL, Robert Gleason	BUG1c	
RUNIAK, Nicholas	S1c	New Jersey
RUSH, Richard Perry	S1c	Texas

USS Arizona (BB-39) Casualty List   --continued

RUSHER, Orville Lester	MM1c	Missouri
RUSKEY, Joseph John	CBMP	California
RUTKOWSKI, John Peter	S1c	New York
RUTTAN, Dale Andrew	EM3c	Florida
SAMPSON, Sherley Rolland	EM3c	Minnesota
SCHNEIDER, William Jacob	PFC,USMC	
SCHRANK, Harold Arthur	BKR1c	Texas
SCHROEDER, Henry	BM1c	New Jersey
SCHUMAN, Herman Lincoln	SK1c	California
SCHURR, John	EM2c	Kansas
SCILLEY, Harold Hugh	SF2c	Montana
SCOTT, A. J.	S2c	
SCOTT, Crawford Edward	PFC,USMC	
SCOTT, George Harrison	PFC,USMC	
SCRUGGS, Jack Leo	MUS2c	California
SEAMAN, Russell Otto	F1c	Iowa
SEELEY, William Eugene	S1c	Connecticut
SEVIER, Charles Clifton	S1c	California
SHANNON, William Alfred	S1c	Idaho
SHARBAUGH, Harry Robert	GM3c	Pennsylvania
SHARON, Lewis Purdie	MM2c	California
SHAW, Clyde Donald	S1c	Ohio
SHAW, Robert K.	MUS2c	Texas
SHEFFER, George Robert	S1c	Indiana
SHERRILL, Warren Joseph	Y2c	Texas
SHERVEN, Richard Stanton	EM3c	North Dakota
SHIFFMAN, Harold Ely	RM3c	Michigan
SHILEY, Paul Eugene	S1c	Pennsylvania
SHIMER, Melvin Irvin	S1c	
SHIVE, Gordon Eshom	PFC,USMC	California
SHIVE, Malcolm Holman	RM3c,USNR	California
SHIVELY, Benjamin Franklin	F1c	Michigan
SHORES, Irland Jr.	S1c	Alabama

171

USS Arizona (BB-39) Casualty List --continued

SHUGART, Marvin John	S1c	Colorado
SIBLEY, Delmar Dale	S1c	New York
SIDDERS, Russell Lewis	S1c	Ohio
SIDELL, John Henry	GM2c	Illinois
SILVEY, Jesse	MM2c	Texas
SIMENSEN, Carleton Elliott	2LT,USMC	
SIMON, Walter Hamilton	S1c	New Jersey
SIMPSON, Albert Eugene	S1c	
SKEEN, Harvey Leroy	S2c	Arizona
SKILES, Charley Jackson Jr.	S2c	Virginia
SKILES, Eugene	S2c	
SLETTO, Earl Clifton	MM1c	Minnesota
SMALLEY, Jack G.	S1c	Ohio
SMART, George David	COX	Montana
SMESTAD, Halge Hojem	RM2c	Minnesota
SMITH, Albert Joseph	LTJG	Virginia
SMITH, Earl Jr.	S1c	Missouri
SMITH, Earl Walter	FC3c	Florida
SMITH, Edward	GM3c	Illinois
SMITH, Harry	S2c,USNR	California
SMITH, John A.	SF3c	Ohio
SMITH, John Edward	S1c	California
SMITH, Luther Kent	S1c	Tennessee
SMITH, Mack Lawrence	S1c	Arkansas
SMITH, Marvin Ray	S1c	Texas
SMITH, Orville Stanley	ENS	Oklahoma
SMITH, Walter Tharnel	MATT2c	Mississippi
SNIFF, Jack Bertrand	CPL,USMC	
SOENS, Harold Mathias	SC1c	California
SOOTER, James Fredrick	RM3c	
SORENSEN, Holger Earl	S1c	New Mexico
SOUTH, Charles Braxton	S1c	Alabama
SPENCE, Merle Joe	S1c	Tennessee

<u>USS Arizona (BB-39) Casualty List</u> --continued

SPOTZ, Maurice Edwin	F1c	Illinois
SPREEMAN, Robert Lawrence	GM3c	Michigan
SPRINGER, Charles Harold	S2c	California
STALLINGS, Kermit Braxton	F1c	North Carolina
STARKOVICH, Charles	EM3c	Washington
STARKOVICH, Joseph Jr.	F2c	Washington
STAUDT, Alfred Parker	F3c	Washington
STEFFAN, Joseph Philip	BM2c	Illinois
STEIGLEDER, Lester Leroy	COX	Ohio
STEINHOFF, Lloyd Delroy	S1c	California
STEPHENS, Woodrow Wilson	EM1c	Washington
STEPHENSON, Hugh Donald	S1c	New York
STEVENS, Jack Hazelip	S1c	Texas
STEVENS, Theodore R.	AMM2c	California
STEVENSON, Frank Jake	PFC,USMC	New York
STEWART, Thomas Lester	SC3c	Arkansas
STILLINGS, Gerald Fay	F2c	
STOCKMAN, Harold William	FC3c	Idaho
STOCKTON, Louis Alton	S2c	California
STODDARD, William Edison	S1c	Louisiana
STOPYRA, Julian John	RM3c	Massachusetts
STORM, Laun Lee	Y1c	California
STOVALL, Richard Patt	PFC,USMC	
STRANGE, Charles Orville	F2c	
STRATTON, John Raymond	S1c	Indiana
SUGGS, William Alfred	S1c	Florida
SULSER, Frederick Franklin	GM3c	Ohio
SUMMERS, Glen Allen	Y1c	Washington
SUMMERS, Harold Edgar	SM2c	Ohio
SUMNER, Oren	S2c	New Mexico
SUTTON, Clyde Westly	CCSTDP	California
SUTTON, George Woodrow	SK1c	Kentucky
SWIONTEK, Stanley Stephen	FLDCK	Illinois

USS Arizona (BB-39) Casualty List   --continued

SWISHER, Charles Elijah	S1c	California
SYMONETTE, Henry	OC1c	California
SZABO, Theodore Stephen	PVT,USMCR	
TAMBOLLEO, Victor Charles	SF3c	Maryland
TANNER, Russell Allen	GM3c	Washington
TAPIE, Edward Casamiro	MM2c	California
TAPP, Lambert Ray	GM3c	Kentucky
TARG, John	CWTP	California
TAYLOR, Aaron Gust	MATT1c	California
TAYLOR, Charles Benton	EM3c	Illinois
TAYLOR, Harry Theodore	GM2c	Indiana
TAYLOR, Robert Denzil	COX	Iowa
TEELING, Charles Madison	CPRTP,USNR	California
TEER, Allen Ray	EM1c	California
TENNELL, Raymond Clifford	S1c	Texas
TERRELL, John Raymond	F2c	Arkansas
THEILLER, Rudolph	S1c	California
THOMAS, Houston O'Neal	COX	Texas
THOMAS, Randall James	S1c	West Virginia
THOMAS, Stanley Horace	F3c	
THOMAS, Vincent Duron	COX	California
THOMPSON, Charles Leroy	S1c	Illinois
THOMPSON, Irven Edgar	S1c	Ohio
THOMPSON, Robert Gary	SC1c	California
THORMAN, John Christopher	EM2c	Iowa
THORNTON, George Hayward	GM3c	Mississippi
TINER, Robert Reaves	F2c	Texas
TISDALE, William Esley	CWTP	California
TRIPLETT, Thomas Edgar	S1c	California
TROVATO, Tom	S1c	California
TUCKER, Raymond Edward	COX	Indiana
TUNTLAND, Earl Eugene	S1c	North Dakota
TURNIPSEED, John Morgan	F3c	Arkansas

USS Arizona (BB-39) Casualty List --continued

TUSSEY, Lloyd Harold	EM3c	North Carolina
TYSON, Robert	FC3c	Louisiana
UHRENHOLDT, Andrew Curtis	ENS,USNR	Wisconsin
VALENTE, Richard Dominic	GM3c	California
VAN ATTA, Garland Wade	MM1c	California
VAN HORN, James Randolph	S2c	Arizona
VAN VALKENBURGH, Franklin	CAPT(CO)	Minnesota
VARCHOL, Brinley	GM2c	Pennsylvania
VAUGHAN, William Frank	PHM2c	
VEEDER, Gordon Elliott	S2c	Idaho
VELIA, Galen Steve	SM3c	Kansas
VIEIRA, Alvaro Everett	S2c	Rhode Island
VOJTA, Walter Arnold	S1c	Minnesota
VOSTI, Anthony August	GM3c	California
WAGNER, Mearl James	SC2c	California
WAINWRIGHT, Silas Alonzo	PHM1c	New York
WAIT, Wayland Lemoyne	S1c	
WALKER, Bill	S1c	Texas
WALLACE, Houston Oliver	WT1c	Arkansas
WALLACE, James Frank	S1c	Wisconsin
WALLACE, Ralph Leroy	F3c	Oregon
WALLENSTIEN, Richard Henry	S1c	
WALTERS, Clarence Arthur	S2c	California
WALTERS, William Spurgeon Jr.	FC3c	New Mexico
WALTHER, Edward Alfred	FC3c	
WALTON, Alva Dowding	Y3c	Utah
WARD, Albert Lewis	S1c	Oklahoma
WARD, William E.	COX	Illinois
WATKINS, Lenvil Leo	F2c	Kentucky
WATSON, William Lafayette	F3c	Florida
WATTS, Sherman Maurice	HA1c	Arkansas
WATTS, Victor Ed	GM3c	Texas
WEAVER, Richard Walter	S1c	Nevada

USS Arizona (BB-39) Casualty List   --continued

WEBB, Carl Edward	PFC,USMC	
WEBSTER, Harold Dwayne	S2c	Colorado
WEEDEN, Carl Alfred	ENS	California
WEIDELL, William Peter	S2c	Minnesota
WEIER, Bernard Arthur	PVT,USMC	Illinois
WELLER, Ludwig Fredrick	CSKP	California
WELLS, Floyd Arthur	RM2c	
WELLS, Harvey Anthony	SF2c	California
WELLS, Raymond Virgil Jr.	S1c	Missouri
WELLS, William Bennett	S1c	Missouri
WEST, Broadus Franklin	S1c	South Carolina
WEST, Webster Paul	S1c	Arkansas
WESTCOTT, William Percy Jr.	S1c	Indiana
WESTERFIELD, Ivan Ayers	S1c	California
WESTIN, Donald Vern	F3c	Oregon
WESTLUND, Fred Edwin	BM2c	California
WHISLER, Gilbert Henry	PFC,USMC	
WHITAKER, John William Jr.	S1c	Louisiana
WHITCOMB, Cecil Eugene	EM3c	Michigan
WHITE, Charles William	MUS2c	
WHITE, James Clifton	F1c	Texas
WHITE, Vernon Russell	S1c	South Carolina
WHITE, Volmer Dowin	S1c	Mississippi
WHITEHEAD, Ulmont Irving Jr.	ENS	Connecticut
WHITLOCK, Paul Morgan	S2c	Texas
WHITSON, Ernest Hubert Jr.	MUS2c	California
WHITT, William Byron	GM3c	Kentucky
WHITTEMORE, Andrew Tiny	MATT2c	Tennessee
WICK, Everett Morris	FC3c	Oregon
WICKLUND, John Joseph	S1c	Minnesota
WILCOX, Arnold Alfred	QM2c	Iowa
WILL, Joseph William	S2c	Colorado
WILLETTE, Laddie James	S2c	Michigan

USS Arizona (BB-39) Casualty List   --continued

WILLIAMS, Adrian Delton	S1c	Louisiana
WILLIAMS, Clyde Richard	MUS2c	Oklahoma
WILLIAMS, George Washington	S1c	Virginia
WILLIAMS, Jack Herman	RM3c	South Carolina
WILLIAMS, Laurence "A"	ENS,USNR	Ohio
WILLIAMSON, Randolph Jr.	MATT2c	
WILLIAMSON, William Dean	RM2c,USNR	California
WILLIS, Robert Kenneth Jr.	S1c	Louisiana
WILSON, Bernard Martin	RM3c,USNR	New York
WILSON, Comer A.	CBMP	Alabama
WILSON, Herschel Woodrow	F2c	Ohio
WILSON, John James	S1c	California
WILSON, Neil Mataweny	CWO	California
WILSON, Ray Milo	RM3c,USNR	Iowa
WIMBERLY, Paul Edwin	GM3c	Tennessee
WINDISH, Robert James	PVT,USMC	Missouri
WINDLE, Robert England	PFC,USMC	Illinois
WINTER, Edward	WO,USNR	Washington
WITTENBERG, Russell Duane	PVT,USMC	
WOJTKIEWICZ, Frank Peter	CMMP	California
WOLF, George Alexanderson Jr.	ENS,USNR	Pennsylvania
WOOD, Harold Baker	BM2c	Colorado
WOOD, Horace Van	S1c	Texas
WOOD, Roy Eugene	F1c	Arizona
WOODS, Vernon Wesley	S1c	Texas
WOODS, William Anthony	S2c	New York
WOODWARD, Ardenne Allen	MM2c	California
WOODY, Harlan Fred	S2c	
WOOLF, Norman Bragg	CWTP	Alabama
WRIGHT, Edward Henry	S2c	Illinois
WYCKOFF, Robert Leroy	F1c	New Jersey
YATES, Elmer Elias	SC3c	Nebraska
YEATS, Charles Jr.	COX	Illinois
YOMINE, Frank Peter	F2c	Illinois

USS Arizona (BB-39) Casualty List   --continued

YOUNG, Eric Reed	ENS	Colorado
YOUNG, Glendale Rex	S1c	
YOUNG, Jay Wesley	S1c	Utah
YOUNG, Vivan Louis	WT1c	Virginia
ZEILER, John Virgel	S1c	Colorado
ZIEMBRICKE, Steve A.	S1c	New York
ZIMMERMAN, Fred	Cox	North Dakota
ZIMMERMAN, Lloyd McDonald	S2c	Missouri
ZWARUN, Jr. Michael	S1c	New Jersey

It is *NOT* the Congressional Medal of Honor

The Medal of Honor is the highest award the United States of America can give for military valor. Because it is conferred by the President in the name of the Congress, it is commonly, but erroneously, called the Congressional Medal of Honor (CMH).

It is bestowed on an individual who distinguishes themselves "conspicuously by gallantry and intrepidity at the risk of their life above and beyond the call of duty."

The award was conceived in the 1860s and first presented in 1863. In their provisions for judging whether an individual is entitled to the Medal of Honor, each of the armed services has set up regulations that permit no margin of doubt or error.

The deed of the person must be proven by the incontestable evidence of at least two eyewitnesses; it must be so outstanding that it clearly distinguishes his gallantry beyond the call of duty from lesser forms of bravery; it must involve the risk of life; and it must be the type of deed which, if it had not been done, would not subject the individual to any justified criticism.

A history of the Medal of Honor, with a list of all recipients since 1863 is available from the Superintendent of Documents, U.S. Government Printing Office, Washington, D.C. 20402, for a fee.

U.S. CAPTURED FRENCH SHIPS BEFORE ENTERING WAR

The first action against foreign ships in U.S. ports was on May 15, 1941, *seven months before Pearl Harbor*, when armed U.S. troops boarded and took into protective custody the luxury passenger liner Normandie and 10 other French ships. The U.S. renamed her the SS Lafayette. However, the magnificent ship burned at dockside in New York in February 1942 and had to be scrapped.

★ ★

U.S. SUB SANK WORLD'S LARGEST AIRCRAFT CARRIER

The largest aircraft carrier of any navy became part of the Japanese fleet on November 11, 1944, when the 59,000-ton Shinano (with a 30-centimeter-thick deck over concrete) went on line. However, this ship recorded the briefest period of sea duty of any major ship in the war. The American submarine Archerfish (SS-311) torpedoed and sank her on November 29 in the Kumano Sea. This was the largest submarine kill of the war.

★ ★

U.S. DESTROYERS CAPTURED GERMAN U-BOAT

The capture of the German U-boat 505 was the first time since 1814 that U.S. naval forces had boarded and taken an enemy ship. The submarine surfaced after being damaged by depth charges during an attack by U.S. antisubmarine surface ships, including the destroyer escorts Chatelain (DE-149) and Pillsbury (DE-227). The U-boat's captain, believing reports from his crew that the submarine was sinking, surfaced. A party from the Pillsbury boarded and secured U-505. It was taken in tow by the Guadalcanal (CVE-60), which later passed the job onto a fleet tug, and is now on permanent display at the Museum of Science and Industry in Chicago, Ill.

★ ★

UNIQUE AND HISTORIC DEFEAT FOR JAPAN

The first naval defeat ever sustained by Japan came at the hands of the U.S. in the Battle of Midway.

ONLY CHAPLAIN TO RECEIVE MEDAL OF HONOR
The only chaplain in the war to receive the Medal of Honor was Joseph O'Callahan, USN, who earned the distinction for heroism aboard the aircraft carrier USS Franklin (CV-13) during the invasion of the Philippines in 1944.

★ ★ ★ ★ ★ ★ ★ ★ ★ ★ ★ ★ ★ ★ ★ ★ ★ ★ ★ ★

U-BOAT ACE ACCIDENTALLY SHOT BY GERMAN SENTRY
Germany's second most successful U-boat captain, Wolfgang Luth, was accidentally shot and killed by a sentry when he failed to properly identify himself near the headquarters of Admiral Karl Doenitz. Luth commanded four different U-boats in the war, made 14 patrols, and sank 44 enemy ships, just one short of Otto Kretschmer's record.

★ ★ ★ ★ ★ ★ ★ ★ ★ ★ ★ ★ ★ ★ ★ ★ ★ ★ ★ ★

PLANES FROM BIG 'E' SUNK FIRST JAPANESE SUB
The first Japanese submarine sunk by U.S. aircraft fire after the Pearl Harbor attack was I-70 on December 10, 1941, by aircraft from the USS Enterprise (CV-6).

★ ★ ★ ★ ★ ★ ★ ★ ★ ★ ★ ★ ★ ★ ★ ★ ★ ★ ★ ★

USMC PILOTS SANK FIRST JAPANESE SURFACE SHIP
The first Japanese surface ship sunk by U.S. aircraft attack in the war was the destroyer Kisaragi, by U.S. Marine aircraft defending Wake Island on December 11, 1941. The battle took place four days after Pearl Harbor.

★ ★ ★ ★ ★ ★ ★ ★ ★ ★ ★ ★ ★ ★ ★ ★ ★ ★ ★ ★

SEVEN GERMAN "BEAVER" U-BOATS SUNK IN ONE DAY
The greatest number of U-boats sunk on a single day by the Allies was seven, on July 7, 1944. These were, however, the German one-man submarines, called Biber (beaver). Slightly under 30 feet In length, the Biber U-boats were credited with sinking at least a dozen merchant vessels and nine navy ships.

FIRST JAPANESE SHIP SUNK BY U.S. NAVAL FIRE

The first Japanese ship sunk by the U.S. Naval fire after the attack on Pearl Harbor was the merchant ship Atsutasan Maru, by the submarine Swordfish (SS-193) on December 16, 1941.

★ ★ ★ ★ ★ ★ ★ ★ ★ ★ ★ ★ ★ ★ ★ ★ ★ ★ ★ ★

BRITISH PASSENGER LINER FIRST SHIP SUNK IN WAR

The first ship sinking in the war occurred on September 1, 1939, the day Germany invaded Poland. The British passenger liner Athenia, with 1,400 people aboard, was torpedoed and sunk by U-30 west of Scotland while en route to Canada. Twenty-eight Americans were among the 118 passengers killed in the attack. Although Berlin had issued specific orders that warnings be given to civilian ships, the commander of U-30 failed to do so. Germany denied responsibility even after it later discovered that U-30 had mistaken the Athenia for an armed merchant cruiser.

★ ★ ★ ★ ★ ★ ★ ★ ★ ★ ★ ★ ★ ★ ★ ★ ★ ★ ★ ★

GERMAN NAVY STUCK IT TO THEIR RUSSIAN PALS

The first order authorizing the German navy to seek and destroy Soviet submarines, under the cloak of claiming to mistake them for British ships, was issued on June 15, 1941. The German directive called for the "annihilation of Russian submarines without any trace, including their crews." It specifically mentioned submarines found south of the Aland Islands. This was a week before Germany invaded Russia and at a time when the two countries were still at peace.

★ ★ ★ ★ ★ ★ ★ ★ ★ ★ ★ ★ ★ ★ ★ ★ ★ ★ ★ ★

WORST U.S. NAVAL DEFEAT WAS AT SAVO ISLAND

The worst U.S. naval defeat ever in a fair fight was the 32-minute-long August 9, 1942, Battle of Savo Island. The U.S. Navy lost three heavy cruisers and one destroyer, 1,270 men killed, and 709 wounded. A fourth cruiser, the Australian HMAS Canberra, was also lost Japan sustained negligible damage to their ships, lost 35 men, and reported another 57 wounded. The battle resulted in the greatest number of ships of the same class sunk in a single action when three heavy cruisers of the USS New Orleans-class were destroyed in ten minutes: USS Vincennes (CA-44); USS Quincy (CA-39); and USS Astoria (CA-34).

★ ★

WORST NAVAL DEFEAT OF ALLIES WAS IN JAVA SEA

The worst naval defeat sustained by the Allies during the war was the February 27 to March 1, 1942, Battle of the Java Sea. The Japanese Imperial Navy sank 10 U.S., British, and Dutch ships during the engagement (plus four of their own by accident!).

★ ★

FIRST SUBMARINER TO RECEIVE MEDAL OF HONOR

The first member of the U.S. Submarine Service to receive the Medal of Honor (posthumously) was Commander Howard Gilmore of the USS Growler (SS-215) in 1943. Gilmore had ordered his officers to clear the bridge of the submarine while he remained on deck to maneuver the Growler to safety after it had rammed a Japanese gunboat. Injured in the exchange of gunfire that followed, Gilmore gave his last order to the officer of the deck: "Take her down." With her captain remaining topside, the Growler commenced her dive. It was seriously damaged but managed to escape to safety.

★ ★

DESTROYER SANK MOST SUBS IN SHORTEST TIME

The destroyer escort USS England (DE-635) holds the record for sinking the greatest number of Japanese submarines in the shortest time period, five enemy subs in eight days during May 1944: I-16, May 19; RO-106, May 22; RO-104, May 23; RO-116, May 24; RO-108, May 26. The England extended that to six submarines in 12 days, also a record, when she sank RO-105 on May 31. The England's first kill of the series, a Japanese I-class submarine, was larger than the destroyer escort herself. The six submarines were part of a group of 25 the Japanese sent in advance of its fleet as scouts for what would become known as the Battle of the Philippine Sea. Seventeen Japanese submarines were sunk.

★ ★ ★ ★ ★ ★ ★ ★ ★ ★ ★ ★ ★ ★ ★ ★ ★ ★ ★

U.S. SUBS SANK MAJORITY OF JAPANES TONNAGE

More than half of the total Japanese merchant marine tonnage lost in the war was due to U.S. submarines, bringing Japan to the edge of starvation.

★ ★ ★ ★ ★ ★ ★ ★ ★ ★ ★ ★ ★ ★ ★ ★ ★ ★ ★

ONLY ONE BRITISH AIRCRAFT CARRIER SURVIVED WAR

The only British aircraft carrier to make it through the war was HMS Furious. She had originally been a cruiser before being converted.

★ ★ ★ ★ ★ ★ ★ ★ ★ ★ ★ ★ ★ ★ ★ ★ ★ ★ ★

BIG SURPRISE WHEN THEY CAME THROUGH THE HAZE

The only naval action against the Allies during the Normandy invasion on June 6, 1944, was from a trio of German E-boats from the 5th Flotilla under the command of Lieutenant Commander Heinrich Hoffmann. The three little boats broke through a haze off the beaches at Normandy and suddenly found themselves face to face with the greatest naval armada ever assembled (more than 5,000 ships). Hoffmann's sailors fired 18 torpedoes and quickly retreated. Their effort resulted in 30 casualties sustained in the sinking of a Norwegian destroyer, Svenner.

★ ★ ★ ★ ★ ★ ★ ★ ★ ★ ★ ★ ★ ★ ★ ★ ★ ★ ★

REALLY NOT SOMETHING TO BRAG ABOUT

The Japanese ship that sank *the most Japanese ships* was the heavy cruiser Mikuma. Some sources credit her with sinking four Japanese transports on February 28, 1942, while attempting to hit the cruiser USS Houston (CA-30) during a follow-up engagement to the Battle of the Java Sea. (NOTE: In his book But Not in Shame, John Toland cites Japanese sources as saying the four transports were accidentally sunk by torpedoes from the heavy cruisers Mikuma and

Mogami. However, in The Two-Ocean War, naval historian Samuel Eliot Morison disputes this, claiming that the cruisers were too far away to score with torpedoes and that Panjang Island lay between them and the transports).

★ ★ ★ ★ ★ ★ ★ ★ ★ ★ ★ ★ ★ ★ ★ ★ ★ ★ ★

GERMANY'S TOP U-BOAT ACE CAPTURED IN 1941

Germany's most successful U-boat commander was Otto Kretschmer, who sank 45 ships during 16 patrols as commander of U-23 and U-99. He was the first U-boat commander to sink more than a quarter-million tons of enemy shipping. On March 17, 1941, after an engagement with the destroyers HMS Walker and HMS Vanoc, Kretschmer and his crew were captured after scuttling their boat by Royal Navy Captain Donald MacIntyre. Twenty percent of the German U-boat fleet was lost in March 1941 as a result of British air and naval fire. In addition to Kretschmer, the toll included several other veteran U-boat commanders.

★ ★ ★ ★ ★ ★ ★ ★ ★ ★ ★ ★ ★ ★ ★ ★ ★ ★ ★

WOMAN WAS ON SHIP THAT HOLDS CROSSING RECORD

The first Canadian woman to serve at sea during the war was Fem Blodgett, who earned the distinction in June 1941 when she became a radio operator on the Norwegian cargo ship Mosdale. The Mosdate holds the record for wartime crossings of the Atlantic, having made the dangerous passage 98 times.

★ ★ ★ ★ ★ ★ ★ ★ ★ ★ ★ ★ ★ ★ ★ ★ ★ ★ ★

GERMAN MINES TOOK HEAVY TOLL IN TWO MONTHS

On November 23, 1939, the British discovered the first German magnetic mine in the Thames estuary. It was defused by Lieutenant Commander J.G.D. Ouvry. In November and December of 1939, 59 Allied and neutral ships representing 203,513 tons were sunk by German magnetic mines. The German magnetic mines remained on the seafloor and were activated by the magnetic field generated by a ship passing overhead. They were a great improvement over moored, contact mines, which could be located by minesweepers, their cables cut, and then the mines themselves destroyed by small-arms fire. Britain overcame the magnetic mines through the use of an electric cable around ships' hulls, thereby countering the magnetic field.

★ ★

JAPANESE SHIP SUNK BY GERMAN MINES IN THAMES

Ironically the first ship sunk by indiscriminate mine warfare was the Japanese passenger ship Terukuni Maru which hit a German-laid mine in the Thames estuary on November 21, 1939.

★ ★

1940 ATTACK WAS PROTOTYPE FOR PEARL HARBOR

The first successful attack by aircraft against ships was the November 11, 1940, raid by 20 British Swordfish torpedo biplanes from the aircraft carrier Illustrious against the Italian naval base at Taranto. The British planes came in at under 40 feet above sea level. The Royal Navy lost two planes versus severe damage to nearly half of the Italian battle fleet A trio of capital ships, Conte di Cavour, Littorio, and Duilio, remained out of action for much of the war. The success of the attack was not lost on Admiral Yamamoto.

★ ★

SOUVENIRS COST U.S. SUB SKIPPER HIS COMMAND

The only U.S. submarine skipper relieved of command of a Japanese submarine was Hiram Cassedy. Cassedy had been assigned to accept the surrender at sea of one of three Japanese I-class submarines designed and built to torpedo the Panama Canal. Cassedy violated strict orders not to take souvenirs when he passed out swords to his officers. Admiral William F. Halsey removed him from command of his boat and the Japanese sub.

★ ★

ONLY SHIPS TO BE SUNK TWICE IN WORLD WAR II

The first major warship to be sunk by aircraft bombing in the war was the 8,350-ton German cruiser Kőnigsberg, which was sunk at dock in Bergen, Norway, on April 10, 1940, by two bombs from British Blackburn Skuas. She was also the only German ship to be sunk twice during the war. Salvaged and restored, she was sunk again on September 22, 1944. A similar fate befell the Italian cruiser Gorizia, also sunk twice during the war. She was scuttled and first sunk off La Spezia on September 8, 1943. Salvaged and restored, she was sunk by the Allies in June 1944.

★ ★ ★ ★ ★ ★ ★ ★ ★ ★ ★ ★ ★ ★ ★ ★ ★ ★ ★ ★

FIRST U.S. SHIP SUNK BY MINES ON EAST COAST

The first ship lost from German mining of ship lanes along the East coast of the U.S. was the merchant ship SS Robert C. Tutle on June 15, 1942. Weeks earlier a pair of German U-boats loaded with mines intended for placement in New York harbor were sunk before they could complete their mission.

★ ★ ★ ★ ★ ★ ★ ★ ★ ★ ★ ★ ★ ★ ★ ★ ★ ★ ★ ★

GERMAN'S ONE AIRCRAFT CARRIER NEVER GOT IN WAR

The only German aircraft carrier was the Graf Zeppelin. Her keel was laid in 1938, and she was launched later that year. However, the Zeppelin was still not finished when Germany surrendered in 1945. During construction there were serious differences between the Kriegsmarine and Luftwaffe about the type of aircraft the Graf Zeppelin would carry.

★ ★ ★ ★ ★ ★ ★ ★ ★ ★ ★ ★ ★ ★ ★ ★ ★ ★ ★ ★

JAPANESE FLEET AT MIDWAY WAS THEIR LARGEST EVER

The largest fleet assembled in Japanese naval history was the one it moved against the U.S. in the Battle of Midway, June 4-6, 1942. The total fleet consisted of more than a hundred ships, including 11 battleships and eight aircraft carriers. By the time it was over the tide of the war in the Pacific had turned in favor of the U.S. *Four of the six Japanese carriers that participated in the attack on Pearl Harbor were sunk:* Akagi, Kaga, Soryu and Hiryu. The 36,500-ton Akagi, which had been the flagship on December 7, became the first Japanese ship to be scuttled in the war. It was sunk by friendly fire after receiving serious damage at Midway. Japan also lost the heavy cruiser Mikuma and 332 aircraft. U.S. losses included the aircraft carrier USS Yorktown (CV-5) and the destroyer USS Hammann (DD-412) The resounding American victory over a numerically superior enemy force a scant six months after the shock of Pearl Harbor was due to the U.S. Navy's ability to read Japanese codes and use the information to gain a tactical advantage.

★ ★ ★ ★ ★ ★ ★ ★ ★ ★ ★ ★ ★ ★ ★ ★ ★ ★ ★ ★

LOPSIDED RESULTS: ONE PLANE FOR FIVE SHIPS
The British lost only one Swordfish torpedo biplane while at the same time sinking five Italian ships during the Battle of Cape Matapan off the southern tip of Greece, March 28, 1941. The Italians lost more than 2,400 sailors aboard the cruisers Pola, Zara, and Mume plus two destroyers.

★ ★ ★ ★ ★ ★ ★ ★ ★ ★ ★ ★ ★ ★ ★ ★ ★ ★ ★ ★

WHERE DID YOU GUYS LEARN TO DRIVE?
The only underwater collision between two U.S. submarines was on February 25, 1945, when the USS Hoe (SS-258) and USS Flounder (SS-251) apparently needed more room to navigate than they had off Indochina. Neither sub sank.

★ ★ ★ ★ ★ ★ ★ ★ ★ ★ ★ ★ ★ ★ ★ ★ ★ ★ ★ ★

"BIG BEN" SURVIVED MOST DEVASTATING ATTACK
The USS Franklin (CV-13) sustained the most devastating attack against any ship in U.S. history that didn't sink. Seriously damaged and considered lost during the invasion of the Philippines in 1944, "Big Ben,"* as she was affectionately known to her crew, received two direct hits from a Japanese dive bomber. One 500-pound bomb penetrated to the hangar deck, igniting gasoline reservoirs, which in turn caused tremendous explosions of stored ammunition. Scores of fully fueled aircraft, their bomb racks loaded, were blown apart, killing everyone there. Violent explosions also consumed all aircraft waiting to take off on the flight deck. In all, over 800 of the Franklin's crew were killed and nearly 400 others injured. When the

ship was dead in the water and all but written off as lost by nearly everyone else, the commanding officer, Captain Leslie E. Gehres, responded to a question with the famous reply- "Abandon? Hell, we're still afloat" Gehres was the first U.S. Navy enlisted man to rise through the ranks and eventually be named commander of an aircraft carrier. He received one of the 19 Navy Crosses crew members were awarded. Even when the still burning, stricken ship was finally taken in tow, Japanese planes repeatedly attacked her.

* Contrary to popular belief the Franklin, despite the "Big Ben" nickname, was not named in honor of Benjamin Franklin but rather for the Civil War engagement, the Battle of Franklin (Tennessee).

★ ★

USS LAFFEY (DD-724) "THE SHIP THAT WOULD NOT DIE"

The USS Laffey (DD-724), nicknamed *The Ship That Would Not Die*, experienced the most extensive Japanese aircraft attack against any U.S. ship in the war when it was attacked by 22 planes, including several kamikaze, struck by two bombs, and heavily strafed while on radar picket duty 30 miles northwest of Okinawa on April 16,1945. The Laffey shot down eight enemy planes and damaged six more before they crashed on board. The Laffey is the only surviving destroyer of the USS Alan M. Sumner class and is open for public viewing as part of the Patriot's Point Naval and Maritime Museum in Charlestown, S.C. (*See Appendix section for Historic World War II ship memorials*).

★ ★

3,000 DIED IN GREATEST LOSS OF LIFE ON ONE WARSHIP

The largest single loss of life involving a warship in history was the sinking of the 72,809-ton battleship Yamato, one of the two largest battleships in the world. Only 269 personnel from the 3,292 member crew survived. Yamato was sunk after three hours of bombing and torpedo attacks by aircraft from U.S. Task Force 58 during the Okinawa campaign in April 1945. Those lost included Admiral Seiichi Ito, the last Japanese admiral to command a major naval force in battle against the U.S. Navy. Ito was killed on April 8,

1945, while leading the 10-ship action in the East China Sea. Six of the Japanese ships were lost in the battle. Of the 900 U.S. aircraft involved, only 10 were lost.

★ ★ ★ ★ ★ ★ ★ ★ ★ ★ ★ ★ ★ ★ ★ ★ ★ ★ ★ ★

INDIANAPOLIS (CA-35) WAS GREATEST U.S. LOSS AT SEA

The largest single loss of U.S. Navy personnel at sea, 883 lives, was in the sinking of the cruiser USS Indianapolis (CA-35) on July 30, 1945. The Indianapolis was operating under secret orders while participating in Operation Bronx Shipments, the delivery of components for the atom bomb to Tinian Island on July 26, when she was hit by a pattern of six torpedoes fired by Japanese submarine I-58. The cruiser sank in 12 minutes. Because of the fact that the Indianapolis had been operating under secret orders with her route, destination, and mission classified, it took longer than would be expected for her to be noticed as missing and more than 96 hours before the 316 survivors were picked out of the sea. Ironically, more members of the Indianapolis crew died from shark attacks than had been killed in the torpedoing and sinking.

★ ★ ★ ★ ★ ★ ★ ★ ★ ★ ★ ★ ★ ★ ★ ★ ★ ★ ★ ★

U.S. OFFICER COURTMARSHALLED FOR LOOSING SHIP

The only U.S. Navy officer court-martialed for losing a ship in the war was Captain Charles McVay, commanding officer of the USS Indianapolis (CA-35). Torpedoed on July 30, 1945, the Indianapolis was the last major U.S. ship sunk in the war. At McVay's trial, the commander of the submarine that sank the Indianapolis testified that zigzagging would not have prevented him from sinking the ship.

★ ★ ★ ★ ★ ★ ★ ★ ★ ★ ★ ★ ★ ★ ★ ★ ★ ★ ★ ★

BLIND MAN'S BLUFF AT BATTLE OF CORAL SEA

The first naval battle in which opposing ships never saw each other was the Battle of the Coral Sea, May 3-8, 1942. (The battle actually took place in its Northern bight, the Solomon Sea.) The battle was an exchange between carrier aircraft against opposing ships. The Japanese sank the carrier USS Lexington (CV-2), the destroyer USS

Sims (DD-409), the fleet oiler USS Neosho (AO-23), a Pearl Harbor survivor, and damaged the carrier USS Yorktown (CV-5). U.S. naval flyers sank the destroyer Kikuzuki and three other ships plus the aircraft carrier Shoho, which holds the record time of any Japanese ship in the war for going to the bottom: 10 minutes. Each side lost about 30 planes. Although Japan lost five ships versus three for the U.S., the Americans' ships represented the greater tonnage loss. The Battle of the Coral Sea is generally regarded as Japan's first naval defeat of the war because their intention to invade Australia was thwarted. (NOTE: The Lexington was not actually sunk by the Japanese but so badly damaged that the American destroyer USS Phelps (DD-360) administered the *coup de grace* afterward)

★ ★ ★ ★ ★ ★ ★ ★ ★ ★ ★ ★ ★ ★ ★ ★ ★ ★ ★ ★

ONLY FLEET AIRCRAFT CARRIER SUNK BY SUBMARINE

The only submarine credited with sinking a fleet aircraft carrier was Japan's I-19, which sank the USS Wasp (CV-7) near Espiritu Santo on September 15, 1942. The American carrier had to be finished off by friendly destroyer fire. Commander of I-19 was Takaichi Kinashi, Japan's leading submarine officer. The U.S. also lost two escort carriers to submarines: USS Liscome Bay (CVE-56), off Tarawa, November 24, 1943, and USS Block Island (CVE-21), on May 29, 1944, off the Madeira Islands.

★ ★ ★ ★ ★ ★ ★ ★ ★ ★ ★ ★ ★ ★ ★ ★ ★ ★ ★ ★

BIG "E" EARNED ALL-TIME BRAGGING RIGHTS

The USS Enterprise (CV-6) earned more battle stars (20) in World War II than any warship in U.S. history. Aircraft from the Big E sank 71 enemy ships and destroyed 911 enemy aircraft Despite her record, the Enterprise was sold for scrap after the war. On January 18, 1946, she made port along the South Wall of the U.S. Naval Base in Bayonne, N.J., and never went to sea as a fighting ship again. Enterprise was decommissioned at 1: 47 p.m., February 17, 1947, and became a member of the Atlantic Reserve Fleet Each Memorial Day for the next decade the Big E was the most visited of the several World War II warships in reserve at Bayonne. In 1957 the Navy announced plans to sell the Enterprise for scrap. Admiral William F. Halsey used his influence to delay the order while efforts were made to raise private funds to preserve her. But this was not to be. In the summer of 1958 the Enterprise, with the assistance of tugboats, left the navy base, passed under Bayonne Bridge, and slowly moved up Newark Bay and the Hackensack River. She made her final port at the old Federal Shipyard site in Kearney, N.J. In early 1959 men with torches and pneumatic hammers did what the Japanese Imperial Navy had not been able to do, and the Enterprise ceased to exist.

★ ★ ★ ★ ★ ★ ★ ★ ★ ★ ★ ★ ★ ★ ★ ★ ★ ★ ★ ★

THE IMPORTANCE OF CALCULATED FOLLOWUP
The first Battle of Narvik (Norway) on April 10, 1940, resulted in Britain and Germany each losing two destroyers. However, after the engagement broke off, five German ships that had participated in the sea battle were tracked and eventually destroyed by the British.

★ ★ ★ ★ ★ ★ ★ ★ ★ ★ ★ ★ ★ ★ ★ ★ ★ ★ ★ ★

HEY SAILOR, DID YOU SHAVE TODAY, OR EVER?
The youngest person to serve aboard a U.S. Navy ship in combat was 12-year-old Calvin Graham, who won a Bronze Star and Purple Heart on USS South Dakota (BB-57) before the Navy found out he had incorrectly reported his age when he enlisted.

★ ★ ★ ★ ★ ★ ★ ★ ★ ★ ★ ★ ★ ★ ★ ★ ★ ★ ★ ★

LARGEST AMPHIBIOUS OPERATION OF THE WAR
The largest amphibious operation in the war was Operation Husky, the invasion of Sicily on July 10, 1943, in which 1,375 ships were directly involved plus an additional 36 ships used in support covering operations. The planning was made particularly difficult because it was not until the middle of May (when the North Africa campaign ended) that Allied planners knew exactly how many divisions they would have. During the initial assault seven divisions, one armored combat team, two commando brigades, and

an assault brigade were to be put ashore against an enemy who was, at least on paper, almost equal in numbers. The D-Day invasion of Normandy exceeds the invasion of Sicily only if follow-up amphibious landings are counted.

★ ★

USS TORSK (SS-423) LAST SUB TO SINK A SHIP IN WAR

USS Torsk (SS-423) is credited with being the last U.S. submarine to fire a torpedo and sink a combatant enemy ship on August 14, 1945, the day before the Pacific war ended. The Torsk, commissioned in December 1944, is now a submarine memorial exhibit open to the public in Baltimore, Md. (*See Appendix for listing of World War II ship memorial sites*).

★ ★

NO U.S. BATTLESHIP NAMED FOR STATE OF MONTANA

The only one of the 48 contiguous United States that never had a battleship named after it was Montana (Hawaii and Alaska became states long after the U.S. stopped building battleships). A widely held, but incorrect, story is that this was "punishment" because Rep. Janet Rankin (R- Montana) was the only Member of Congress to vote "no" to declaration of war against Japan on December 8, 1941, and had also voted "no" against war with Germany in 1917. However, work was started on a battleship to be named Montana during World War I. And in World War II a Montana-class of battleships was in progress, but in both cases the wars ended before the ships were finished. The names and hull numbers of the cancelled WWII ships would have been: USS Montana (BB-67); USS Ohio (BB-68); USS Maine (BB-69); USS New Hampshire (BB-70); and USS Louisiana (BB-71). The five Montana class ships would have been 65,000 tons and 903 ft. in length.

★ ★

USS BATFISH (SS-310) RACKED UP THREE FOR THREE

USS Batfish (SS-310) is the only submarine to sink three enemy submarines in three days. In February 1945, on her sixth war patrol, the Batfish encountered and sank three of the four known Japanese submarines around the Philippines. The Batfish is now a memorial exhibit in Muskogee, Okla. *(See Appendix for listing of all World War II memorial ships sites open to visitors).*

★ ★ ★ ★ ★ ★ ★ ★ ★ ★ ★ ★ ★ ★ ★ ★ ★ ★ ★ ★

PHILIPPINE SEA WAS BIGGEST AIRCRAFT CARRIER FIGHT

The greatest aircraft carrier engagement of the war was the Battle of the Philippine Sea. The Allies' fleet was spearheaded by 15 aircraft carriers against nine aircraft carriers for the Japanese. In overall fleet sizes the Allies had a distinctive 2-1 advantage with 112 warships against Japan's 55 ships.

★ ★ ★ ★ ★ ★ ★ ★ ★ ★ ★ ★ ★ ★ ★ ★ ★ ★ ★ ★

FIRST "BABY FLATTOP" WAS CONVERTED CARGO SHIP

The first ship designated as an escort aircraft carrier (Baby Flattop) was the SS Mormacmail a converted cargo ship. It entered U.S. Navy service as the USS Long Island (CVE-1).

★ ★ ★ ★ ★ ★ ★ ★ ★ ★ ★ ★ ★ ★ ★ ★ ★ ★ ★ ★

UNWANTED DISTINCTION OFF NEW JERSEY COAST

The first U.S. ship sunk in U.S. coastal waters was the USS Jacob Jones (DD-130) a destroyer, which was torpedoed by German U-boat 578 off New Jersey on February 28, 1942.

★ ★ ★ ★ ★ ★ ★ ★ ★ ★ ★ ★ ★ ★ ★ ★ ★ ★ ★ ★

A DUAL BETWEEN EQUALS: SUB vs. SUB IN PACIFIC

The first U.S. submarine to sink a Japanese submarine was the USS Gudgeon (SS-211), under the command of Lieutenant Commander Joseph Grenfell, which, on January 27, 1942, sank I-173

★ ★ ★ ★ ★ ★ ★ ★ ★ ★ ★ ★ ★ ★ ★ ★ ★ ★ ★ ★

FORT STEVENS, OREGON, SHELLED BY JAPANESE SUB

The first Japanese attack on a military base on the U.S. mainland occurred at Fort Stevens, Oregon, on June 22, 1942, when a Japanese submarine fired at the coastal outpost. There were no casualties. The last time a United States mainland military outpost had been fired on by a foreign power was by the British during the War of 1812. The first Japanese attack against Canada was in June 1942, when a submarine fired on a radio station on Vancouver Island.

★ ★

MAKASSAR STRAIT WAS FIRST BIG NAVAL BATTLE
The first major U.S. naval engagement in the Pacific was the Battle of Makassar Strait on January 24, 1942. Four American destroyers intercepted and engaged a Japanese invasion force headed for the petroleum farms at Balikpapan, Borneo. The outnumbered U.S. destroyers sank four Japanese troop transports, inflicting heavy casualties.

★ ★

HEDGHOGS DIDN'T SINK A SUB UNTIL 1944
The first submarine sunk as a result of Hedgehog fire (cluster bombs) was I-175 on February 5, 1944. Hedgehogs and a smaller version called Mouse-traps were adopted by the U.S. Navy in 1942. They consisted of clusters of bombs that broke into a pattern after being fired from a surface ship.

★ ★

1942 SAW FIRST U.S. MAINLAND ATTACK BY JAPANESE
The first U.S. civilian facility on the mainland to come under enemy attack during the war was the oil fields located west of Santa Barbara, Calif. They were fired on by Japanese submarine I-17 on February 23, 1942.

★ ★

FIRST ALLIED WARSHIP SUNK BY SUBMARINE
The first Allied warship sunk by a submarine was British fleet carrier HMS Courageous on September 17, 1939, by U-29 under the command of Otto Schuart. According to Royal Navy records, 519 members of the 22,500-ton ship's crew perished when it went to the

bottom of the sea in the Western Approaches off southwestern Ireland. The aircraft carrier was on antisubmarine duty at the time. After the sinking the Royal Navy removed fleet carriers from this duty.

★ ★

FIRST BRITISH NAVAL VICTORY WAS OVER ITALY IN '41

The first British naval victory over an Axis power was in mid-March 1941, against the Italians in the Mediterranean.

★ ★

LAST BRITISH SHIP SUNK IN PACIFIC WAS OFF CEYLON

The aircraft carrier HMS Hermes was the last British warship sunk in the Pacific war. The Hermes was lost off Ceylon on April 9, 1942, as a result of Japanese aircraft fire. This is not to be confused with the British destroyer also named Hermes, which was given to the Greeks, then captured and put into service by the Germans.

★ ★

DANZIG WAS FIRST CITY UNDER NAVAL BOMBARDMENT

The first city to come under naval bombardment in the war was Danzig, by the German battleship Schleswig-Holstein on September 1, 1939, the day war broke out in Europe.

★ ★

LAST JAPANESE BATTLESHIP AFLOAT AT END OF WAR

The only Japanese battleship still floating at the time of the surrender was the 42,785-ton Nagato. In terms of size, the 725-foot-long warship was the 19th-largest battleship in the war. (NOTE: *See appendix listing of the 20 largest battleships.*)

★ ★

WISHFUL THINKING "SUNK" U.S. BATTLESHIP SIX TIMES

The battleship most often reported sunk by the Japanese was USS North Carolina (BB-55), which was said to have been destroyed six times during her 40 months at sea. Runner-up was USS South Dakota (BB-57), said to have gone to the deep five times.

★ ★ ★ ★ ★ ★ ★ ★ ★ ★ ★ ★ ★ ★ ★ ★ ★ ★ ★ ★

HOSPITAL SHIPS WERE IN HARMS WAY TO OFTEN
Italy lost eight hospital ships during the war, the greatest number of any combatant nation.

★ ★ ★ ★ ★ ★ ★ ★ ★ ★ ★ ★ ★ ★ ★ ★ ★ ★ ★ ★

FIRST U.S. SUBMARINE TO SINK JAPANESE DESTROYER
The first U.S. submarine to sink a Japanese destroyer was S-44, which sank the Kako on August 10, 1942.

★ ★ ★ ★ ★ ★ ★ ★ ★ ★ ★ ★ ★ ★ ★ ★ ★ ★ ★ ★

LARGEST NAVAL ARMADA WAS FOR NORMANDY
The largest naval armada assembled in the war was the massive fleet collected for the Normandy invasion. American records say 5,000 ships were involved, whereas the British state a more conservative 4,500.

★ ★ ★ ★ ★ ★ ★ ★ ★ ★ ★ ★ ★ ★ ★ ★ ★ ★ ★ ★

U.S. MERCHANTMAN SUNK BY SUICIDE TORPEDO IN '44
The only U.S. ship sunk by Japanese Kaitens (one-man suicide torpedoes) was the merchantman SS Mississinewa in October 1944.

★ ★ ★ ★ ★ ★ ★ ★ ★ ★ ★ ★ ★ ★ ★ ★ ★ ★ ★ ★

LIBERTY SHIPS BUILT IN RECORD TIME
The record for building a Liberty ship was four days, 15 hours. The first one launched just 10 days after the keel was laid, was the SS Joseph N. Teal in October 1942.

★ ★ ★ ★ ★ ★ ★ ★ ★ ★ ★ ★ ★ ★ ★ ★ ★ ★ ★ ★

FIRST, LAST LIBERTY SHIPS BUILT, AND ONLY TWO LEFT
The first of 2,751 Liberty ships built was the SS Patrick Henry in September 1941. The last was the SS Benjamin Warner in 1944. Two Liberty ships exist as memorials open to the public: the SS

John W. Brown and SS Jeremiah O'Brien. (See Appendix for a listing of all World War II ship memorials available for visits).

★ ★ ★ ★ ★ ★ ★ ★ ★ ★ ★ ★ ★ ★ ★ ★ ★ ★ ★

FIRST BLACK TO COMMAND A LIBERTY SHIP
The first black to take command of a Liberty ship was Captain Hugh Mulzac, skipper of the SS Booker T. Washington.

★ ★ ★ ★ ★ ★ ★ ★ ★ ★ ★ ★ ★ ★ ★ ★ ★ ★ ★

FIRST U.S. NAVY SHIP NAMED HONORING A BLACK
The first U.S. Navy ship named in honor of a black American was the destroyer escort USS Harmon (DE-678) on July 25, 1943. Leonard Roy Harmon was killed in action aboard the San Francisco (CA-38) during the Battle of Guadalcanal, and was posthumously awarded the Navy Cross for risking his life for shipmates.

★ ★ ★ ★ ★ ★ ★ ★ ★ ★ ★ ★ ★ ★ ★ ★ ★ ★ ★

FIRST COMMISSIONED BLACK OFFICER IN U.S. NAVY
The first black American commissioned in the U.S. Navy was Ensign Bernard Robinson in June 1942.

★ ★ ★ ★ ★ ★ ★ ★ ★ ★ ★ ★ ★ ★ ★ ★ ★ ★ ★

FIRST U.S. NAVAL AIR OFFENSIVE IN PACIFIC
The first U.S. naval-air offensive in the Pacific was the February 1, 1942, attack against Japanese air and naval bases in the Marshall and Gilbert islands. The U.S. force consisted of two aircraft carriers, five cruisers, and 10 destroyers.

★ ★ ★ ★ ★ ★ ★ ★ ★ ★ ★ ★ ★ ★ ★ ★ ★ ★ ★

MILLIONAIRES YACHT FIRST INTEGRATED U.S. NAVY SHIP
The first fully integrated U.S. Navy ship, with blacks serving as officers as well as ratings, was the IX-99, an armed weather ship operating in the Atlantic and credited with an assist in sinking a U-boat. Prior to her war years IX-99 was the legendary four-masted barque SY Sea Cloud, owned by Post Cereals heiress Marjorie Merriweather Post. Returned to her owner after the war, and

resuming her original name, Sea Cloud eventually became a 68-passenger, 5-star, luxury cruise ship. Built in Germany in 1931, Sea Cloud remains in service to this day. Her five chevrons for World War II service are displayed proudly on the bridge. She is believed to be the only ship that saw combat in World War II which civilians can book passage on today.

★ ★ ★ ★ ★ ★ ★ ★ ★ ★ ★ ★ ★ ★ ★ ★ ★ ★ ★ ★

GERMAN WEATHER SHIP HAD ENIGMA CODE MACHINE
The first capture of an Enigma coding machine took place on May 7, 1941, when British sailors from HMS Somali boarded and captured the 139-foot-long steam-powered German weather ship Munchen in the North Atlantic. Armed with a single machine gun, the crew of the German ship abandoned the vessel after a number of near hits by the Somali. Because the Munchen's sea cocks had been rendered inaccessible when her ballast was replaced by concrete (for strength against icebergs), no effort was made to scuttle the ship.

★ ★ ★ ★ ★ ★ ★ ★ ★ ★ ★ ★ ★ ★ ★ ★ ★ ★ ★ ★

CAPTURED U-BOAT NETTED ENIGMA CODE MACHINE
The first German U-boat captured by the Allies was U-110 on May 9, 1941, by the Royal Navy's HMS Bulldog and HMS Broadway in the North Atlantic. More significantly, however, was the fact that the British had obtained their second Enigma coding machine in 72 hours. But the submarine sank while in tow the following day.

★ ★ ★ ★ ★ ★ ★ ★ ★ ★ ★ ★ ★ ★ ★ ★ ★ ★ ★ ★

BREAKING GERMAN ENIGMA, JAPANESE PURPLE CODES
The two most significant intelligence breakthroughs in the war were the ability of the U.S. to read Japanese Purple code traffic and Britain's reading of Germany's Enigma code traffic. Credit for the Purple intelligence is generally given to U.S. Army Colonel William Friedman, who spent three years attempting what many critics considered a two-pronged impossible task: (a) to determine the operating principles of and then replicate the mechanical encoding and decoding devices the Japanese were using without ever having

seen one, and (b) once that was done, to discover the correct cryptographic sequences used. However, it was the genius of a civilian cryptanalyst, Harry Larry Clark, who triggered the actual breakthrough.

★ ★ ★ ★ ★ ★ ★ ★ ★ ★ ★ ★ ★ ★ ★ ★ ★ ★ ★ ★

FIRST U.S. SHIP CAPTURED BY GERMANS
The first U.S. ship captured after the war began in Europe was the merchant ship City of Flint, by the German pocket battleship Deutschland.

★ ★ ★ ★ ★ ★ ★ ★ ★ ★ ★ ★ ★ ★ ★ ★ ★ ★ ★ ★

HOW WE GOT THE PT-BOAT DESIGN FROM ENGLAND
The first U.S. Navy PT boat (#9) arrived in New York from Great Britain two days after World War II had begun in September 1939. It had been purchased there by Henry R. Sutphen, executive vice president of the Electric Boat Company, which had its Elco Naval Division in Bayonne, N.J. Sutphen used his British-purchased boat as a model for the hundreds of others made at the Bayonne facility. The Navy took delivery of this original boat from Elco in June 1940 and designated it PT-9. By the time Pearl Harbor was attacked, several companies were offering designs in what were unofficially called the "Plywood Derby's of 1941". The most famous of all Elco boats was future President John F. Kennedy's PT-109.

★ ★ ★ ★ ★ ★ ★ ★ ★ ★ ★ ★ ★ ★ ★ ★ ★ ★ ★ ★

U.S. PT-BOATS PACKED THE MOST PUNCH PER POUND
Pound for pound, the most heavily armed vessels in the U.S. Navy were the deadly and highly maneuverable PT boats.

★ ★ ★ ★ ★ ★ ★ ★ ★ ★ ★ ★ ★ ★ ★ ★ ★ ★ ★ ★

FLETCHER LOST TWO U.S. AIRCRAFT CARRIERS
The only U.S. Navy admiral to have the unfortunate distinction of having two aircraft carriers lost while he was aboard them is Admiral Frank J. Fletcher. He was on the USS Yorktown (CV-5) at Midway and the USS Lexington (CV-2) in the Battle of the Coral

Sea. Fletcher, who had been awarded the Medal of Honor in 1914 for action in the Vera Cruz campaign, was also on the USS Saratoga (CV-3) when she was hit by, and survived, a Japanese torpedo attack.

★ ★

LAST HIGH NOON ON THE HIGH SEAS
The last surface-to-surface engagement of the war was on March 30, 1945 at Okinawa when the USS Irwin (DD-794) sank two Japanese torpedo/patrol crafts.

★ ★

FIRST U.S. AIRCRAFT CARRIER HAD BEEN COAL SHIP
The Navy's first aircraft carrier, USS Langley (CV-1), had been converted from the 5,500-ton fleet collier USS Jupiter (AC.3). The Jupiter, and a sister ship that had been lost in an accident in 1918, were coal-carrying supply ships that became obsolete with the introduction of oil as an energy source for the fleet.

★ ★

BATTLECRUISER HULLS BECAME U.S. CARRIERS
The first two U.S. aircraft carriers to be converted from battle cruiser hulls were the USS Lexington (CV-2) and USS Saratoga (CV-3). The conversions were provided for in the Washington Naval Disarmament treaty after World War I. The U.S. was permitted to convert two existing hulls into aircraft carriers of 33,000 tons each. In reality both topped out at just over 36,000 tons when "legal" modifications were added.

★ ★

HIGHEST U.S. CASUALTY RATE WAS FOR SUBMARINERS
The branch of the U.S. military that sustained the highest casualty rate was the submarine service, with 22 percent. For every U.S. surface-ship sailor lost in the war, six U.S. submarines lost their lives. One out of every seven submariners died: 3,505 officers and enlisted men. It was the heaviest ratio of any branch of the U.S.

armed services, including the Marines. One out of every five submarines was lost. In the euphemistic parlance of submariners, there are 49 World War II submarines "still out on patrol" in the Pacific, while three are still on patrol in the Atlantic.

★ ★ ★ ★ ★ ★ ★ ★ ★ ★ ★ ★ ★ ★ ★ ★ ★ ★ ★ ★

FIRST U.S. SUBMARINE SUNK AT CAVITE, PHILIPPINES

The first U.S. submarine sunk in the war was the Sealion (SS-195), at Cavite Naval Station in the Philippines. on December 19, 1941. The Sealion had been in port for overhauling and was badly damaged during the December 10 raid by Japanese aircraft. She was sunk by U.S. Navy depth charges after being stripped of useful equipment.

★ ★ ★ ★ ★ ★ ★ ★ ★ ★ ★ ★ ★ ★ ★ ★ ★ ★ ★ ★

GERMAN U-BOATS WERE DEADLY DUTY

The 785 submarines Germany lost in the war was greater than the collective total of all other major combatant nations: Japan lost 129; Italy, 107; Britain, 74; the U.S., 52; the Soviet Union, 50.

★ ★ ★ ★ ★ ★ ★ ★ ★ ★ ★ ★ ★ ★ ★ ★ ★ ★ ★ ★

U.S. SUBMARINE SUNK ITSELF WITH "BOOMRANG"

The only known instance in which a U.S. submarine sank itself involved the USS Tullibee (SS-00) on March 26, 1944. The Tullibee, in the waters off Palau in the Carolines, fired two torpedoes at a Japanese transport. One of the torpedoes turned and made a complete circle, hitting and sinking the Tullibee.

★ ★ ★ ★ ★ ★ ★ ★ ★ ★ ★ ★ ★ ★ ★ ★ ★ ★ ★ ★

FIRST KAMIKAZE ATTACK, FIRST AND LAST SHIPS SUNK

The first kamikaze attacks ever took place during the Battle for Leyte Gulf on October 25, 1944. The first ship sunk as a result of a kamikaze attack was the 6,730-ton escort carrier USS St.-L6 (CVE-63) a few minutes before 11 a.m. The first U.S. ship crashed by a kamikaze had been the escort carrier USS Santee (CVE-29) at 7:40 a.m. The last U.S. ship sunk by a kamikaze was the destroyer USS

Callaghan (DD-792), off Okinawa on July 28, 1945. By war's end kamikazes would sink or damage more than 300 ships, causing more than 15,000 U.S. casualties.

★ ★

U.S. SANK FIRST GERMAN U-BOAT FROM THE AIR
The first U-boat sunk by the U.S. was U-656, which was torpedoed from the air of Cape Race, Newfoundland, by Ensign William Tepuni while piloting a Navy Lockheed-Hudson on March 1, 1942.

★ ★

FIRST U-BOAT SUNK BY U.S. SURFACE SHIP
The first U-boat sunk by a U.S. Navy surface ship was U-85, on April 15, 1942, off Wemble Shoal near Hatteras, by Lieutenant Commander H. W. Howe of the destroyer USS Roper (DD-147).

★ ★

FIRST U-BOAT SUNK IN WORLD WAR II
The first German U-boat sunk was U-39, by British destroyers in the Atlantic, on September 14, 1939. At the outbreak of war Germany had 45 battle-ready U-boats out of a fleet of 57. Nine others were under construction. By February 1943, during the Battle of the Atlantic, Germany had 409 U-boats in active service. They reached their peak in May 1943 when there were 425 at large.

★ ★

ONLY U.S. SUBMARINE TO SINK A BATTLESHIP
The only U.S. submarine credited with sinking a battleship was the USS Sealion II (SS-310), which torpedoed Japan's 36,610-ton Kongo off Foochow, China, on November 21, 1944.

★ ★

FIRST U.S. SUBMARINE SUNK IN ATLANTIC
The first U.S. submarine sunk in the Atlantic was S-26, off Panama on January 24, 1942. The last U.S. submarine sunk in the Atlantic was the Dorado (SS-526), on October 12, 1943.

ONLY U.S. SUBMARINE SUNK BY JAPANESE SUBMARINE
The only U.S. submarine to be sunk by a Japanese submarine was the USS Corvina (SS-226), which was sunk off Truk on November 16, 1943, by I-176.

★ ★ ★ ★ ★ ★ ★ ★ ★ ★ ★ ★ ★ ★ ★ ★ ★ ★ ★ ★

LAST SUBMARINE TO SINK A SUBMARINE
The last submarine to sink another submarine was the USS Spikefish (SS-404) which sank I-873 on August 13, 1945, one day before Japan agreed to surrender. Spikefish picked up the sole Japanese survivor.

★ ★ ★ ★ ★ ★ ★ ★ ★ ★ ★ ★ ★ ★ ★ ★ ★ ★ ★ ★

FIRST U.S. SHIP SUNK BY JAPANESE SUBMARINE
The first U.S. ship sunk by a Japanese submarine was SS Cynthia Olson, by I-26, approximately 750 miles off the U.S. West Coast on December 7, 1941. This submarine was also responsible for the greatest loss of life involving members of one family when the five Sullivan brothers died during the sinking of the USS Juneau (CL-52) in the naval battle of Guadalcanal, November 12-15, 1942.

★ ★ ★ ★ ★ ★ ★ ★ ★ ★ ★ ★ ★ ★ ★ ★ ★ ★ ★ ★

LAST U.S. AIRCRAFT CARRIER SUNK IN WORLD WAR II
The last U.S. aircraft carrier sunk in the war was the 622 ft. USS Princeton (CVL-23), on October 24, 1944, during the Battle of the Sibuyan Sea, which was the first of the four major engagements that constitute the Battle for Leyte Gulf. She was the fourth U.S. ship to carry the name Princeton, but had originally been laid down as the Tallahassee (CL-61), in 1941.

★ ★ ★ ★ ★ ★ ★ ★ ★ ★ ★ ★ ★ ★ ★ ★ ★ ★ ★ ★

I DIDN'T SHUT THE DOOR. . . DID YOU SHUT THE DOOR?
The only known instance in which a submarine sank when a crew-member failed to secure one of its torpedo doors was Japan's loss of I-169 off the Island of Truk. The sub was forced to make an emergency dive to escape attacking U.S. aircraft.

LAST U.S. SUB SUNK DAY ATOM BOMB WAS DROPPED
The last U.S. submarine sunk was the Bullhead (SS-332), on August 6, 1945, the day the atom bomb was dropped on Hiroshima.

★ ★ ★ ★ ★ ★ ★ ★ ★ ★ ★ ★ ★ ★ ★ ★ ★ ★ ★ ★

ITALIAN SUBMARINE WAS FIRST SUNK BY AIRCRAFT FIRE
The first submarine sunk by aircraft fire was Italy's Argonauta, by an RAF Sunderland on June 28, 1940.

★ ★ ★ ★ ★ ★ ★ ★ ★ ★ ★ ★ ★ ★ ★ ★ ★ ★ ★ ★

AN AMERICAN CASUALTY DURING DIEPPE RAID
The first American casualty, other than Air Force, in the war in Europe was Lieutenant Colonel Loren B. Hillsinger, during the August 19, 1942, raid on Dieppe, France. He was aboard the destroyer HMS Berkley and lost a leg when the ship was bombed.

★ ★ ★ ★ ★ ★ ★ ★ ★ ★ ★ ★ ★ ★ ★ ★ ★ ★ ★ ★

THE DEMISE OF THE GERMAN COMMERCE RAIDERS
The last of the 10 armed German commerce raiders to be sunk by the Allies was the Michel (Shiff-28). It was torpedoed by the submarine USS Tarpon (SS-175) off Japan in October 1943. Raiders accounted for 133 Allied ship sinkings, totaling 830,000 tons. The Michel, which had been preying on Allied shipping in both the Atlantic and the Pacific, was the first and only German raider sunk by a United States submarine in the Pacific.

★ ★ ★ ★ ★ ★ ★ ★ ★ ★ ★ ★ ★ ★ ★ ★ ★ ★ ★ ★

NAVY WAS SAFEST PLACE FOR BRITS TO SERVE
The Royal Navy sustained the lowest number of British combat fatalities, 50,758 compared to the 69,606 lost by the Royal Air Force and the 144,079 army personnel reported killed or missing.

FACT: Though the USS Wisconsin's (BB-64) hull number suggests she was the last U.S. battleship completed, she actually went into service some two months before the USS Missouri (BB-63).

The city of Honolulu sustained approximately $500,000 worth of damage during the Japanese attack. However, it was determined afterward that the approximately 40 explosions that rocked the city were from U.S. anti-aircraft fire.   *–U.S. Army photo*

===

FACT: Three U.S. Navy men whose names would later be linked forever with World War II were involved in the first successful Atlantic crossing by flying boats. Marc Mitscher, Patrick Bellinger and John C. Towers were members of the crews of three 68-ft. long NC-4 aircraft (nicknamed Nancys) that departed Rockaway Beach, N.Y, May 18, 1919. Only one of the planes completed the trip. The plywood and fabric craft had a wingspan of 128 ft., the largest aircraft in the world at the time. Years later Bellinger would tell the world America was at war with his famous *"Air Raid Pearl Harbor, this is no drill."* Mitscher would achieve fame as a carrier task force commander, and Towers would become one of the most vocal members of Congress to fight for a U.S. Navy Air Force.

World War II
Historic Naval Ship Memorials

Ships have always held a fascination for sailors and non-sailors alike. Enshrined warships from past conflicts going as far back as the American Revolution fascinate each generation viewing them. It is therefore not surprising that U.S. Navy World War II fighting ships' memorials draw increasing numbers of visitors each year.

Battlefield memorials mark the very spots where this nation first won its independence and then more than four score years later preserved it. Bunker Hill, Yorktown, Saratoga, Lexington, Bull Run and Gettysburg, are but a few. However it is not possible to mark historic locations on the high seas. So we've done the next best thing. We've preserved the ships. Not all of them, to be sure, and probably far too few. As you move through the pages of this section it is worth reflecting for a moment that these World War II warships have been saved from being scrapped in almost all cases by what began as the determined efforts of small groups of people.

AN IMPORTANT NOTE BEFORE VISITING:

Locations, admissions, hours of operation, additional ships and other things may have changed since publication. What follows is intended as a representative listing of United States World War II ships open as memorials. *It is not meant to be a complete list.* Some memorial sites have two or more ships. For the most current information we recommend the *HISTORIC NAVAL SHIPS ASSOCIATION* website. Every ship mentioned here, plus many others, is on the HNSA site, replete with website links to specific ships. Go to: http://www.maritime.org/hnsa-guide.htm

THE ARIZONA (BB-39) MEMORIAL

Located exactly where it was on December 7, 1941, Battleship Row, Ford Island, Pearl Harbor, Oahu, Hawaii. The USS Arizona Memorial spans the sunken bull of the battleship which is resting in thirty-eight feet of water. The U.S. Navy conducts daily free tours on a first-come, first-served basis, which also include a documentary film about the Japanese attack. At present there are also four civilian tour boats making daily tours for a nominal fee, but they do not debark passengers at the memorial itself, something the Navy tour does. Navy tour passengers can visit the three sections of the memorial: the museum room, which houses mementos of the ship; the assembly area, capable of accommodating 200 persons for ceremonies; and the shrine room, where names of the 1,177 U.S. personnel killed on the ship are engraved on a marble wall. The civilian boats tour the harbor and play tapes that explain the action on the morning of the attack and pause alongside the memorial for a moment of silence.

Well over one million people visit the USS Arizona Memorial annually. It is the most popular tourist attraction in Hawaii.

The USS *Arizona* was launched at the New York Navy Yard on June 19, 1915, and commissioned on October 17, 1916. She was a member of the honor escort that brought President Woodrow Wilson to France for the 1918 Paris Peace Conference. Throughout the 1920s she was the mightiest ship of the U.S. fleet and was modernized between the wars. On April 2, 1940, she was assigned to duty at Pearl Harbor. She left the U.S. west coast for the last time in 1941, reaching Pearl Harbor on July 8, 1941.

The ship is no longer in commission, but in memory of the men who lost their lives on the "Day that will live in infamy" the Navy has granted special permission for the American flag to fly over the USS *Arizona*.

★ USS Becuna (SS-319), USS Olympia in Philadelphia

Located at Penn's Landing, Delaware Avenue and Spruce Street, Philadelphia, Pennsylvania, the Olympia and Becuna (SS-319), officially became a part of Independence Seaport Museum in January, 1996. Coined the Historic Ship Zone, visitors can step into our nation's past with self-guided explorations of each vessel. The acquisition of the 1892 cruiser Olympia and World War II submarine Becuna is the first phase of a long range effort to add to the collection of historic ships.

Purchases made in the ship's store help to preserve these two historic ships. One particularly interesting item is souvenir coins made from the Olympia's propellers.

The World War II submarine USS Becuna is a guppy-class boat that was commissioned on May 27, 1944. She served as the submarine flagship of the Southwest Pacific Fleet under General Douglas MacArthur. The Becuna earned four battle stars and a Presidential Unit Citation in five war patrols. After a postwar refit, she continued to see active duty in the Atlantic and Mediterranean during the Korean and Vietnam wars. She was decommissioned on October 1, 1969. The Becuna is the last of her type open for public exhibit.

Naval buffs and military historians need little introduction to the USS Olympia. Launched on November 5, 1892, and retired on September 1, 1922, she played a part in all the major American actions that marked this country as a world power.

Commodore Dewey, eyeball-to-eyeball with the Spanish fleet off the Philippine Islands on May 1, 1898, uttered the historic "You may fire when you are ready, Gridley," thus exploding the Battle of Manila Bay into history. She delivered the peace-keeping force to Murmansk, Russia, in 1918, served as flagship for U.S. Navy ships in the eastern Mediterranean, flagship for the North Atlantic Squadron and was as a training ship for Annapolis midshipmen.

★ USS Bowfin (SS-287) in Hawaii

Located at 11 Arizona Memorial Drive, Honolulu, Hawaii. The USS Bowfin (SS-287) one of only 15 U.S. WWII submarines still in existence today. She is nicknamed the "Pearl Harbor Avenger,"

Children under six years of age are not permitted aboard the Bowfin. No federal or state funds are used for the maintenance. The exhibit is operated by the Pacific Fleet Submarine Memorial Association as a memorial to the 52 U.S. submarines and 3,505 submariners of World War II who are considered "still on patrol." Visitors are provided with lightweight radio wands which receive transcribed narratives at stations throughout the submarine. Additionally, tour guides are in the boat to answer questions. The gift shop offers fairly priced items and the volunteer staff is pleasant.

The USS Bowfin was launched at Portsmouth, New Hampshire, on December 7, 1942, the first anniversary of the Pearl Harbor attack. She was commissioned on May 1, 1943. During her nine war patrols between August 1943 and August 1945, the USS Bowfin sank 179,946 tons of enemy shipping (44 ships), and one of her commanders, Walter T. Griffith, ranks as the seventh-highest-scoring American submarine commander in the war (see our listing of the leading submarine and U-boat commanders elsewhere in this book). Griffith is credited with sinking seventeen enemy ships while serving on the USS Bowfin and USS Bullhead. The Bowfin earned eight battle stars and both the Presidential Unit Citation and the Navy Unit Commendation.

The Bowfin saw a variety of assignments after World War II and was not decommissioned until December 1971. Rather than see this fierce fighting boat sold for scrap and possibly end up being recycled into razor blades, a small group in Hawaii formed the association that persuaded the U.S. Navy to give them the boat, and the result is this exhibit.

★ USS Croaker (SS-246) <u>in Buffalo, N.Y.</u>

Located at the Buffalo & Erie County Naval & Military Park. One Naval Park Cove, Buffalo, New York 14202. Prior to 1988 the USS Croaker was on exhibit in Groton, Connecticut.

USS Croaker was commissioned at the U.S. Naval Submarine Base, Groton, Connecticut, on April 21, 1944. She participated in six war patrols in the Pacific and is credited with sinking 11 Japanese ships: a cruiser; four tankers; two freighters; two escort craft; a minesweeper and an ammunition ship.

After World War II the Croaker returned to Connecticut and was a member of the fleet until 1971. She is maintained by the Submarine Memorial Association, Inc., which was also involved in obtaining the world's first nuclear-powered submarine, the USS Nautilus, as a permanent national monument exhibit at Groton, near the USS Croaker, till the Croaker moved to Buffalo in 1988.

★ USS Intrepid (CV-11) <u>in New York City</u>

Located at Pier 86 on West 46th Street in New York City. The Intrepid Sea-Air-Space Museum offers considerably more than an exciting visit to one of the only two U.S. World War II aircraft carriers open to visitors, since it combines exhibits that feature other areas of interest noted in its name.

Built in 1943 in Newport News, Virginia, at a cost of $44 million, the Intrepid carried 360 officers and 3,008 enlisted men during wartime service. She was nicknamed the Fighting I but because she was the most frequently hit United States Navy ship in the war she became known as the Evil I. Her combat record would easily fill several pages. Planes from her decks sank the two largest battleships (72,809 tons) ever built, the Yamato and Musashi. In the 1960s the USS Intrepid was the primary recovery ship for NASA during two Project Mercury and Project Gemini space missions.

The museum section of the exhibit (on the hangar deck) features four theme halls: the United States Navy Hall uses special effects to recreate the excitement of carrier aviation and puts an emphasis on the modern peacekeeping Navy; Intrepid Hall takes visitors back to the action of World War II; Pioneer Hall details man's early probes into the sky with flight; Technologies Hall covers the great advances in sea, air and space that had a profound influence on the 20th Century.

The Flight Deck includes many historic aircraft. The Intrepid Sea-Air-Space Museum opened to the public in the summer of 1982, and new onboard exhibits are being added regularly. It is also worth nothing that over the years other ships have been added to this memorial exhibit.

★ *USS Kidd (DD-661)* in Louisiana

Located in Baton Rouge, Louisiana and adjacent to the USS Kidd (DD-661) on the banks of the Mississippi, is the Nautical Center of the Louisiana Naval War Memorial, housing many attractions for the history or naval enthusiast, including several one-of-a-kind artifacts, and is located just walking distance from Louisiana Arts & Sciences Museum.

Also at this site is the USS Baton Rouge (SSN-689), a nuclear-powered *Los Angeles*-class attack submarine. The Louisiana Naval War Memorial Commission says that a good number of the 200,000 annual visitors to the Arts and Sciences Center also visit the Kidd and the museum. A gift shop and snack bar are on the grounds.

Commissioned in April 1943, and named for Rear Admiral Isaac C. Kidd who was killed manning a machine gun on his flagship, the USS Arizona (BB-39), the Kidd saw action in every major World War II naval campaign in the Pacific and earned four battle stars. Engagements she was involved in included Okinawa, Leyte, the Gilberts, Marshalls and the Philippines. Her nickname is the Pirate of the Pacific. She earned four battle stars during the Korean War.

The USS Kidd was decommissioned in 1964 and became part of the Atlantic Reserve Fleet until 1982, when ownership was transferred to the Louisiana Naval War Memorial Commission.

In the Nautical Center, you'll find the USS Kidd Exhibition with an eight-foot model used to build all 175 *Fletcher*-class destroyers. Another display honors those who died April 11, 1945, during an attack by a Japanese *kamikaze*. Pieces of the actual plane can be found in another exhibit

★ *USS Ling (SS-297)* in New Jersey

Located on the coastline of Borg Park on the Hackensack River at 78 River Streets (intersection with Court St.), Hackensack, New Jersey. Operated and maintained by the Submarine Memorial Association, a not-for-profit corporation operating the New Jersey Naval Museum. The museum is open to the public, and guided tours of the USS LING are available on Saturdays 10 A.M. to 5 P.M. Closed Sundays and major holidays. Weekday tours by arrangement. Call (201) 342-3268.

In addition to the Ling, other exhibits include: The Patrol Boat Riverine: Hundreds of these boats were in use in Vietnam, but only a few are still around. Many have been sold to foreign navies, stripped for parts or destroyed. The PBR in New Jersey is the only one in the Northeastern United States! Japanese Kaiten is a World War II suicide torpedo (Kaiten means Turned Towards Heaven); German Seahund *(means sea-dog)* WWII German 2 man, 39 ft. long coastal defense submarine. The Seehund was used for shallow water and coastal defense at the end of WWII. Two torpedoes could be launched from external rails on each side of the boat.

The museum contains a number of different and unique items ranging from a SEAL delivery vehicle to personal photos and effects. There is a gift shop and exhibit of nautical items of interest. Money raised through the boat tours and the gift shop is used by the non-profit Submarine Memorial Association to maintain the exhibits, which, besides the USS Ling, include several missiles, torpedoes, mines and anchors. The boat is heated for winter touring.

The USS Ling was commissioned on June 8, 1945, and managed to get in one Atlantic war patrol before the war ended. She is the last of the fleet-type submarines that patrolled American shores in the war years and was built by the Cramp Shipbuilding Company and outfitted at the Boston Navy Yard.

The Ling was decommissioned on October 26, 1946, and became part of the New London Group, Atlantic Reserve Fleet, until she was reactivated as a Submarine Naval Reserve training vessel in 1960. In December 1962, the Ling was converted from an SS to an AGSS submarine and served as one of the most elaborate and authentic training aids in the world.

She was decommissioned for a second, and final, time in December 1971. She arrived at her present berth on January 13, 1973.

While on active service, the Ling carried a complement of ninety-five officers and men and an armament capacity of twenty-four torpedoes.

★ *USS Massachusetts (BB-59)* in Massachusetts

Located at Battleship Cove, Fall River, Massachusetts, at Exit 5, I-95. The battleship is the main attraction of an exhibit that includes five other ships and a marine museum.

The museum contains 131 beautifully executed ship models ranging in size from a half inch to twelve feet long. At several locations visitors can press a button and hear background information about the particular exhibit being viewed.

The other ships at Battleship Cove include the destroyer USS Joseph R Kennedy (DD-850); the submarine USS Lionfish (SS-298); a PT boat; the gunboat Asheville; and the bow of the cruiser USS Fall River (CA-131).

The USS Massachusetts holds the distinction of being the first battleship to fire 16-inch guns at the enemy in World War II, in the Atlantic, against the Germans, and the last to fire them, this time in the Pacific, against Japanese. From that first volley until the last, she traveled over 225,000 miles and participated in thirty-five battles. Her nickname is Big Mamie.

The USS Massachusetts is the official state memorial to those who gave their lives in all branches of the service during World War II. The memorial area contains the names of the more than 13,000 Bay State residents who died in the war.

The destroyer USS Joseph R Kennedy is the official state memorial to the more than 4,500 who died in the Korean and Vietnam conflicts.

★ *USS Missouri (BB-63)* in Pearl Harbor, Hawaii

Berthed at Ford Island in Pearl Harbor and open to the public at this site since January 29, 1999. Of all the ships in this section the battleship USS Missouri is the last one to have been the property of the U.S. Navy, preserved as part of the mothball fleet.

If Congress had approved funding for reactivation of this mighty battleship during 1983, the 887 ft. long Missouri would have joined her sister ship, the USS New Jersey (BB-62), as a World War II survivor in the active fleet.

The USS Missouri was built at the New York Naval Shipyard and was launched on January 29, 1944. She was commissioned on June 11 of that year and remained in service until being decommissioned on February 26, 1955. She transited the Panama Canal and entered the western Pacific in January 1945.

The Missouri participated in operations against Okinawa, Iwo Jima and the Japanese mainland. She was President Truman's favorite ship (he was from Missouri, if you didn't recall).

It was on her decks, while Tokyo Bay on September 2, 1945, that the instrument of surrender was signed by the representatives of the Japanese government, thus ending World War II.

Truman could have used any number of other large ships (battleships or aircraft carriers in the area) for the historic surrender, but, according to a popular and widely held story, he had the Missouri steam to Tokyo Bay so that the ceremonies could take place on her decks. Thereby assuring his state's namesake ship a place in history.

Between 225,000 and 250,000 people reportedly visit the USS Missouri annually.

★ *USS North Carolina (BB-55)*   in North Carolina

At the time of the Pearl Harbor attack, USS North Carolina (BB-55) was having a post shakedown overhaul in Portland Maine. She is now on exhibit in Wilmington, North Carolina as a battleship memorial dedicated to the 10,000 state residents who died in World War II.

A sound-and-light spectacular titled "The Immortal Showboat" (from her nickname) is presented nightly at 9 P.M. in the summer. It depicts her World War II record, replete with the majestic roar of the 16-inch guns.

The 729-ft. long USS North Carolina was the third U.S. Navy ship to bear that name. Her keel was laid at the Brooklyn Navy Yard on

Navy Day, October 27, 1937, and she was launched on June 13, 1940, and commissioned on April 9, 1941. Her gross wartime tonnage was 44,800 tons.

During her forty months in combat zones in World War II, the Showboat was reported sunk six times Tokyo Rose.

She participated in the following Asiatic-Pacific campaigns: Guadalcanal and Tulagi; eastern Solomons; Gilbert Islands; Tarawa; Makin; Marshalls; Kwajalein; Roi; Namur; Guam; Saipan; Palau; Yap; Ulithi; Woleai; Satawan; Ponape; New Guinea; Aitape; Tanahmerah Bay; Humboldt Bay; Marianas; Tinian; Philippines; Iwo Jima; Honshu; Nansei; Shoto; Okinawa; Kerama-retto; Kyushu and the Inland Sea, among others.

★ USS Texas (BB-35) in Texas

Located at Battleground Road, San Jacinto State Park, La Porte, Texas. A snack bar is nearby as are several restaurants. Approximately 240,000 people from all over the world visit the "Grand Old Lady" annually.

The effort to preserve the Texas was the first such undertaking to create a ship-and-shore memorial to a state's naval namesake and encouraged other groups to create similar exhibits. Fleet Admiral Chester W. Nimitz was present at the dedication ceremonies when the USS Texas went on public display as a memorial in 1948. It was the first World War II era ship to become a memorial.

Commissioned in 1914 at Norfolk, Virginia, as a Dreadnought-class battleship, USS Texas saw action in both world wars. In World War II she made her combat debut in Operation Torch, the North African invasion, and participated in Operation Overlord, the D-Day invasion of Normandy. In the Pacific she made her presence felt at Iwo Jima and Okinawa. She is the third U.S. Navy ship named for the State of Texas.

After the Japanese surrender, the USS Texas was one of the ships in the Magic Carpet Fleet that had the richly pleasant tasks of returning U.S. servicemen to the United States.

Also enshrined at San Jacinto State Park along with the USS Texas is the USS Cabrilla (SS-288), a World War II submarine that sank 38,767 tons of enemy shipping during six of her eight war patrols.

The San Jacinto State Park is a short drive by freeway from downtown Houston.

★ *USS Yorktown (CV-10)* in South Carolina

Located at Patriots Point, Charleston Harbor, South Carolina. the Fighting Lady is the main attraction at this exhibit that includes three other ships and several aircraft. There is a gift shop and restaurant. The ship's theater regularly shows the movie *The Fighting Lady.*

The aircraft carrier USS *Yorktown* received the traditional champagne christening on April 15, 1943, at Newport News, Virginia. First Lady Mrs. Eleanor Roosevelt did the honors. Some ten months later the *Yorktown* celebrated the 7,000th landing on her decks. Her total landings in World War II alone were 31,170. The Fighting Lady earned fifteen battle stars during which time she set records for the fastest launches and recoveries of aircraft and the heaviest flying schedules. She also set a record in shooting down 14 enemy aircraft, while her planes accounted for 458 enemy planes in the air and 695 on the ground. She earned a presidential unit citation and several other awards. Among the major naval campaigns the Yorktown (CV-10) saw action in were: Truk, the Marianas, the Philippines, Iwo Jima, and Okinawa.

At 899-ft. long and 33,800 gross tons the USS Yorktown (CV-10) was named to honor those who served on her namesake, the 809.5-ft. long, 29,100 gross ton USS Yorktown (CV-5), sunk at Midway.

Besides this great carrier, visitors can also see the destroyer USS Laffey (DD-724), hit by more Japanese kamikaze planes than any other ship in one battle; the World War II submarine USS Clamagore (SS-343); the world's first nuclear-powered merchant ship, the Savannah; plus a grouping of military aircraft, including a B-25 and eight others.

★ *USS Hazard (AM-240)* in Nebraska

Located at the Greater Omaha Marina, 2000 North 25th Street, East Omaha, Nebraska.

In addition to the minesweeper USS *Hazard,* the Greater Omaha Marina also exhibits the post-World War II submarine USS *Marlin* (SST-2) and a McDonnell Douglas A-4 Skyhawk.
There is a restaurant and lounge, golf-driving range, trailer campgrounds, three boat-launch ramps. The *Hazard* is the largest ship that has traveled this far inland, making the trek from Orange, Texas, to Omaha - a distance of 2,000 miles - in 29 days. She now rests at the marina on the Missouri River.

The USS *Hazard* was launched on May 21, 1944, at Winslow, Washington, and commissioned on October 31, 1944. She saw active service in World War II screening convoys and sweeping for mines at Eniwetok, the Philippines, Okinawa, Keramaretto, the East China Sea, the Yellow Sea and Jinsen, Korea.

★ *USS Pampanito (AG SS-383)* in California

Located at Fisherman's Wharf in San Francisco, California. The Pampanito was built at Portsmouth Naval Shipyard, New Hampshire, and commissioned on 6 November 1943. She is credited with sinking five enemy ships totaling 27,288 tons on six war patrols. She rescued 73 Australian and British POW's after she and the USS Sealion sank two Japanese ships that were transporting them to labor camps.

★ *Other World War II Ships Open to Visitors*

For details, visit the Historic Naval Ships Assn. Website:
http://www.maritime.org/hnsa-guide.htm

USS Alabama (BB-60)	Mobile, AL
USS Hornet (CV-12)	Alameda, CA
SS Jeremiah O'Brien	San Francisco, CA
SS Red Oak Victory (AK-235)	Richmond, CA
SS Lane Victory	San Pedro, CA
Auxilliary Schooner Brilliant	Mystic, CT
LCVP (Higgins Boat)	Washington, DC
Motor Whaleboat	Washington, DC
SS American Victory	Tampa, FL
U-505 (captured)	Chicago, IL
USCGC Taney (WHEC-37)	Baltimore, MD
USS Torsk (SS-423)	Baltimore, MD
USS Cassin Young (DD-793)	Boston,MA
USS Silversides (SS-236)	Muskegon, MI
USS LST-393	Muskegon, MI
USCGC McLane (WMEC-146)	Muskegon, MI
USS New Jersey (BB-62)	Camden, NJ
USS Slater (DE-766)	Albany, NY
USS The Sullivans (DDG-537)	Buffalo, NY
USS Little Rock (CL-92)	Buffalo, NY
USAT LT-5	Oswego, NY
USS Cod (SS-224)	Cleveland, OH
USS Batfish (SS-310)	Muskogee, OK
USS Requin (SS-481)	Pittsburgh, PA
USS Lexington (CV-16)	Corpus Christi, TX
Admiral's Barge	Fredericksburg, TX
USS Cavalla (SS-244)	Galveston, TX
USS Stewart (DE-238)	Galveston, TX
PT 309	Keniah, TX
PT 619	Memphis, TN
USS Wisconsin (BB-64)	Norfolk, VA
USS Cobia (SS-245)	Manitowoc, WI

THE REMARKABLE USS UTAH (BB-31/AG-16)

The following copy has been excerpted from, and is used here with permission of William Hughes, creator and moderator of The Official USS Utah Association web site: http://members.home.net/wmhughes/ussutah.html

The UTAH has been almost forgotten. Seldom honored by public visits, it rests in the waters of Pearl Harbor as a distant memory of America's most remembered day, a sad epitaph for a fine battleship.

The UTAH was assigned to the Atlantic Fleet in March 1912. For the next two years the battleship was assigned to regular duties in the Atlantic Fleet.

Once World War I was underway, the UTAH became a training ship for gunnery and engineering for new recruits. On September 10, 1918, the UTAH moved to Bantry Bay, Ireland to protect convoys and secure approaches to the British Isles. The war ended that year. The UTAH served as honor escort for the transport GEORGE WASHINGTON carrying President Woodrow Wilson to the Versailles Peace Conference. Also in the honor escort was the USS ARIZONA (BB-39).

For the next 12 years the UTAH served with distinction in the Atlantic Fleet. The UTAH was one of those condemned as a battleship and was designated to be removed from service in order to comply with the London treaty. In 1934 she was saved from demolition when the Navy decided to remove the armament and convert Utah to an experimental mobile target ship. On July 1, 1931, UTAH was redesignated a miscellaneous auxiliary ship, and the hull was reclassified from BB-31 to AG-16. Conversion took nearly a year, but as a result the UTAH became one of the most sophisticated technical marvels of the period.

Certainly the installation of the radio-controlled steering and steaming apparatus bears witness to the scientific advances of the

1930s. The mechanism allowed the UTAH to be controlled from another ship or aircraft. The ship could steam at varying rates of speed, alter course and lay smoke screens. It could maneuver as a ship would during battle. All this was accomplished by electric motors that could open and close throttle valves, position the steering gear and regulate the supply of oil to the boilers in order to generate smoke for laying down screens. A Sperry "metal mike" or gyro pilot kept the ship on course. The UTAH was placed in full commission on April 1, 1932. Although the UTAH could operate without the touch of human hands, it did have to be monitored (at least every four hours). In the past it had taken 500 men, including officers and seamen, to operate the vessel.

The UTAH broke new ground in the field of remote control (which) was used for space exploration and guided missiles more than a generation later.

The UTAH was changed over in August 1935 to an antiaircraft training ship for the Pacific Fleet, a status ultimately more important than the category of mobile target ship. Thus the UTAH embarked on a new phase of training that would occupy the remaining years of the ship's life until its demise on December 7, 1941.

In April 1940, the UTAH (received) a 5-inch 25-gun battery, considered by many as the best antiaircraft weapon in existence. From Washington the UTAH sailed for Hawaiian waters to conduct an advanced antiaircraft gunnery school. Trainees arrived aboard from the battleships WEST VIRGINIA, COLORADO, NEW MEXICO, and OKLAHOMA and the cruisers NEW ORLEANS, PHOENIX, NASHVILLE, and PHILADELPHIA. For several weeks the crews practiced loading and controlling the 5-inch batteries, 50-caliber machine guns, and 1.1 -inch guns.

It set sail for the last time for Hawaii on September 14, 1941. For the weekend of December 6-7, the UTAH returned to Pearl Harbor and moored at berth F-ll on the west side of Ford Island.

ELVIS PRESLEY AND
THE USS ARIZONA MEMORIAL

In 1943, less than two years after the Japanese surprise attack on Pearl Harbor, there already was a growing interest in creating a "Shrine of Pearl Harbor." The original concept was totally different from the eventual USS *Arizona* Memorial, but the fact that support for a memorial was so close to the tragic events of December 7, 1941 and that the U.S. was still embroiled in the war, indicated that Americans did indeed want to "Remember Pearl Harbor."

Other proposals for a memorial followed until in 1949 the future State of Hawaii established the Pacific War Memorial Commission (PWMC) for the purpose of organizing and overseeing efforts for various war memorials in Hawaii.

Eventually, a platform was constructed across the hull of the sunken USS Arizona (BB-39) in March of 1950. Permission was granted to erect a flagpole on the Arizona wreckage and for a flag to be raised and lowered there daily.

By May, 1956 the United States Navy became involved with the PWMC. Their combined efforts led to Congress passing Public Law 85-344 in 1958, which in effect made it possible to move ahead with an actual memorial, and $150,000 in federal funding was approved on September 6, 1961. The actual cost of the USS Arizona Memorial would be more than $500,000. The difference came from various sources, including $50,000 from the State of Hawaii.

But perhaps the single event that gained the most publicity and most likely inspired other contributions, was a 1961 sold-out concert by Elvis Presley at the Bloch Arena in Pearl Harbor (for which Presley did not take a fee). It raised $65,697. The PWMC also had help from the then popular TV show, "This Is Your Life", which helped raise $95,000. Public donations accounted for the rest of the needed funds.

Admiral Ernest J. King, replaced Admiral Harold R. Stark as Chief of Naval Operations (CNO) in March 1942, hardly three months after the Pearl Harbor attack. The dour-faced King was an advocate for the U.S. concentrating all efforts to defeat Japan before Germany. But FDR thought otherwise. *–U.S. Navy photo*

APPENDICES

PROFILE OF U.S. SERVICEMEN (1941-1945)

The average base pay for enlisted personnel was $71.33 per month For officers it was $203.50 per month.

38.8 percent (6,332,000) of U.S. servicemen and women were volunteers while 61.2 percent (11,535,000) were draftees. Of the 17,955,000 men examined for induction, 35.8 percent (6,420,000) were rejected as physically or mentally unfit.

The average duration of service in the military was 33 months and 73 percent served overseas for an average of 16.2.

Out of every 1,000 who served in combat, 8.6 were killed in action, 3 died from other causes, and 17.7 received nonfatal wounds.

38.8 percent of enlisted personnel were in non-combat, rear echelon assignments in administrative, technical, support, or manual labor.

PRISONERS OF WAR IN WORLD WAR II

Prisoners held by the Allies (excluding those in the USSR)
German 630,000; Italian 430,000; Japanese 11,600.
Allied prisoners held by Germany:
American 90,000; French 765,000; Italian 550,000;
British 200,000; Yugoslav 125,000.
Allied prisoners held by Japan:
American 15,000; British 8,000; Dutch 22,000

The Atom Bombing of Hiroshima Was Not The Deadliest U.S. Air Raid Against Japan in WW II

Many people incorrectly believe that the atomic bombs the United States dropped on Hiroshima or Nagasaki were the deadliest bombings in history. In fact they were not, nor were they the deadliest raids in World War II, nor even the deadliest in the Pacific Theater for that matter. The bombings that caused the greatest loss of life were the incendiary bombs.

On the night of March 9-10, 1945, an attack force of 279 U.S. B-29s delivered unequaled destruction of a population center: Tokyo. The Superfortresses dropped 1,665 tons of napalm bombs which upon impact exploded and rained down an adhering, glue-like fire as much as a hundred feet in all directions. In less than 30 minutes the incendiaries created an inferno which consumed 83,793 people.

The various causes of death were incineration, suffocation, or scalding, primarily of those forced into boiling canals and rivers. Another 41,000 victims were injured. More than a million people lost their lives in the 1944-1945 Allied air attacks as 15.8 square miles of central Tokyo were completely destroyed.

The three Deadliest Air Raids on Japan in World War II

Tokyo, March 9-10	incendiary raid	83,793 deaths
Hiroshima, Aug. 6	atomic bomb attack	70,000 deaths
Nagasaki, Aug. 9	atomic bomb attack	20,000 deaths

==

FACT: James Jones, the future best-selling author, was a 17-year-old private in the United States Army, stationed on Oahu, Hawaii, on December 7, 1941. A decade later his novel *From Here to Eternity* would fictionalize, but otherwise accurately describe, the everyday routine and concerns of Army life in Hawaii up to and at the time of the attack.

U.S. Navy World War II Fleet Aircraft Carriers

The 1944-45 edition of Jane's Fighting Ships stated that the strength of the postwar 1946 U.S. Navy would be 18 battleships, 27 fleet aircraft carriers, and 79 escort aircraft carriers. The prewar rivalry between "the Gun Club" dreadnought admirals and the advocates of naval air power was over. The pendulum had swung dramatically in Hawaii on a December Sunday in 1941. The U.S. had eight aircraft carriers red the war. By September 1945 the Navy had added 113 more of all types, including Fleet (CV), Light Fleet (CVL), and Escort (CVE). Listed here are only the Fleet (CV) carriers.

A trio of large Fleet Aircraft Carriers (CVB) of 45,000 tons and 986 feet in overall length were laid down in 1943 and 1944 but were also not completed before the end of the war. They included USS Midway (CVB-41), USS Franklin D. Roosevelt (CVB-42), and USS Sea (CVB-43). Orders for three others were cancelled in 1945.

Hull No.	Carrier	Completed	Tonnage	Length
CV-1	USS Langley	1922	12,903	519
CV-2	USS Lexington	1927	49,500	909.5
CV-3	USS Saratoga	1927	49,500	909.5
CV-4	USS Ranger	1934	14,500	769
CV-5	USS Yorktown	1937	29,100	809.5
CV-6	USS Enterprise	1938	29,100	809.5
CV-7	USS Wasp	1940	18,500	741
CV-8	USS Hornet	1941	29,100	809.5
CV-9	USS Essex	1942	33,800	899
CV-10	USS Yorktown (2)	1943	33,800	899
CV-11	USS Intrepid	1943	33,800	899
CV-12	USS Hornet (2)	1943	33,800	899
CV-13	USS Franklin	1944	33,800	899
CV-14	USS Ticonderoga	1944	33,800	899
CV-15	USS Randolph	1944	33,800	899
CV-16	USS Lexington (2)	1943	33,800	899

Hull No.	Carrier	Completed	Tonnage	Length
CV-17 USS Bunker Hill		1943	33,800	899
CV-18 USS Wasp (2)		1943	33,800	899
CV-19 USS Hancock		1944	33,800	899
CV-20 USS Bennington		1944	33,800	899
CV-21 USS Boxer		1945	33,800	899
CV-31 USS Bon Homme Richard		1944	33,800	899
CV-36 USS Antietam		1945	33,800	899
CV-38 USS Shangri-La		1944	33,800	899
CV-39 USS Lake Champlain		1944	33,800	899

*CV-32	USS Leyte	*These last seven Essex-class*
*CV-33	USS Kearsarge	*carriers were commissioned*
*CV-34	USS Oriskany	*after hostilities ended. The*
*CV-37	USS Princeton (2)	*class originally called for 36*
*CV-40	USS Tarawa	*carriers. Twelve others were*
*CV-45	USS Valley Forge	*cancelled in March and*
*CV-47	USS Philippine Sea	*August, 1945.*

How the U. S. and Japan Named Warships

United States Navy

Battleships	States of the Union
Heavy cruisers	major cities, also territories or possessions
Light cruisers	smaller cities
Carriers	famous ships and battles from the Revolution
Destroyers	distinguished U.S. naval personnel
Submarines	fish, marine life (till 1971)

Imperial Japanese Navy

Battleships	ancient provinces and regions
Heavy cruisers	mountains, mountain ranges
Light cruisers	swift rivers, famous big rivers
Carriers	mythical flying animals, or birds of prey
Destroyers	weather descriptions (i.e. Winds of Spring)
Submarines	I, Ro, or Ha (A, B, C, and numbers)

U. S. Fleet & Escort Carriers Lost in WW II

CARRIER	LOCATION	FROM	DATE
Hornet	Solomon Islands	aircraft	Oct. 26, 1942
Lexington	Coral Sea	aircraft	May 8, 1942
Princeton	Philippines	aircraft	Oct. 24, 1944
Wasp	Espiritu Santo	submarine	Sept. 15, 1942
Yorktown	Midway	aircraft	June 7, 1942
Bismarck Sea	Iwo Jima	kamikaze	Feb.21,1945
Block Island	Madeira Islands	submarine	May 29, 1944
Gambier Bay	Timor Island	surface ship	Oct. 25, 1944
Liscome Bay	Tarawa	submarine	Nov. 24, 1943
Ommaney Bay	Philippines	kamikaze	Jan. 4, 1945
St. Lo	Philippines	kamikaze	Oct. 25, 1944

Japanese Fleet & Escort Carriers Lost in WW II

CARRIER	LOCATION	FROM	DATE
Akagi	Midway	aircraft	June 4, 1942
Chitose	Luzon, Philippines	aircraft	Oct. 25, 1944
Chiyoda	Luzon, Philippines	ships, aircraft	Oct. 25, 1944
Hiryu	Midway	aircraft	June 5, 1942
Hiyo	Philippine Sea	aircraft	June 20, 1944
Kaga	Midway	aircraft	June 4, 1942
Ryujo	Malaita Island,	aircraft	Aug. 24, 1942
Shinano	Honshu	submarine	Nov. 29, 1944
Shoho	Coral Sea	aircraft	May 7, 1942
Shokaku	Yap Island	submarine	June 19, 1944
Soryu	Midway	air and sub	June 4, 1942
Taiho	Yap Island	submarine	June 19, 1944
Unryu	East China Sea	submarine	Dec. 19, 1944
Zuiho	Luzon, Philippines	aircraft	Oct. 25, 1944
Zuikaku	Luzon, Philippines	aircraft	Oct. 25, 1944
Chuyo	Honshu, Japan	submarine	Dec. 4, 1943
Kaiyo	Beppu Bay,Japan	aircraft	July 24, 1945
Jinyo	Yellow Sea	submarine	Nov. 17, 1944
Otaka	Luzon, Philippines	submarine	Aug. 18, 1944
Unyo	South China Sea	submarine	Sept. 16, 1944

Admiral Chester W. Nimitz replaced Admiral Husband E. Kimmel as Commander in Chief U.S. Pacific Fleet (CINCPAC) shortly after the Pearl Harbor attack and America's entry into the war. *—U.S. Navy photo*

Top 20 U.S. Navy Submarine Commanders

It is interesting to note that the top U.S. submarine commander, Richard H. O'Kane, would rank seventh among the top 20 German U-boat commanders (based on the number of ships sunk).

Commander and Submarine(s)	Ships Sunk	Patrols
Richard H. O'Kane; Tang	31	5
Eugene B. Fluckey; Barb	25	5
Slade D. Cutter; Seahorse	21	4
Samuel D. Dealey; Harder	20.5	6
William S. Post, Jr.; Gudgeon, Spot	19	7
Reuben T. Whitaker; S-44, Flasher	18.5	5
Walter T. Griffith; Bowfin, Bullhead	17	5
Dudley W. Morton; R-5, Wahoo	17	6
*John E. Lee; S-12, Grayling, Croaker	16	10
William B. Sieglaff; Tautog, Tench	15	7
Edward E. Shelby; Sunfish	14	5
Norvell G. Ward; Guardfish	14	5
Gordon W. Underwood; Spadefish	14	3
John S. Coye, Jr.; Silversides	14	6
Glynn R. Donaho; Flying Fish, Picudo	14	7
George E. Porter, Jr.; Bluefish, Sennet	14	6
Royce L. Gross; Seawolf, Boarfish	13.5	7
*Henry G. Munson; S-38, Crevalle, Rasher	13	9
Robert E. Dornin; Trigger	13	3
Charles O. Triebel; S-15, Snook	13	8

* Gross tonnage was considered in the ranking only when two or more commanders sank an equal number of ships.

* With three different submarine commands each, John E. Lee and Henry G. Munson commanded the most submarines to earn a spots in the top 20 ranking.

Top 20 Kriegsmarine U-boat Commanders

Commander and U-boat(s)	Ships Sunk	Patrols
Otto Kretschmer; U-23, U-19	45	16
Wolfgang Luth; U-9, U-138, U-43, U-181	44	14
Jochim Schepko; U-3, U-19, U-100	39	14
Erich Topp; U-57, U-552	35	13
Victor Schutze; U-25, U-103	34	7
Heinrich Liebe; U-38	30	9
Karl F. Merten; U-68	29	5
Gunther Prien; U-47	29	10
Jochim Mohr; U-124	29	6
Georg Lassen; U-160	28	4
Carl Emmermann; U-172	27	5
Herbert Schultze; U-48	26	8
Werner Henke; U-515	26	6
Heinrich Bleichrodt; U-48, U-109	25	8
Robert Gysae; U-98, U-177	25	8
Klaus Schoh; U-108	24	8
Reinhard Hardegen; U-147, U-123	23	-
H. L. Willenbroch; U-5, U-96, U-256	22	10
Engelbert Endrass; U-46, U-567	22	9
Ernst Kals; U-130	19	5

* Otto Kretschmer, Germany's most successful U-boat commander, credited with sinking 45 ships during 16 patrols as commander of U-23 and U-99, was the first U-boat commander to sink more than a quarter-million tons of shipping. On March 17, 1941, Kretschmer and his crew were captured by British destroyers HMS Walker and HMS Vanoc after scuttling their boat. Twenty percent of the U-boat fleet was lost in March 1941 as a result of British air and naval fire. In addition to Kretschmer, the toll included several other veteran U-boat commanders on the above list.

Top 50 Fighter "Aces" in World War II

The U.S. and most other nations recognized the term "ace" as it applied to pilots who scored a minimum of five victories (or kills). As difficult as that was, the aces of all nations would fill several pages. The U.S., Great Britain, Canada, Australia, and the other Allies for the most part included only aircraft shot down in flight as a victory. Some countries counted planes on the ground, cars, trains, and so on; hence some of the celestial numbers. Fighter pilots listed here are those who were aces five times over or more, meaning a minimum of 25 victories. However, 38 German aces are credited with 100 victories or more each. In the interest of brevity, only the German superaces with 250 or more victories each have been listed.

Fighter Ace	Country	Number of Victories
Erich Hartmann	Germany	352
Gerhard Barkhorn	Germany	301
Gunther Rall	Germany	275
Otto Kittel	Germany	267
Walther Nowotny	Germany	255
Hiroyishi Nishizawa	Japan	87*
Shoichi Sugita	Japan	80*
Hans H. Wind	Finland	75
Saburo Sakai	Japan	64*
Ivan Kozhedub	USSR	62
Alek Pokryshkin	USSR	59
Grigorii Rechkolov	USSR	58
Hiromichi Shinohara	Japan	58
Nikolai Gulaev	USSR	57
Waturo Nakamichi	Japan	55

***Some reports credit Nishizawa with 103 kills and Sugita with 120. Sakai is credited with 80 kills in other works. However, this author is satisfied that the figures given here are the most frequently accepted. The discrepancies are pointed out because they do exist.

Fighter Ace	Country	Number of Victories
Takeo Okumura	Japan	54
Nooshi Kanno	Japan	52
Kirill Yevstigneev	USSR	52
Satoshi Anabuki	Japan	51
Yosuhiko Kuroe	Japan	51
Dimitrii Glinka	USSR	50
Atexandr Klubov	USSR	50
Ivan Pilipenko	USSR	48
Arsenii Vorozheikin	USSR	46
Niki Skomorokhov	USSR	46
Vasilii Kubarev	USSR	46
J. Pattle	S. Africa	41
Richard I. Bong	U.S	40
Thomas B. McGuire	U.S	38
J. E. Johnson	Gr. Britain	38
Cretian Galic	Yugoslavia	36
A. G. Malon	S. Africa	35
David McCampbell	U.S.	34
P. H. Closterman	France	33
B. Finucane	Ireland	32
G. F. Beurling	Canada	31.5
Frances S. Gabreski	U.S.	31
J. R. D. Graham	Gr. Britain	29
R. R. S. Tuck	Gr. Britain	29
C. R. Caldwell	Australia	28.5
Gregory Boyington	U.S.	28
J. Frontisek	Czech	28
Robert S. Johnson	U.S.	28
J. H. Lacey	Gr. Britain	28
C. F. Gray	New Zealand	27.5
Chas. H. MacDonald	U.S.	27
George E. Preddy	U.S.	26
E. S. Lock	Gr. Britain	26
Joseph E. Foss	U.S.	26
Robert M. Hanson	U.S.	25

The 10 Fastest Fighter Planes in World War II

Between 1939-45, 64 different fighter planes were employed by Allied and Axis nations. Ranked by speed, here are the 10 fastest.

Aircraft	Country	Mph	Range (mi)
1-Messerschmitt-263 (rocket)	Germany	596	NA
2-Messerschmitt-262 (jet)	Germany	560	650
3-Heinkel He-162A	Germany	553	606
4-P-51-H	U.S.	487	850
5-Lavochkin La-11	USSR	460	466
6-Spitfire XIV	Britain	448	460
7-Yakovlev Yak-3	USSR	447	506
8-P-51-D Mustang	U.S.	440	2,300
9-Tempest VI	Britain	438	740
10-Focke-Wulf FW-190-D	Germany	435	560

If the list continued, other fighters would rank:

(12) P-47-D Thunderbolt	U.S.	428 mph
(14) F4U Corsair	U.S.	417 mph
(16) P-38 Lightening	U.S.	414 mph
(19) Messerschmitt 109G	Germany	400 mph

HIGHEST U.S. AIRCRAFT PRODUCTION IN WORLD WAR II

P-47 Thunderbolts was produced in greater numbers than any other U.S. fighter between July, 1940 and August, 1945. The top five U.S. military aircraft produced in that period were: B-24, (18,188); P-47, (15,579); P-51, (14,490); P-40, (13,700); B-17, (12,677).

FACT: Between 1939-1945 Germany lost 95,000 aircraft, almost double Japan's 49,485 lost. Among the Allies, the U.S. reported the most, 59,296. Britain lost 33,090. No other combatant nation lost more than 7,200 (The Soviets did not release figures).

Allied and Axis Tanks in World War II by Size

Country/Tank	Tons	Length	Number built
1-German; PzKpfw Tiger II	74.8	33.9	485
2-German; PzKpfw Elephant	74.8	22.3	90
3-German; PzKpfw Tiger I	62.7	27.9	1,350
4-Soviet; KVIA Kliment	52	22	10,000
5-German; PzKpfw Panther	50	33.1	384
6-German; PzKpfw V	49.3	29	3,740
7-Soviet; JSH Joseph Stalin	45.3	32.2	Unknown
8-British; Mark IV Churchill	43.1	24.5	5,640
9-U.S.; M26 Pershing	41.1	28.10	2,428
10-U.S.; M4A3 Sherman	37.1	19.3	49,000
Soviet; T34/85	34.5	20.2	Unknown
Soviet; SU85	32.4	26.8	Unknown
U.S.; M3 (Lees & Grants)	31	18.6	4,924
British; Mark VIII Cromwell	30.8	20.10	1,000+
Soviet; T34/76	29.7	21.7	40,000
British; Mark IIA Matilda	29.7	18.5	2,987
German; PzKpfw III	24.5	17.9	5,650
British; Mark VI Crusader	22.1	19.7	5,300
German; PzKpfw IV	19.7	19.4	6,000
British; Mark III Valentine	17.9	17.9	8,275
German; PzKpfw Chaser	17.6	20.7	1,577
Japanese; 97 Chi-Ho	15.6	18.1	1,000+
Italian; model Mi3/40	15.4	16.2	2,000
U.S.; M3al Stuart	14.3	14.10	4,621
Japanese; 89B Chi-Ro	12.8	18.1	1,000+
Italian; model 11/39	10.8	15.6	100
Soviet; T26	10.1	15.3	4,500
German; PzKpfw II	9.35	15.9	650
Japanese; 95 Ho-Go	7.5	14.4	2,464
British; Mark Via	5.7	13.2	1,000+
Italian; L3	3.4	10.5	2,500

THE SCORE SHEET ON WORLD WAR II TANKS

- The major warring nations used no less than 31 different tank models in combat between 1939-45, as per the facing page;

- Using that unofficial ranking, the largest Japanese tank would be 22 on the list, while the three largest American tanks come in at 9; 10; and 13 positions;

- Germany had the three largest, and four of the five largest. The largest by far was the German Tiger II. At 33.9 feet, and tipping the scales at 74.8 tons, it required a five-man crew. The second largest tank, the German Elephant, also at 74.8 tons was only 22.3 feet long.

- Only two tanks required six man crews: the German Elephant and the U.S. M3. Several tanks had five-man crews.

- The smallest tank on the list was the Italian L3, which, at 3.4 tons and 10.5 feet, accommodated a two-man crew.

- The 49,000 U.S. Shermans were the greatest single type, while the 90 German Elephants produced were reportedly the smallest number made in any series.

U.S. POPULATION AND MILITARY STRENGTH

	Civilian Population	Armed Forces Total	Overseas
July 1940	131,658,000	464,000	168,000
July 1941	131,595,000	1,807,000	281,000
July 1942	130,942,000	3,918,000	940,000
July 1943	127,499,000	9,240,000	2,494,000
July 1944	126,708,000	11,689,000	5,512,000
July 1945	127,573,000	12,355,000	7,447,000
Jan. 1946	133,782,000	6,907,000	3,462,000
July 1946	138,385,000	3,004,000	1,335,000

GERMANY'S KAMIKAZE PILOTS HAD PARACHUTES

Apparently Hitler and Goering thought the Japanese idea of suicide planes had enough merit that they instituted a similar program in the Luftwaffe. In March 1945 a request went out for volunteers for Sonderkommando units. And some 300 stepped forward. Their job would be to fly one-way suicide missions against Allied bombers. Training consisted of a 10-day's of instructions at a Luftwaffe air base near Magdeburg. The volunteers were taught fighter-ramming techniques, i.e.: approaching a target by coming at it with the sun directly behind you; the pilot was urged to fire throughout the approach and go into its ramming dive aiming at the enemy fuselage just forward of the bomber's tail.

The main effort of the training, however, was psychological motivation through lectures and films. Unlike their Japanese counterparts in the Pacific, the German kamikaze pilots were given the opportunity to bail out of their aircraft if that was possible. Approximately 200 German kamikaze pilots were routed to four groups known as Sonderkommando Elbe, with units named after winged attack birds like Falcon, Eagle, Condor, etc. The Elbe group's first, and perhaps final, action was on April 7, 1945. Unbeknownst to them, Hitler would be dead and the war in Europe would be over in less than a month). To the marshal tempo of military and patriotic music, along with encouraging propaganda broadcast through their radio headsets, they commenced their mission. Normal communications between pilots were not possible since their radio transmitters had been disabled. Contradictory information exists on exactly how many German kamikaze pilots were killed. However, Allied records indicate that 169 German fighters were shot down on April 7 by the U.S. Eighth Air Force. Out of 1,300 airborne Allied bombers that same day, 22 were lost. The other kamikaze pilots were stationed in Prague, but there is no record of them ever having seen action.

The Two Largest Battleships Ever Built

Japan had the biggest and most powerful ships of the war. In 1937 the Imperial Navy ordered two giant battleships, the Yamato and the Musashi, in total violation of the Washington and London naval-treaties, because of their size and armament. Each ship was 862 feet long. Carrying crews up to 2,500 men strong, the ships had a range of 7,200 miles and could hit a top speed of 27 knots.

Above all, the guns on the Yamato and the Musashi made the ships unique. They possessed 18.1 inch guns. Nothing afloat was comparably equipped. The ships had nine of the giant guns apiece, each of which could hurl a shell 35 miles and pierce 16 inches of steel plate. A single hit was deemed sufficient to knock out a carrier, and it was assumed one 18.1 inch shell could kill a concentrated battalion of ground soldiers.

For all this, the ships were flops. They were already obsolete when commissioned. Of the two others in the class (ordered later), one was converted to a carrier (Shinano) after the Battle of Midway. Construction of the other (hull number 111) was simply halted.

The Yamato's record illustrates the point. Although it saw considerable action (the Battles of Midway, Philippine Sea, and Leyte Gulf), it is believed to have sunk only one ship, the destroyer Hoel in the Battle of Samar. But in this action, the Yamato's smaller, conventional guns provided the kill, not the 18.1 inchers. While it carried 1,080 giant shells, it fired only 81 and probably none of them hit anything. And this was the only time the Yamato ever fired the big guns. U.S. aircraft finally sank the Yamato on April 7, 1945.

The Musashi's record was even less impressive, having been sunk in the 1944 Battle of Leyte Gulf. Their contribution to the Japanese war effort was practically nil.

COMBAT STATISTICS OF JAPANESE KAMIKAZES

The Japanese "suicide planes", as they were commonly called, were, for all intents and purposes, much more of a psychological weapon than the military force that could repeal certain defeat for Japan. Though nothing can lessen the horror that they killed and maimed U.S. Navy Personnel, their deeds fell far short of breaking American resolve. From their first flights on Oct. 25, 1944, until the end of the war a total of 1,228 Japanese kamikaze corps pilots plunged to their deaths in suicide missions. This unprecedented planned program of human sacrifice was Japan's final act of desperation to negate the overwhelming U.S. naval force that was pounding its way inexorably toward the home islands. The kamikazes took a frightful toll in American lives, but they did not stop or delay the inevitable defeat of the empire. Nonetheless, to sailors on these ships the destruction was awesome.

U.S. Navy Ships Hit by Kamikazes

Sunk		*Damaged*
0	Fleet carriers	16
0	Light carriers	3
3	Escort carriers	17
0	Battleships	15
0	Heavy cruisers	5
0	Light cruisers	10
13	Destroyers	87
1	Destroyer escorts	24
0	Submarines	1
2	High-speed minelayers	15
0	Light minelayers	13
5	Landing ships - tanks	11
1	Mine sweepers	10
9	Auxiliaries and small craft	61
34 Total		Total 288

Women defense workers on their way to work in Honolulu, Hawaii, on 10 August 1945, join U.S. servicemen celebrating the news that Japan had accepted the Potsdam Agreement, which called for "unconditional surrender." A day earlier the U.S. had dropped the second atomic bomb on a Japanese city, Nagasaki. Had the Japanese continued to wage war the target of a third atomic bomb was Tokyo. The other option would have been an actual invasion of the Japanese home islands which is estimated would have cost tens of thousands of American lives. The war that began with the destruction of U.S. battleships in Pearl Harbor would end on a U.S. battleship in Tokyo Bay with the surrender ceremonies in September. *–U.S. Army photo*

Bibliography
Primary sources

Aster, Sidney. *1939. The Making of the Second World War.* New York: Simon and Schuster, 1974.

Bauer, Eddy. *Illustrated World War II Encyclopedia* (24 vols.). Monaco: Jaspard Polus, 1966. English translation printed in the United States by H. S. Stuttman, Inc.

Buchanan, A. Russell. *The United States and World War II.* New York: Harper & Row, 1964.

Clark, Blake. *Remember Pearl Harbor!* Hawaii: Mutual, 1987

Collier, Basil. *Japan at War.* London: Sidgwick and Jackson, 1975.

Dulles, Allen W. *The Craft of Intelligence.* New York: Harper & Row, 1963.

Elson, Robert. *Prelude to War.* New York: Time/Life, 1976.

Feis, Herbert. *The Road to Pearl Harbor,* N.Y.: Atheneum, 1964

Fuller, J. F. C. *The Second World War, 1939-1945.* New York: Duell, Sloan & Pearce, 1949.

Kahn, David, *The Codebreakers.* New York: Macmillan, 1967.

Kimmel, Husband E. *Admiral Kimmel's Story.* Chicago: Henry Regnery, 1955.

King, Ernest J., and Whitehill, W M. *Fleet Admiral King.* New York: Norton, 1952.

LaForte, Robert S. and Marcello, Ronald E. *Remembering Pearl Harbor*. New York: Ballentine, 1992.

Lawson, Ted W. *Thirty Seconds over Tokyo*. New York: Random House, 1943.

Layton, Edwin T. *And I Was There*. New York: Morrow, 1985

Leahy, W. *I Was There*. New York: Whittlesey, 1950.

Lewin, Ronald. *The American Magic*. New York: Farrar, Straus & Giroux, 1982.

Lord, Walter. *Day of Infamy*. New York: Henry Holt, 1957.

---*Incredible Victory*. New York: Harper & Row, 1967.

Morison, Samuel E. *The History of United States Naval Operations in World War II* (14 vols.). Boston: Little, Brown, 1947-62.

Prange, Gordon, *At Dawn We Slept*. N.Y.: McGraw-Hill, 1981.

---*The Pearl Harbor Papers*. Virginia: Brassey's, 2000.

---*Pearl Harbor: The Verdict of History*. N.Y. McGraw Hill, 1987.

---*Dec. 7, 1941*. New York: McGraw-Hill, 1988.

Richardson, James O. *On the Treadmill to Pearl Harbor,* Washington, D.C. 1973 Dept. of the Navy

Toland, John. Infamy. N.Y.: Random House, 1981

Secondary sources

Aldeman, Robert H. and Walton, George. *The Devil's Brigade* Philadelphia: Chilton, 1966.

Ambrose, Stephen E. *The Supreme Commander: The War Years of General Dwight D. Eisenhower*. New York: Doubleday, 1970.

Angelucci, Enzo. *Airplanes from the Dawn of Flight to the Present Day*. New York: McGraw-Hill, 1973.

Aron, Robert. *De Gaulle Before Paris. The Liberation of France, June-August 1944*. New York: Putnam, 1962.

Baron, Richard; Baum, A.; and Goldhurst, R. *Raid! The Untold Story of Patton's Secret Mission*. New York: Putnam, 1981.

Bazna, Elyesa. *I Was Cicero*. New York: Harper & Row, 1962.

Bekker, Cajus. *The Luftwaffe War Diaries*. N. Y.: Doubleday, 1968.

---*Hitler's Naval War*. New York: Doubleday, 1974.

Belote, James H., and Belote, William M. *Corregidor. The Saga of a Fortress.* New York: Harper & Row, 1967.

Benford, Timothy B. *World War II Flashback.* New York: Longmeadow Press, 1991.

---*The Ultimate World War II Quiz Book.* New York: Barnes & Noble, 1987.

---*The World War II Quiz & Fact Book.* N.Y.: Harper & Row, 1983.

Blair, Clay, Jr. *Silent Victory.* New York: Lippincott, 1975.

Boyington, Gregory. *Baa Baa Black Sheep.* N.Y.: Putnam, 1958.

Bradley, Omar N. *A Soldier's Story.* New York: Henry Holt, 1951.

Brown, Anthony Cave. *Bodyguard of Lies.* New York: Harper & Row, 1975.

Bullock, Alan. *Hitler - A Study in Tyranny.* New York: Harper & Row, 1963.

Butcher, Harry. *My Three Years with Eisenhower.* New York: Simon and Schuster, 1946.

Calvocoressi, Peter, and Wint, Guy. *Total War.* New York: Pantheon, 1972.

Carell, Paul. *The Foxes of the Desert.* New York: Dutton, 1961.

Catton, Bruce. *The War Lords of Washington.* New York: Harcourt Brace, 1948.

Churchill, Winston S. *The Second World War.* Boston: Houghton Mifflin, 1948-53.

Clark, Alan. *Barbarossa: The Russian-German Conflict, 1941-1945.* New York: Morrow, 1965.

Collins, Larry, and Lapierre, Dominique. *Is Paris Burning?* New York: Simon and Schuster, 1965.

Cortesi, Lawrence. *Operation Bismarck Sea.* Canoga Park, California: Major Books, 1977.

Daley, Robert. *An American Saga: Juan Trippe and His Pan American Empire.* New York: Random House, 1980.

Dean, John R. *The Strange Alliance: The Story of Our Efforts at Wartime Cooperation with Russia.* New York: Viking, 1947.

De Gaulle, Charles. *War Memoirs.* New York: Simon and Schuster, 1964.

Deighton, Len. *Blitzkrieg.* New York- Knopf, 1980.

243

Delmer, Sefton. *The Counterfeit Spy.* N.Y.: Harper & Row, 1971.

Dissette, Edward, and Adamson, Hans Christian. *Guerrilla Submarines.* New York: Bantam Books, 1980.

Dulles, Allen W. *The Secret Surrender.* New York: Harper & Row, 1966.

Eisenhower, Dwight D. *Crusade in Europe.* N.Y.: Avon, 1968.

Epstein, Helen. *Children of the Holocaust.* N.Y.: Putnam, 1979.

Essame, Hubert, and Belfield, E. M. G. *Normandy Bridgehead* New York: Ballantine, 1970.

Farago, Ladislas. *The Broken Seal.* N.Y.: Random House, 1967.

----*The Game of the Foxes.* New York: McKay, 1971.

Fleming, Peter. *Operation Sea -Lion.* New York: Simon and Schuster, 1957.

Ford, Corey. *Donovan of OSS.* Boston: Little, Brown, 1970.

Friedheim, Eric and Taylor, Samuel W. *Fighters Up.* Philadelphia: Macrae-Smith, 1945.

Gavin, James M. *On to Berlin.* New York: Viking, 1978.

Goebbels, Joseph. *Diaries of Joseph Goebbels, 1942-1943.* New York: Doubleday, 1948.

Goralski, Robert. *World War II Almanac, 1939-1945.* New York: Putnam, 1981.

Hirsch, Phil. *War.* New York: Pyramid Books, 1964.

Hughes, Terry, and Costello, John. *The Battle of the Atlantic.* New York: Dial, 1977.

Innis, W Joe, with Bunton, Bill, *In Pursuit of the Awa Maru.* New York: Bantam Books, 1981.

Irving, David. *The German Atomic Bomb.* New York: Simon and Schuster, 1968.

--- *The Trail of the Fox.* New York: Dutton, 1977.

Jackson, Stanley. *The Savoy- The Romance of a Great Hotel.* London: Frederick Muller, 1964.

Jackson, W G. F. *The Battle for Italy.* London: Batsford, 1967.

Johnson, Frank D. *United States PT Boats of World War II.* Poole, Dorset, U.K.: Blandford Press, 1980.

Kaufman, Louis; Fitzgerald, B.; and Sewell, T.; *Mo Berg Athlete, Scholar, Spy.* Boston: Little, Brown, 1974.

Keegan, John. *Who Was Who in World War II.* New York: Thomas Y. Crowell, 1978.

Keil, Sally Van Wagenen. *Those Wonderful Women in Their Flying Machines.* New York: Rawson, Wade, 1979.

Kitchen, Ruben P., Jr. *Pacific Carrier.* N.Y.: Zebra Books, 1980.

Kowalski, Isaac. A *Secret Press in Nazi Europe.* New York: Shengold, 1978.

Kramarz, Joachim. *Stauffenberg:* London: Deutsch, 1967.

Kurzman, Dan. *The Race for Rome.* New York: Doubleday, 1975.

Le Vien, Jack, and Lord, John. *Winston Churchill. The Valiant Years.* New York: Bernard Geis, 1962.

Longmate, Norman. *If Britain Had Failed.* New York: Stein & Day. 1974.

McClendon, Dennis E. *The Lady Be Good.* Fallbrook, Calif. Aero Publishers, Inc., 1982.

McKee, Alexander. *Last Round Against Rommel.* New York: New American Library, 1964.

Manchester, William. *American Caesar. Douglas MacArthur, 1880-1964.* Boston: Little, Brown, 1978.

Manvell, Roger, and Fraenkel, Heinrich. *The Canaris Conspiracy.* New York: McKay, 1969.

Marshall, Samuel. *Night Drop.* Boston: Little, Brown, 1962.

Mason, David. *Who's Who in WW II.* Boston: Little, Brown, 1978.

---*U-Boat.- The Secret Menace.* New York: Ballantine, 1968.

Michel, Henri. *The Shadow War.* New York: Harper & Row, 1973.

Michel, Jean. *Dora: The Nazi Concentration Camp Where Modern Space Technology Was Born and 30,000 Prisoners Died.* New York: Holt, Rinehart and Winston, 1980.

Mikesh, Robert C. *Japan's World War II Balloon Bomb Attacks on North America* Washington: Smithsonian Institution, 1973.

Mollo, Andrew. A *Pictorial History of the SS.* New York: Bonanza, 1979.

Montagu, Ewen. *The Man Who Never Was.* Philadelphia: Lippincott, 1954.

Morella, Joe; Epstein, Edward Z.; and Griggs, John. *The Films of World War II.* New York: Citadel/Lyle Stuart, 1975.

Murphy, Robert. *Diplomat Among Warriors*. New York: Doubleday, 1964.

Page, Geoffrey. *Tale of a Guinea Pig*. New York: Bantam, 1981.

Patton, George S., Jr. *War As I Knew It*. Boston: Houghton Mifflin.

Payne, Robert. *The Life and Death of Adolf Hitler*. New York: Praeger, 1973.

Pearcy, Arthur. *DC-3*. New York: Ballantine, 1975.

Peniakoff, Vladimir. *Popski's Private Army*. N.Y.: Bantam, 1980.

Popov, Dusko. *Spy-Counterspy*. N.Y.: Grosset & Dunlap, 1974.

Preston, Antony. *Aircraft Carriers*. N.Y.: Grosset & Dunlap, 1979.

Rayner, D. C. *Escort*. London: William Kimber & Company, 1955.

Ryan, Cornelius. *The Longest Day*. New York: Simon and Schuster, 1959.

---*A Bridge Too Far*. New York: Simon and Schuster, 1974.

---*The Last Battle*. New York: Simon and Schuster, 1966.

Schaeffer, Heinz. *U-Boat 977*. New York: Norton, 1953.

Sherrod, Robert. *Tarawa*. New York: Duell, Sloan & Pearce. 1944.

Shirer, William L. *The Rise and Fall of the Third Reich*. New York: Simon and Schuster, 1960.

Simms, Edward H. *American Aces*. N.Y.: Harper & Brothers, 1958.

Speer, Albert. *Inside the Third Reich*. New York: Avon, 1970.

Stagg, J. M. *Forecast for Overload*. New York: Norton, 1972.

Steichen, Edward. *U.S. Navy War Photographs*. New York: Crown Publishers, 1956-1980.

Strong, Sir Kenneth. *Intelligence at the To*p. New York: Doubleday, 1969.

Sulzberger, C. L. *The American Heritage Picture History of World War II*. New York: American Heritage, 1966.

Sunderman, James F. *World War II in the Air*. New York: Franklin Watts, 1962.

TerHorstorst, Jerald F., and Albertazzie, Ralph. *The Flying White House*. New York: Coward, McCann & Geoghegan, 1979.

Thomson, David. *Europe Since Napoleon*. N.Y.: Knopf, 1960.

Toland, John, *The Last 100 Days*. N.Y.: Random House, 1965.

---*The Rising Sun*. N.Y.: Simon and Schuster, 1971.

Townsend, Peter. *Duel of Eagles.* N.Y.: Simon and Schuster, 1971.

Tregaskis, Richard. *Guadalcanal Diary.* New York: Random House, 1943.

Truman, Harry S. *Memoirs.* New York: Doubleday, 1958.

Whiting, Charles. *Hitler's Werewolves.* New York: Bantam, 1973.

---*The Hunt for Martin Bormann.* New York: Ballantine, 1973.

---*Patton.* New York: Ballantine, 1971.

Wiener, Jan G. *The Assassination of Heydrich.* New York: Pyramid, 1969.

Williams, Eric. *The Wooden Horse.* New York: Bantam, 1980.

Winterbotham, Frederick W *The Ultra Secret.* New York: Harper & Row, 1974.

Young, Desmond. *Rommel, the Desert Fox.* New York: Harper & Brothers, 1950.

Award-winning author and best-selling novelist TIMOTHY B. BENFORD is president of Benford Associates, Inc., an international public relations agency specializing in the tourism industry. A former newspaper and magazine editor, several of his books have also been published in Spanish, French, and Polish. The novel, Hitler's Daughter, won the West Coast Review of Books Porgie Award and was made into a USA Network Movie of The Week. Benford continues to write extensively about myriad subjects including history, numismatics, classic cars, World War II, and travel for publications in the U.S., Canada, and the U.K. He resides in Mountainside, N.J. with his wife Marilyn.

Most of Tim Benford's books remain in print. For information and availability contact him c/o American Book Publishers at: **AmericanBP@aol.com**